Private International Law in Japan

Private International Law in Japan

Second Edition

Jun Yokoyama

This book was originally published as a monograph in the International Encyclopaedia of Laws/Private International Law.

Founding Editor: Roger Blanpain
General Editor: Frank Hendrickx
Volume Editor: Bea Verschraegen

Wolters Kluwer

Published by:
Kluwer Law International B.V.
PO Box 316
2400 AH Alphen aan den Rijn
The Netherlands
E-mail: international-sales@wolterskluwer.com
Website: lrus.wolterskluwer.com

Sold and distributed in North, Central and South America by:
Wolters Kluwer Legal & Regulatory U.S.
7201 McKinney Circle
Frederick, MD 21704
United States of America
Email: customer.service@wolterskluwer.com

Sold and distributed in all other countries by:
Air Business Subscriptions
Rockwood House
Haywards Heath
West Sussex
RH16 3DH
United Kingdom
Email: international-customerservice@wolterskluwer.com

ISBN 978-94-035-1942-5

e-Book: ISBN 978-94-035-1971-5
web-PDF: ISBN 978-94-035-1960-9

The Author

Jun Yokoyama was born in 1949, in Matsuyama, Japan. He studied in Tokyo and received his law degrees from Hitotsubashi University. He was Professor of Hitotsubashi University, Tokyo, Japan from 1990 to 2013 and has been Professor of Seikei University, Tokyo, Japan since 2013. He was Delegate of Japan for the 18th session of the Hague Conference on private international law and for the Special Commission of the Hague Conference concerning the Convention on the international protection of adults, Chairman of the International Family Law Committee of the International Law Association, and a member of the Legislative Council for the Minister of Justice of Japan. Among his publications are 'International Family Law' and 'Private International Law'.

The Author

Table of Contents

List of Abbreviations

A. Law Reports

Hanji	Hanreijiho (Law Case Reports)
Hanta	Hanreitaimuzu (Law Times Report)
Kagetsu	Kateisaiban-geppou (Monthly Report on the Family Court Cases)
Kinyu Homu	Kinyu Homu Jijou (Financial Law Bulletin)
Kosai Minshu	Koutou Saibansho Minji Horeishu (High Courts Reports (civil cases))
Minshu	Saikosaibansho Minji Saibanreishu (Report on the Civil Cases of the Supreme Court)
Shimbun	Horitsu-shimbun (Newsletter for Lawyers)

B. Legal Sources

AGR	Act on General Rules for Application of Laws 2006
APFM	Act on Procedure in Family Matters
ARAFIP	Act on Recognition and Assistance for Foreign Insolvency Proceedings
CCP	Code of Civil Procedure
CEA	Civil Execution Act
CISG	United Nations Convention on Contracts for the International Sales of Goods of 1980
Horei	Act on General Rules for Application of Laws 1898
PSLA	Personal Status Litigation Act
UCP	Uniform Customs and Practice for Documentary Credits

C. States and Organizations

DPRK	Democratic People's Republic of Korea
ICSID	International Center for Settlement of Investment Disputes
JCAA	Japan Commercial Arbitration Association
ROK	Republic of Korea

List of Abbreviations

UCP	Uniform Customs and Practice for Documentary Credits
US	United States
D. Periodicals	
J.A.I.L.	Japanese Annual of International Law
J.Y.B.I.L.	Japanese Yearbook of International Law

General Introduction

§1. Historical Development

1. In the middle of the nineteenth century, the newly established Japanese government tried to systematize its legal system in place of the feudal law. The codification of private law was necessary for that purpose.[1] The government also needed a set of choice-of-law rules to convince foreign powers that there was no problem in acknowledging Japanese courts' jurisdiction over their citizens in Japan.

2. The Treaty of Nanking, with which the Opium War ended, was followed by a separate commercial agreement signed between China and Britain on 18 October 1843. This agreement established the treaty port system accompanied by the provision on extraterritoriality designed to ensure that British residents in China would be subject only to their own law administered through British consular courts. This privilege is unequal in that the provision does not grant equivalent rights to Chinese residents in Britain. In the 1850s, Britain and the other Western powers succeeded in transplanting the treaty port system from China to Japan. It turned out that it took almost forty years for Japan to abolish the extraterritoriality in spite of the Japanese government's struggling for its abandonment. It is only natural that those Western powers would not agree to do it for such a prolonged period of time. Britain and other foreign powers feared that they would take a step in the dark, when they abandoned their citizens to the jurisdiction of an oriental developing country, an action for which there was no precedent.[2] It was not until 16 July 1894 that Japan concluded a treaty with Britain to abolish the extraterritoriality on condition that Japanese law should be reformed in line with European legal systems.[3] The codification of private international law was an essential part of such law reform, along with the Civil Code and the Code of Civil Procedure (CCP), because disputes upon which the British consular courts had enjoyed powers to adjudicate, namely disputes in which British people were involved, were dealt with by the Japanese courts after the treaty took effect. It was on 16 July 1898, exactly four years after the conclusion of that treaty, that a set of choice-of-law rules called the *Horei* was put in force.

1. *See*, Hiroshi Oda, *Japanese Law* 17 (3rd ed., Oxford University Press 2009).
2. F.C. Jones, *Extraterritoriality in Japan* 155 (Yale University Press 1931).
3. Treaty of Commerce and Navigation between Great Britain and Japan signed on 16 Jul. 1894.

The very date of 16 July 1898 was also the earliest date on which, in accordance with the treaty,[4] Japan could notify to Britain its readiness to bring the treaty into force.

3. Most of the choice-of-law rules as contained in the *Horei* were bilateral.[5] Foreign laws are applicable on equal terms with Japanese law. The preference of the bilateral formula was inspired by the draft of German private international law prepared by *Albert Gebhardt*.[6] The *Horei* had its predecessor afterwards called the 'Former *Horei*', which had been enacted in 1880, modelled upon provisions of the French, Italian, and Belgian Civil Codes at that time. This Former *Horei*, which was never put in force, was also formulated in the bilateral way. Whereas Japan was undoubtedly outside *von Savigny's* community of law of nations, such consistent preference of the style may be explained when we look at the backgrounds of the legislation. Those who were engaged in drafting the choice-of-law rules could not help being sensitive about the concerns of the United States (US) and the European powers, *inter alia*, Britain as to what would take place after they yielded their citizens to the jurisdiction of Japanese courts. It was feared that unilateral choice-of-law rules, which would delimit only the sphere of application of the Japanese substantive law, would not be able to sweep away their concerns. The Japanese drafters had to make it clear that Japanese courts were ready to apply foreign laws on equal terms with Japanese law. We should add that the Japanese legislator probably must have felt bilateral choice-of-law rules were not bad. Such rules stand upon the assumption that the substantive law rules of the forum are on an equal footing with those of the foreign countries, irrespective of how much developed they may be. In view of the very fact that the Japanese Civil Code, which constituted most of the Japanese substantive law rules, just got off the ground at that time, it seems that the bilateral choice-of-law rules looked satisfactory to the Japanese legislator, too. In this sense, those rules were believed to serve the governmental interests of Japan.

4. Subject to a few minor modifications, the *Horei* remained as principal Japanese choice-of-law rules for about a century since its enactment. It was not until 1989 that substantial amendments were made to it. The choice-of-law rules on family mainly underwent considerable revision. The aim was twofold. First, the connecting criteria of those rules had to be modified to conform to the principle of gender equality. Articles 14–17 of the *Horei* had provided for the husband-oriented choice-of-law rules: the personal effects of marriage, the matrimonial regime, and the divorce were governed by the *lex patriae* of the husband. Unlike Germany and Italy, there were no Japanese court decisions declaring that the husband (or father)-oriented choice-of-law rules were unconstitutional. In response to the doubts about their constitutionality raised by some members of the Diet, the Japanese Ministry of

---

4. Article 21 of the Treaty.
5. *See*, Masato Dogauchi, *Historical Development of Japanese Private International Law*, in Basedow/Baum/Nishitani, 27 et seq. *See also*, Yoshiaki Sakurada, *The Origin and Evolution of Private International Law in Japan*, 56 *J.Y.B.I.L.*164 et seq. (2013).
6. The two Japanese scholars, *Nobushige Hozumi* and *Saburo Yamada*, were in charge of preparing the draft. For their contribution to the enactment of the *Horei*, *see*, Aki Kitazawa, *Nobushige Hozumi and Saburo Yamada*, 56 *J.Y.B.I.L.*181 et seq. (2013).

Justice expressed its view that the interests to be protected under the Constitution, particularly, its Article 14 declaring the equality under the law, had nothing to do with the choice-of-law rules but the substantive law rules. For example, a divorced wife might be in the financially better position under the ex-husband's national law than under her own national law. However, the Ministry of Justice had to admit the fact that the husband's national law was more familiar to him than to the wife, and that, in terms of the expectations of the parties as regards the applicable law, some inequality existed.

5. Second, the court practice preceding the reform revealed that the nationality of the husband had failed to work well as a connecting criterion. For example, the choice-of-law rule pursuant to which the divorce should be governed by the national law of the husband frequently induced judges to have recourse to the principle of the *ordre public*. Particularly, when Philippine law prohibiting divorce was referred to as the law governing divorce, judges did not hesitate to do so. As mentioned below with respect to the *ordre public*, the elements of the reported cases are almost identical: a Japanese wife habitually resident in Japan petitioned for divorce from a Philippine husband also habitually resident in Japan. It is true that the prohibition of divorce by Philippine law triggered the application of the *ordre public* clause. The prohibition of divorce undoubtedly looked extraordinary to judges in Japan, where around 90% of marriages are dissolved by agreement. More important is the fact, however, that the great majority of Philippine-Japanese spouses established their matrimonial homes in Japan. Whereas the nationality of husband proved to indicate a weak link with the Philippines, the spouses' link with the forum (*Inlandsbeziehung*) seemed sufficient in most cases. Such links with the forum were found to yield a new connecting criterion, namely, the common habitual residence of the spouses. The Legislative Council of 1989 expected this connecting criterion to make it as unnecessary as possible for judges to resort to the *ordre public* clause. The experience of more than three decades seems to endorse this expectation. There has been no reported case in which the application of Philippine law was excluded on the ground of the *ordre public* after the revised *Horei* came into force.

6. In the 1990s, Japan was in serious economic depression. Many companies went bankrupt. Banks and other financial institutions had bad loans, namely, uncollectable loans. In coping with such economic depression, the government adopted a series of schemes to revitalize the national economy. One of them was to promote the liquidation of assets. Given that claims might be subject to foreign laws, the enactment of a new choice-of-law rule on the assignment of credit was felt necessary, because the provision of the *Horei* on the voluntary assignment of credit obviously derived from the French case law in the nineteenth century. Whereas the Ministry of Justice seems to have originally intended to take a patchwork quilt approach to the problem, it did not take much time for the Ministry to realize that not only the provision in question but also the other provisions, which had been put outside the range of the previous revision in 1989, should undergo thorough revision. Consequently, the *Horei* on the whole became subject to the revision, with the result that, in 2006, the Act on General Rules for Application of Laws (AGR) was enacted in replacement of the *Horei*.[7]

§2. International and Supranational Legal Framework

7. Apart from the public international law rules as mentioned below, there is no agreement providing international and supranational legal framework for Japan to make legislative or judicial activities within.

§3. Nature and Scope

8. A set of choice-of-law rules are said to aim at designating a legal system applicable to legal problems of private law nature. In this sense, they have been distinguished from substantive law rules, including the ones specifically envisaging international situations, for example, the UN Convention on Contracts for the International Sales of Goods (CISG). The Private International Law (PIL) in a wider sense comprises rules on issues relating to civil procedure, *inter alia*, the international jurisdiction of Japanese courts, and the recognition and enforcement of foreign decisions in Japan.

9. Japanese rules on nationality and aliens are not regarded as pertaining to PIL at least so much as in French authors' textbooks.

10. Japan is a unitary state with unitary legal system in territorial and personal terms. It follows that there are neither inter-provincial nor inter-personal choice-of-law rules, whereas, before the end of the Second World War, it had such rules dealing with conflicts of laws between Japanese substantive law and laws prevailing in such areas as the Taiwan Island and the Korean Peninsula.

§4. Characteristics of National Private International Law (JPIL)

11. As mentioned earlier, JPIL as a set of choice-of-law rules was codified in the name of *Horei* in 1898 as a necessary tool for abolishing the treaties which looked unequal to the government at that time. Those choice-of-law rules were bilateral or all-sided. Since then, Japanese courts and academic writers have tried to apply foreign laws on equal terms with Japanese law. They have stood upon the assumption that the ideal choice-of-law rules should not be biased in favour of giving wider scope of application to the *lex fori*.

7. For the enactment of the AGR, *see*, Hironori Wanami, *Background and Outline of the Modernization of Japanese Private International Law*, in Basedow/Baum/Nishitani, 61 et seq.

§5. Domestic Authorities Involved, Interpretation and Application of PIL

I. Courts

12. The Japanese CCP enacted in 1890 was drafted by a German lawyer, *Herman Techow*. It is natural that Article 219 of the said Code was very similar to Article 265 of the German CCP (*Zivilprozessordnung*) at that time. Article 219 CCP read: '[l]ocal customary laws, commercial customs and charters, or the laws in force in foreign countries require proof'. Although the provision itself was abrogated in 1926, the rule according to which the court shall apply the foreign law on its own motion, calling for the cooperation of the parties if necessary, has been believed to keep its validity. The ex officio application of foreign law is mandatory in all kinds of private law matters.

13. There is no provision dealing with the consequences entailed by the court's failure to ascertain the applicable foreign law. There has been no case in which the court applied Japanese law on the ground that the foreign law is presumed to be similar to the *lex fori*. Instead of automatically applying Japanese law as a subsidiary law, Japanese courts have often resorted to the '*johri*' (if literally translated, 'reason') or the general principles of law. It should be noted that the courts seem to have used the notion of *johri* in the three different senses: (1) the general principles of law presumably prevailing in the applicable foreign legal system whose specific rules pertaining to facts of a case are found unascertainable;[8] (2) the general principle of private international law, in other words, the principle of the closest connection;[9] and (3) the general principles which serve justifying an ad hoc solution reached by the court.[10] Experience tells us that the general principles of law which some courts found prevailing in the foreign applicable law are, in reality, hardly distinguishable from those of Japanese law. The *johri* in the second sense, namely, the principle of the closest connection seems to have resulted in the application of Japanese law. In most cases, the *ad hoc* solutions which courts eventually reached seem to be justifiable in the eyes of the Japanese substantive law rules. It may well be that the courts have used the *johri*, whatever meaning it may have, as something justifying the application of Japanese law in failure of ascertaining the applicable foreign law.

14. According to Article 318 CCP, the Supreme Court may accept a final appeal, when the judgment in prior instance is found to involve material matters concerning the construction of laws and regulations. The court practice including that of the Supreme Court and the academic writers' views have held that the 'laws and regulations' of this provision include foreign laws, not only when incorrect application

8. For example, Judgment of the Sapporo District Court, 26 Jun. 1984, 29 *J.A.I.L.* 260 (1986) (Zimbabwean divorce law).
9. For example, Decree of the Nagoya Family Court, 12 Mar. 1982, *Kagetsu* 35-1-105 (North Korean succession law).
10. For example, Judgment of the Osaka District Court, 27 Sept. 1985, *Hanji* 1179-94.

of domestic choice-of-law rules results in erroneous applications of foreign laws but also when inferior courts, which correctly applied choice-of-law rules, erroneously applied governing foreign laws.[11] While the Supreme Court was basically established to cope with the uniformity in construction and interpretation of Japanese law, the need for ensuring a certain uniformity has been felt in cases in which foreign laws are involved.

II. Administrative Agencies

15. The Civil Affairs Bureau of the Ministry of Justice is in charge of handling matters such as the affairs regarding the system of the registration of companies, immovable property, family registration, and nationality. Circulars issued by the director of the Bureau are addressed to the lower echelons of the administration and local government which are not empowered to make a full enquiry into elements of individual circumstances.[12] The circulars are not regarded as a source of law. No breach of a circular by an administrative official entails disputes to be contested in court, but, in practice, they have played an important role in the field of private international law.[13]

---

11. For example, Judgment of the Supreme Court, 18 Mar. 2008, *Hanji* 2006-77. For this judgment, *see*, Keisuke Takeshita, *Improper Application of Foreign Laws and Final Appeal to the Supreme Court*, 55 J.Y.B.I.L. 511 et seq. (2012).
12. For example, one circular addressed to family registrars (issued on 2 Oct. 1989) gives suggestions on how long it would take for a person to have his/her habitual residence in a particular country. It states that the five years continuous sojourn in a country is sufficient to show the establishment of the habitual residence there. Five years' sojourn sounds too long for one's acquisition of habitual residence. It should be noted, however, that, unlike judges, the available range of evidence is limited for family registrars.
13. *See*, Oda, *supra* 45.

Part I. General Principles (Choice of Law Technique)

Chapter 1. Sources of PIL

§1. Public International Law

16. Customary public international law can be taken into account by Japanese courts. For example, the Supreme Court holds that, whereas, with regard to civil jurisdictional immunity of foreign states, the so-called absolute theory of immunity was traditionally recognized as custom in international law, the idea backed by the accumulation of state practices tells that the immunity should not be extended as broadly as to a state's acts in the private law sphere.[14]

§2. Supranational Law

17. Japan participated in the Hague Conference of Private International Law in 1904. Notwithstanding such an early participation, the Conventions signed and ratified by Japan are not so many.[15] Japan is a party to other multinational agreements, such as the 1958 New York Convention on the Recognition and Enforcement of Arbitral Awards. It might be surprising that there have been no bilateral agreements with neighbouring states such as the People's Republic of China and the Republic of Korea (ROK) in the field of PIL.

14. Judgment of the Supreme Court, 2 Apr. 2002, 46 *J.A.I.L.*161 (2003). The law of state immunity is now regulated by the Act on the Civil Jurisdiction of Japan with Respect to a Foreign State, etc. (Act No. 24 of 24 Apr. 2009) which aimed to incorporate 'the United Nations Convention on Jurisdictional Immunities of States and Their Property'(still not in force). It should be noted that the Act applies in relation to the non-contracting states of the Convention.
15. Those Hague Conventions are as follows: Convention of 1 Mar. 1954 on Civil Procedure; Convention of 24 Oct. 1956 on the Law Applicable to Maintenance Obligations towards Children; Convention of 5 Oct. 1961 on the Conflicts of Laws Relating to the Form of Testamentary Dispositions; Convention of 5 Oct. 1961 Abolishing the Requirement of Legalisation for Foreign Public Documents; Convention of 15 Nov. 1965 on the Service Abroad of Judicial and Extrajudicial Documents in Civil or Commercial Matters; Convention of 2 Oct. 1973 on the Law Applicable to Maintenance Obligations; Convention of 25 Oct. 1980 on the Civil Aspects of International Child Abduction.

§3. National Law

18. Japanese law is primarily based on statutory laws. The AGR forms the core of the Japanese choice-of-law rules. The CCP comprises the rules on international jurisdiction (Article 3-2 to 3-11) and the rules on recognition (Article 118) in civil and commercial matters. The Personal Status Litigation Act and the Act on Procedure in Family Matters were revised and, now, contains the new provisions on international jurisdiction in family and succession matters.[16]

Interpretation of Japanese statutes in general has been guided by the preparatory legislative works. This is also the case with Japanese statutes relating to PIL. These legislative works on PIL were, in principle, made by the Legislative Councils whose members were appointed by the Minister of Justice. The conclusion which each Legislative Council reached is, of course, not binding, but views expressed in the proceedings of the Councils have been referred to by judges and academic writers interested in identifying the purpose and the effect of each provision. Their conclusions which left the matter to the development of case law have also been regarded as important as those which turn out to be crystallized into statutory provisions.

§4. Case Law

19. Japan belongs to civil-law rather than common-law jurisdictions. There is no explicit rule adopting the doctrine of *stare decisis*. Nor is the *ratio decidendi* strictly distinguished from the *obiter dicta*. However, it remains true that court judgments, particularly those of the Supreme Court, are often regarded as precedents having the de facto binding force. The judgments of the Supreme Court have played important roles in the development of apposite rules on international jurisdiction, to which the nineteenth century legislator seems to have been indifferent. Furthermore, the Legislative Council tends to leave the development of choice-of-law rules to courts, particularly when academic writers' comparative law research shows no discernible trend to be followed or when their views are fiercely divided with regard to a proposed choice-of-law rule.

§5. Doctrine

20. Scholarly opinions are not a source of law. Court judgments have scarcely referred to them. However, readers of judgments relating to PIL can often identify whose opinions the courts relied on rendering them. Whichever field of law it may be, the importance of the doctrine is ultimately due to the fact that Japanese statutory laws have often been inspired by foreign laws whose current interpretations and applications judges are usually not versed in. It is worth noting that, in cases involving foreign elements, judges are not necessarily familiar with abstract values or interests operating in favour of coordination with legal systems. PIL has been seen as the doctrinal law more than any other law fields.

16. *See*, paras. 406-413 *infra*.

§6. Customary Law

21. Customary law is a source of law. However, it does not seem that Japanese law knows customary rules on choice-of-law rules or on international civil procedure.

Chapter 2. Determination of the Applicable Law

§1. Conflict of Law Rules

I. Types of Conflict of Law Rules

22. JPIL, in principle, consists of hard-and-fast rules. The legislative work is necessarily interwoven with the idea of legal certainty. Furthermore, the legislator has to bear it in mind that the administrative authorities in charge of handling international cases, unlike judges, are not empowered to appraise relevant factors involved in each individual case. For example, the second sentence of Article 27 AGR partly aims to dispense with the family registrars' searching the country with which the divorcing spouses have the closest connection. It is needless to say that no one can expect the registrars to appraise the interests or policies of the states involved.

23. When we take into account political and social backgrounds against which the *Horei* was enacted in the late nineteenth century, it is only fair to say that its legislator had no choice but to adopt the bilateral choice-of-law rules. They were expected to show explicitly that foreign laws were on the same footing with Japanese law. Unilateral choice-of-law rules were few and exceptional. To the present writer's knowledge, there have been no academic writers advocating the unilateralism, either.

II. Connecting Factors

24. There is no connecting factors peculiar to JPIL. It would be sufficient to mention here that JPIL has traditionally given priority to nationality in relation to matters of family and succession. As mentioned below, such preference of nationality originally reflected the patriarchal idea of the household underlying the Japanese Civil Code enacted in 1898.

25. What the legislator of the *Horei* in the late nineteenth century was worried about seems to have been whether the future choice-of-law rules would be detrimental to the traditional family or household institution called '*ie*' endorsed by the Civil Code. In contrast to the nuclear or conjugal family, the household was conceived as a kind of corporate entity which was to perpetuate itself through generations beyond the life span of any single member of the entity and could not operate without its (usually) male head vested with the authority to control its members. The legislator of the *Horei* undoubtedly hated the idea that a foreign law would govern relationships between members of the Japanese household. It was quite fortunate to the legislator that the connecting criterion of the husband's or the father's nationality was in full accord with the patriarchal choice-of-law rules also prevailing in certain European countries at that time. That connecting criterion, in most cases, was expected to lead to the application of Japanese law under which Japanese male household head could control the members of his household. It should be stressed here that the connecting criterion of the husband's or the father's nationality was expected to play a role as the law of his household entity rather than his personal law as individual. What annoyed one of the drafters of *Horei* to the last was that the Civil Code at that time was likely to acknowledge the situation where the household might have its female head in certain situations. When a foreign husband married a Japanese female head, that connecting criterion would entail the application of a foreign law to a Japanese household through the marriage. To avoid this result, the legislator added a unilateral choice-of-law rule to the effect that the personal effects of marriage were governed by Japanese law when a foreign husband married a Japanese female head. In view of such legislative process of the *Horei*, it seems that at least most of the substantive law rules on the household provided in the Civil Code of 1898 were seen as internationally mandatory rules whose necessary sphere of application could be, in most cases, assured by the husband's or father's Japanese nationality which coincided with the connecting criteria of the bilateral choice-of-law rules contained in *Horei*. In this sense, elements of the domestic institution of household are thought to have sneaked into the bilateral choice-of-law rules.

III. Time Factors

26. When statutory choice-of-law rules are enacted with new connecting criteria, transitional provisions are also enacted for the purpose of determining whether events or juridical acts which arose before the new ones are put into force should be subject to the new or previous choice-of-law rules. In principle, the new choice-of-law rule applies retrospectively.[17] However, when such retrospective application is likely to create effects adverse to the legal relationships or the rights acquired under the law designated by previous choice-of-law rule, the new choice-of-law rule applies *ex nunc*. For example, the new one does not apply to contracts validly concluded under the law designated according to the previous choice-of-law rule.[18]

IV. *Dépeçage*

27. JPIL knows no legal technique of *dépeçage* on the basis of the issue-by-issue analysis as prevailing in US.

28. Until 2006, when the AGR was enacted, the governing view was that, apart from its form and a party's legal capacity, a contract should be governed by one single law chosen by the parties. However, there were some judgments of inferior courts which applied English law to the contractual parties' performance on the basis of their express choice, whereas they applied Japanese law to its validity.[19] The current provision, Article 7 AGR, which allows the parties to choose the law governing the contract, says nothing about the possibility of splitting parts of the

17. Article 2 of the Transitional Measures annexed to the AGR.
18. Article 3 of the Transitional Measures annexed to the AGR.
19. Judgment of the Tokyo District Court, 27 May 2002 (unpublished).

contract each of which is governed by a law independent of the law(s) applicable to the other part(s). This silence has been thought not to preclude the parties from choosing a law applicable to each part of their contract.[20] It is also said that the *dépeçage* is not excluded in the absence of the parties' choice of law, either.[21] It remains to be seen, however, on what conditions the *dépeçage* is allowed.

29. Articles 16 and 21 AGR allow the parties to make a subsequent choice of law as regards non-contractual obligations. Whereas the legislator leaves the matter to the development of case law, it is submitted that the *dépeçage* is also permissible for those obligations.

30. Article 26(2) AGR on matrimonial property allows the spouses to designate, with respect to all or some of the immovable properties, the law of the place where these immovable properties are situated, along with and in addition to another applicable law chosen by the spouses or determined pursuant to the objective criterion.

V. Legal Consequences

31. When, in view of the object and statement of a claim, a legal question is found to fall into a specific category of a particular choice-of-law rule, the legal system designated by the rule applies to the legal question, whether domestic or foreign. This is a normal consequence of the application of the bilateral choice-of-law rule containing one single connecting criterion, subject to operations of e.g., *renvoi*, assimilation and *ordre public.*

§2. Relevant Contact and Evasion of the Law

32. The AGR contains no rule explicitly dealing with the phenomenon of the *fraude à la loi.* It does not mean that JPIL is indifferent to avoidance of the application of otherwise applicable mandatory rules. In the process of the enactment of choice-of-law rules, the connecting criteria difficult to be arbitrarily manipulated tend to be adopted. For example, with regard to the choice-of-law rule on succession, a proposed rule enabling the deceased person to designate beforehand the law of his habitual residence was rejected by the Legislative Council, because some members feared that, for example, a Japanese businessman habitually resident in New York might evade the Japanese substantive law rules on compulsory portion by means of choosing New York law for the succession to his property.

33. JPIL has been always aware of the notion of forum shopping as regards direct and indirect jurisdictional rules. It certainly knows the *forum rei sitae*, but on condition that the property of the defendant to be seized is not valued significantly

20. *See*, Koide, 91.
21. *See*, Yokoyama, 173.

modest.[22] In addition, Japanese courts may refuse to exercise the jurisdiction on the ground of the forum non conveniens, particularly when a plaintiff raises the action in an abusive way.[23] As regards foreign divorce decrees, Japanese courts have, from time to time, refused to recognize divorce decrees of foreign courts whose jurisdictions were founded on contacts arbitrarily created by petitioners in the eyes of the Japanese court.[24]

§3. Choice of Law

34. Since the enactment of the *Horei* in 1898, JPIL has allowed parties to a contract to choose the law which would govern their contract (party autonomy).[25] Since 2006 when the AGR was put in force, parties may choose the law applicable to *negotiorum gestio*, unjust enrichment, and tort after the event took place. This extension of the party autonomy to non-contractual obligations was welcomed, because it was expected to enhance the parties' legitimate expectations as to the applicable law.

35. In order to counter-balance the effects of the mutability of the law objectively applicable to the matrimonial property regime, Article 26(2) AGR allows the spouses to choose the law applicable to their matrimonial property. The *professio juris* plays a role of stabilizing their matrimonial property relationships, regardless of any change of their nationality or habitual residence. In contrast, JPIL allows no person to designate the law applicable to the succession to his estate. Foreign people domiciled in Japan on the permanent basis, namely, Korean and Chinese people domiciled there for generations, might expect Japanese law to govern the succession to their property situated in Japan. The Legislative Council discussed the possibility of the *professio juris* in the field of succession law which enables a person to designate Japanese law as a law of habitual residence. However, the number of Korean and Chinese people domiciled in Japan on the permanent basis has been decreasing year by year. This background seems to explain partly the inertia of the Council towards the *professio juris*.

§4. Objective Connecting Factor

I. Principle of the Closest Connection

36. It is in the 1960s that the notion of 'the closest connection' emerged in academic writings and court judgments in Japan. As shown below, the notion was, at

22. Article 3-3(iii) CCP.
23. Article 3-9 CCP.
24. For example, a judgment of the Yokohama District Court, 19 Oct. 1982, *Kagetsu* 36-2-101refused to recognize a Haiti divorce.
25. Article 7 AGR.

that time, used in relation to determination of the *lex patriae* of a Korean or a Chinese person who had been of Japanese nationality until 1951.[26] The ROK and the Democratic People's Republic of Korea (DPRK), both, seemed to regard such former Japanese people as their own nationals. This was also the case with the claims by the People's Republic of China and by Taiwan. Authors and judges had recourse to the criterion of the closest connection in every individual case, in identifying the *lex patriae* of such Korean or Chinese persons.

37. Some provisions of the AGR use the term of the closest connection as a connecting criterion, leaving judges to identify the applicable law in each individual case. The determination of the law applicable to all kinds of tort claims is subject to the escape clause of Article 20 AGR. In light of circumstances established in each individual dispute, the law of the place with which the tort is manifestly more closely connected is applicable in lieu of the law of the place indicated in the preceding choice-of-law rules, in particular, the *lex loci damni*. Article 15 AGR (*negotiorum gestio* and unjustified enrichment) also contains such an escape clause. In applying those provisions, judges are expected to pay due attention to the parties' predictability about the applicable law. Furthermore, Article 8 AGR, which leaves judges to determine the law applicable to the contract in the absence of the choice of law by the parties, allows judges to rebut the presumption based upon the characteristic performance, when the parties' prediction in each contract points to the law other than the presumed one.

38. In addition to such clauses, the provisions of the AGR empower judges to identify the place of the closest connection at the last level in the cascade of the connecting criteria.[27] The provisions aim to ensure the application of the law which is likely to remain within expectations of the spouses in situations where the spouses share neither the *lex patriae* nor the law of the country of the habitual residence.

39. It should be noted here that the AGR contains no general escape clause such as Article 15(1) of the Swiss Private International Law. In family and property matters intertwined with the forum's system of registration, the legislator could not ignore the interests of the third parties who are likely to rely on what are recorded on such registers.

II. Nationality

40. Since the birth of Japanese PIL in the late nineteenth century, nationality has been the primary connecting factor in relation to legal capacity, family, and succession.

---

26. *See*, paras 102–104 *infra.*
27. Article 25 (personal effects of marriage), Art. 26 (matrimonial regime), and Art. 27 AGR (divorce).

41. The main reason why nationality has been used as a connecting factor in Japan seems to be interwoven with the Japanese household registry system, as mentioned above. The first registry system made in 1871 aimed to grasp the entire population in the process of Japan being reshaped as a nation-state.[28] It successfully enabled the government to identify all the members belonging to the registered households as Japanese nationals. Although it was originally designed to serve the administrative purposes such as conscription and taxation, it, as a matter of fact, came to play a role of a civil status registration system during the period of the following two decades. When the Civil Code was enacted in 1898 and the household registration system was formally incorporated into it,[29] the system was elevated to an indispensable element in the formation of the underlying foundation of the family law.[30] Since then, the household register not only has recorded births, deaths, marriages, divorces, and adoptions, but also has set out the relationships between family members. Whereas the register is compiled by household unit and some movements (such as a family member's marriage) necessarily occur within a household unit, the linkage system between the records allows lineage to be traced back through generations. As a consequence, by tracing successive registers relating to a deceased Japanese, one can easily identify whether and to what extent a given person is entitled to succeed as heir to the deceased's estate under Japanese law. For example, submitting a copy of registry to a bank, one can draw the deceased's deposit from the bank without any intervention of courts authenticating his or her heirship. Whereas nationality, in general, is said to be capable of identifying the applicable law with more certainty and more easiness than other connecting factors such as habitual residence, it seems that such certainty and easiness has been understood against the background of the Japanese household registry system and its reliability.[31]

42. The court must identify his or her *lex patriae*, when a person has two or more nationalities. Article 38(1) AGR distinguishes between the two groups of those who are of multiple nationalities. For those who hold foreign nationalities, the law of the nationality of the state in whose territory he or she has the habitual residence is regarded as the *lex patriae*. In the absence of it, the law of the state with which he or she is most closely connected is applicable. However, if a person has the nationality of Japan and of a foreign state, his or her *lex patriae* is always regarded as Japanese law. The preference given to Japanese nationality in this context derives

28. Unlike a western-style civil status register compiled by the individual, the Japanese one was compiled by the household unit which seems to have reflected the customary institution called '*ie*' prevailing at that time.
29. The Civil Code contained no provision defining the 'household'. Each household registry compiled under the Household Registration Act of 1889 made a particular household discernible to everyone's eyes. *See*, Shuhei Ninomiya, *The* Koseki *and Legal Gender Change*, in *Japan's Household Registration System and Citizenship* 170, 175 (David Chapman & Karl Jakob Krogness eds, Routledge 2014).
30. Ken Mukai & Nobuyoshi Toshitani, *The Progress and Problems of Compiling the Civil Code in the Early Meiji Era*, 1 Law in Japan 25, 48 (1967).
31. For the Japanese family registration system, *see*, Noriko Mizuno, *Parent-Child Relationship in the Japanese Civil Code Regarding Medical Technology for Reproductive Treatment*, 52 *J.Y.B.I.L.* 387, 389–398 (2009).

from the concern that, whereas Japanese administrative authorities, particularly in charge of keeping the family registration book, have no difficulty in ascertaining a person's Japanese nationality, the connecting criterion of the closest connection is not compatible with their limited powers of examination.

43. The said rules as laid down in Article 38(1) AGR apply, when the court determines the *lex patriae* common to the spouses as a law governing, e.g., divorce. The same *lex patriae* is not to be conceived as a law of the marital community but as a law which is familiar to each spouse in equal terms. It follows, for example, that, when a husband is a national of state A and a wife possesses the nationalities of the state A and of the state B, the court should, first, determine which the wife's *lex patriae* is. Only if her *lex patriae* is identified as the law of the state A, that law governs their divorce as the same *lex patriae.*

44. Pursuant to Article 38(2) AGR, habitual residence takes the place of nationality for a stateless person as a connecting factor determining his or her personal law. The habitual residence is not deemed to be on the equal footing with nationality in such a cascade of connecting criteria as laid down, e.g., in Article 25 AGR. For example, if a stateless husband is habitually resident in the state A and his wife is of nationality of the state A, it does not follow that the spouses have the same *lex patriae.* The law of state A may apply to the personal effects of marriage as a law of the common habitual residence, if she is also habitually resident in the states A. It should be added that the domiciliary law in the sense of Article 12 of the Convention Relating to the Status of Refugees of 1951 seems to be regarded as the law of his habitual residence.[32]

III. Residence

A. Domicile (of Origin, of Choice, of Dependence)

45. JPIL knows such notion of domicile as prevailing in common-law countries only in one provision, namely, Article 2(iii) of the Act on Governing Laws Relating to the Form of Testamentary Dispositions,[33] which derives from Article 1c) of the Hague Convention on the Conflict of Laws relating to the Form of Testamentary Dispositions.

B. Habitual Residence

46. It is in 1964 that the habitual residence appeared for the first time in Japanese PIL as one of the connecting factors as laid down in Article 2 of the Act on the Law Applicable to the Form of Testamentary Disposition. This connecting factor

32. *See*, Yokoyama, 55.
33. Act No. 100 of 10 Jun. 1964.

seems to have stroke root in JPIL after the ratifications of the two Hague Conventions relating to maintenance obligations, under which the habitual residence plays a primary role in determining the applicable law.[34] In 1989 when the *Horei* was revised, it was adopted as a connecting factor for effects of the mixed marriage and for divorce of such a couple, and for relationships between parents and child. In addition, it was allotted the role to identify the *lex patriae* for a person having more than one nationality and to be the substitute for nationality for a stateless person. Whereas the revised *Horei* kept the notion of habitual residence within the field of personal law, the AGR extends this connecting factor to that of contractual and non-contractual obligations (Articles 8, 15, and 20 AGR).

47. To date, the concept of 'habitual residence' has been used only in the field of private international law. It has no place in other fields of law, for example, tax law or social insurance law. There is no statutory rule aimed at defining the concept of habitual residence. The legislative silence is understandable, because the concept has been believed to be associated with the works of the Hague Conference on Private International Law. In addition, neither the Supreme Court nor inferior courts have had an opportunity to clarify it. Such absence of relevant judgments might be at least partly due to Japan's extremely late ratification of the 1980 Hague Abduction Convention whose application seems likely to raise the question when a child may change his or her habitual residence.

48. The factual aspect of the concept has been stressed in Japan.[35] It is true that it should be as free as possible from elements fictitious or artificial. However, the question whether or not a person's residence in a country qualifies 'habitual' seems to be subject to legal appraisal made in terms of the objectives of the provision. All that the present author can surely say about it are as follows.

49. First, under JPIL, the habitual residence has never been used as a jurisdictional basis but as a connecting factor determining the applicable law. The jurisdictional basis used in relation to the axiom of *actor sequitur forum rei* is the 'domicile' (*ju-sho*), although, normally, the both concepts are likely to overlap each other.[36] Second, the habitual residence serves as a subsidiary connecting factor determining the law applicable to the effects and the dissolution of marriage. In view of nationality being adopted as the primary connecting factor as regards those matters, the term of habitual residence may also be interpreted to connote some stability, even though it is not of permanent nature. Third, under the AGR, the habitual residence is employed outside the personal law field, namely, in relation to the presumptive rule of characteristic performance and as the connecting factor of the choice-of-law

34. The Convention of 24 Oct. 1956 on the Law Applicable to Maintenance Obligations towards Children and the Convention of 2 Oct. 1973 on the Law Applicable to Maintenance Obligations.

35. *See*, Ikehara, 168.

36. Given that the habitual residence is a tool for identifying one applicable law, it is submitted that a person can only have one habitual residence at a time. Whereas the *favor creditoris* as regards maintenance obligations is not entirely inconsistent with the idea according to which the claimant may have at his disposal the applicable laws as many as his habitual residences, such interpretation does not seem to be adopted by the Act on the Law Applicable to Maintenance Obligations.

rule on defamation claim. Fourth, given that the same concept should be understood consistently throughout the provisions of PIL, the place of one's habitual residence may be understood as a tool which stably associate interests of a person concerned with those of local people of the place where that person is a resident: spouses have interests in having as many a chance of remarriage as local people;[37] a merchant has interests in selling goods to foreign customers as easily as he does to local people;[38] a person has interests in keeping his reputation among local people;[39] a claimant has interests in obtaining maintenance as much as people next door.[40] It should be added that, the stable association with local people being required for acquisition of a habitual residence, some Japanese persons kidnapped by the North Korean military agents and forced to reside at its isolated areas seem to retain their habitual residences in Japan.

C. *Temporary Residence*

50. Article 39 AGR regards the temporary residence as a connecting factor subsidiary to the habitual residence when a person concerned is habitually resident nowhere.[41] It sometimes serves to delimit the sphere of application of some overriding mandatory rules. For example, some provisions as contained in the Child Welfare Act apply mandatorily, as far as the child in question is a resident in Japan. It is also used as a jurisdictional ground subsidiary to the domicile when a person concerned is domiciled nowhere in the world.[42]

IV. Registered Office

51. Whereas there has been no statutory basis, JPIL is said to have been faithful to the incorporation theory as regards the fate of legal persons.[43] Whether an entity may have rights and obligations as a legal person is, in principle, determined by the law of the country in which it was registered. In other words, it is immaterial to the question where its principal seat may be situated.

V. *Lex Loci Delicti*

52. According to Article 11 of the *Horei*, the *lex loci delicti* was applicable to obligations arising out of tort. At present, Article 17 AGR refers to the *lex loci damni* in general and to the *lex loci actus* in relation to certain types of cases where

37. Article 27 AGR.
38. Article 8 AGR.
39. Article 19 AGR.
40. Article 2, Act on the Law Applicable to Maintenance Obligations.
41. Article 39 AGR.
42. Article 3-2, CCP; Art. 3-2 of the bill amending the Personal Status Litigation Act.
43. *See*, Commentary I (Nishitani), 157–161.

the *lex loci damni* is likely to be only fortuitously determined. This general choice-of-law rule is followed by the two special rules for product liability (Article 18 AGR) and defamation (Article 19 AGR). The laws applicable pursuant to these three provisions may be displaced in favour of the law referred to by the escape clause (Article 20 AGR). Further, priority is given to the law chosen by parties after the tort took place (Article 21 AGR). In addition, the legislator decided to retain the double actionability rule for all kinds of torts (Article 22 AGR).

VI. *Lex Rei (Cartae) Sitae*

53. The place where an object is located has been a connecting factor of the choice-of-law rule on property rights since the enactment of *Horei*.[44] There is no choice-of-law rule dealing with property rights over registered ships and aircraft.

54. The AGR contains no choice-of-law rule dealing with questions on how rights embedded in negotiable instruments are to be transferred, either. It seems to have been accepted that the *lex cartae sitae* at the time of the transfer governs the question.[45]

§5. Changes in the Connecting Factors: Changes in the *Lex Causae*

55. Apart from property rights over immovable property, connecting factors such as nationality, habitual residence, and *situs* of movables, might move from one country to another. The legislator often takes care of such possibility of movement of a particular connecting factor. One basic idea is that once juridical act or status was validly made or established under one applicable law, another subsequently applicable law should not affect the validity of the existing act or status. When the legislator intends to express such idea as regards a particular matter, choice-of-law provisions explicitly refer to temporal elements. For example, the validity and binding force of a last will are governed by a testator's *lex patriae* at the time when the will was made.[46] In contrast, when a provision lacks the temporal element as regards a particular matter, the legislator often intends to let the applicable law be determined at each relevant time.

56. A choice-of-law rule always designates the *lex causae* as it stands at the time when Japanese judges apply it. When a choice-of-law rule designates a father's *lex patriae* at the child's birth, it means that Japanese judges should not apply the *lex patriae* designated by the father's current nationality but the current law of the state whose nationality he had when the child was born. When the substantive law rules of that country have been amended after the time of the child's birth, the new ones should be applied subject to its relevant transitional provisions.

---

44. Article 13 AGR.
45. *See*, Tameike, 343; Sakurada, 193.
46. Article 37(1) AGR.

§6. Combination of Connecting Factors

57. When a choice-of-law rule contains two or more connecting criteria, the designated legal systems may provide substantive solutions different from each other. On this presupposition, some choice-of-law rules arrange more than one connecting criteria in the alternative, distributive, or cumulative way. These choice-of-law rules imply the preference of a certain substantive value on the level of private international law and such preference overshadows the so-called neutrality of PIL.

58. Such connecting criteria being arranged in the alternative way, the legal system bringing about the result specified by the choice-of-law rule is applicable. For example, if a child is legitimate under a mother's *lex patriae* and not under a father's, the former is applicable. In case that the hypothetical applications of all the legal systems affirm the specified result, all of them apply. In case of all being negative about it, the law producing less negative effect applies. For example, the law whose effect is 'voidable' is preferred to that whose effect is 'void'.

59. According to Article 24(1) AGR, each of the parties must satisfy the substantive requirements of his or her own *lex patriae* in order to celebrate their marriage validly. One of the parties needs to comply only with his or her own personal law, but not the other party's law. In this sense, the distributive application of the two laws is distinguished from the cumulative one. It should be noted that, under the current AGR, only its Article 24(1) affords an example of the distributive application.

60. Some provisions of the AGR designate more than one legal system for one and the same legal question. For example, the adoptee's *lex patriae* as well as the adopter's one cumulatively apply to the question of the third persons' consents necessary for adoption.[47] Unless all the designated laws answer to a particular matter in the affirmative, a legal consequence such as adoption does not follow. In case of all being negative, the law producing more negative effect applies.

61. Whereas the alternative, distributive, and cumulative arrangements of connecting criteria are substantively oriented, their arrangement in cascade is neutral in terms of the substantive value. Article 25 AGR contains three different choice-of-law rules: the effects of the marriage are governed by the same *lex patriae* of the spouses; in the absence of such law, they are governed by the law of the same country in which both spouses have their habitual residence; in the absence of such law, they are governed by the law of the country with which the spouses are most closely connected. The provision applies, by analogy, to the matrimonial property of the spouses (Article 26 (1) AGR) and to the divorce (27 AGR). The arrangement of choice-of-law rules in cascade is also made as regards the relationships between parents and child (Article 32 AGR).

47. Article 31(1) AGR.

Chapter 3. Basic Terms

§1. CHARACTERIZATION (CLASSIFICATION)

62. We sometimes encounter the characterization problem even in relation to the domestic substantive law rules. For example, Article 263 of the Japanese Civil Code reads '[r]ights of common that have the character of co-ownership shall be governed by local custom and shall otherwise be subject to the application of the provisions of this Section.' Unlike the characterization under this substantive law rule, that of the choice-of-law rule is more complex and difficult, because choice-of-law rules are supposed to envisage the applicability of foreign substantive law rules against the background of which the parties make their allegations.

63. The parties sometimes make their allegations as if plural legal questions arose under one legal system, particularly under Japanese law. In such a case, the first step which a judge should take is to untie the bundle of legal questions which fall under the relevant categories different from each other. For example, when one joint heir X alleges that a third party Y to whom another joint heir Z assigned a portion of the estate before a division of the whole inherited estate shall return it to X, the judge should distinguish the part of the allegation concerning the co-ownership between the heirs (subject to the *lex successionis*) from the other part concerning the effect of assignment of the immovable property against the third party (subject to the *lex situs*).

64. Once the allegation is specified meaningfully, the judge proceeds to classify a particular legal question into a pertinent category enlisted in choice-of-law rules. JPIL normally provides no explicit guidance in relation to the problem.[48] Since the views of *Franz Kahn*[49] and *Etienne Bartin*[50] were introduced into the Japanese academic circles in the early twentieth century, the question of characterization has been considered almost synonymous with the question as to what law judges should rely on to decide the classification. The currently prevailing view is that it should be carried out in accordance with the rationales of the Japanese choice-of-law rules themselves, neither the substantive law rules of the *lex fori* nor of the *lex causae*. According to this view, judges are almost invariably expected to pay attention to which connecting criterion corresponding to each category would satisfy certain values such as the parties' justifiable expectations. For example, the *lex contractus* chosen by the parties would enable the debtor to know, at the time of the conclusion of the contract, how long he should keep his receipts and other documents. It follows that questions relating to prescription or limitation of action should fall into a category of the contract rather than the procedure. A Japanese judgment applied the

48. One exception is Art. 5 of Act on the Law Applicable to the Form of Wills which deems a certain limitation of forms of will as pertaining to matters of form. The provision derives from Art. 5 of the Hague Convention on the Conflicts of Laws Relating to the Form of Testamentary Dispositions.
49. Otto Lenel & Hans Lewald, *Abhandlungen zum internationalen Privatrecht von Franz Kahn,* Bd. 1 (München: Duncker & Humblot, 1928), 491 et seq.
50. Etienne Bartin, '*De l'impossibilité d'arriver à la suppression définitive des conflits de lois*', *Journal du droit international privé de M. Clunet,* 1897, 225 et seq.

English Limitation Act 1980 as a part of the *lex contractus*, irrespective of whether the relevant rules on statutes of limitation of the said Act were regarded as procedural in English law.[51]

65. However, it is not that the classification has been carried out completely free from the forum's substantive law rules. For example, a question as to whether the marriage may affect a spouse's name used to be classified into the personal effects of marriage. In contrast, the currently prevailing view is that all the questions relating to the name of a person should be classified into the matter of a person's status to be governed by his or her personal law. This shift of view seems to be intertwined with the abolishment of the household system underlying the Civil Code of 1898 under which the name played a role of identifying the membership of a particular household rather than an individual and under which a married woman normally became a member of the husband's household.

66. To the present author's knowledge, there is no opinion advocating the *lex causae* theory. However, it remains to be seen whether Japanese judges might leave the *lex situs* to determine the nature of property with regard to the term 'immovable property' as contained in Articles 8 and 26 AGR.

§2. Preliminary Question

67. Should the preliminary question be governed by a Japanese choice-of-law rule pertaining to that question or should it be governed by a relevant choice-of-law rule of a foreign law governing the main question? The problem has continued to be one of the most favourites of Japanese academic writers since *George Melchior*'s[52] and *Wilhelm Wengler*'s[53] works had been introduced to Japan in the 1930s. It is not until 1973 that a Japanese court faced a case in which the problem had practical significance in Japan.[54] In the case, a Taiwanese man died intestate leaving his immovable property in Japan. The main question of succession was governed by Taiwanese law as the *lex patriae* of the deceased. A Japanese woman claimed a share of the immovable property as his spouse under Taiwanese law. The deceased's Taiwanese father objected to it, alleging that the marriage between her and the deceased was void. Their alleged marriage, which had been undisputedly celebrated in Japan pursuant to Taiwanese law, did not fulfil the formal requirements pursuant to Japanese substantive law applicable as the *lex loci celebrationis* laid down by the Japanese choice-of-law rule. In contrast, that marriage was valid pursuant to the Taiwanese substantive law applicable as one of the *leges patriae* of the parties under the Taiwanese choice-of-law rule on the formal requirements of marriage. In this

51. Judgment of the Tokyo District Court, 26 Feb. 2002 (unpublished).
52. *Die Grundlagen des deutschen internationalen Privatrechts*, (Berlin: W. de Gruyter, 1932), 245 et seq.
53. '*Die Vorfrage im Kollisionsrecht*', *Rabels Zeitschrift*, 1934, 148 et seq.
54. Judgment of the Tokyo District Court, 26 Apr. 1973, 19 *J.A.I.L.*219 (1975).

case, the preliminary question was something more than purely academic. The following three conditions were certainly satisfied: the main question is governed by the law of a foreign country; a choice-of-law rule of that foreign country for the determination of the preliminary question refers to the law of a country different from that referred to by the corresponding Japanese choice-of-law rule; and the Japanese choice-of-law rule for the determination of the preliminary question leads to a different substantive result from that brought about by the corresponding choice-of-law rule adopted by the foreign country whose law governs the main question. The judge *in casu* simply applied the Japanese choice-of-law rule for the determination of the formal validity of marriage as if he were unaware of the problem of the preliminary question.

68. In 2000, the Supreme Court expressly adopted the view according to which the preliminary question should be governed by the Japanese choice-of-law rule pertaining to that question. In that case, the main question was the succession to be governed by Korean law and the preliminary one was the legitimate parenthood of an heir. The court held as follows: '[i]n a legal relationship with a foreign element, when there is not only a legal question (the main question) before a court but also a preliminary question which needs to be decided in order to solve the main question, and when that preliminary question consists of a different legal relationship from the main question, the law to govern such a preliminary question should be decided by the application of the choice-of-law rules of the forum, that is, the choice-of-law rules of Japan. Neither the substantive law governing the main question nor the law designated by the choice-of-law rules of the country to which the law governing the main question belongs should govern the preliminary question'.[55]

69. Whereas the Court's categorical remarks seem to reflect the view which prevailed in the last century among most of Japanese authors,[56] some recent academic writers are not of the opinion that such *lex fori* method would be valid in every single case. When the Japanese court exercises its jurisdiction to address the issue of succession, the defendant's domicile which founds the jurisdiction of Japanese courts seems to coincide with the last domicile of the deceased. This implies that there exists a fairly strong connection between the forum and the case. In such a case, the parties and the other persons concerned are likely to rely upon the Japanese family register in order to learn more about heirships. Given that the family register sets out the relationships between the family members pursuant to Japanese law including PIL, it may safely be said that all the persons concerned are usually expected to foresee Japanese law, for example, as regards the alleged surviving spouse's family relationship. The remarks made by the Supreme Court as mentioned above should be understood against such a background. Conversely, when the Japanese family register is unlikely to provide adequate information over the heirship, there would be a room for the Japanese court to adopt the view according to which the preliminary question should be governed by the relevant choice-of-law

55. Judgment of the Supreme Court, 27 Jan. 2000, 43 *J.A.I.L.* 197 (2000).
56. For such a view, *see,* Tameike, 227–230; Sakurada, 146.

rule of the foreign law governing the main question. That would be the case where the deceased and the alleged spouse had, for a prolonged period of time, their habitual residence in a foreign country whose law was also the *lex patriae* of the deceased.

70. The drawback inherent in that view is that it disturbs some internal harmony; for example, a woman is regarded as the deceased's wife for the succession and not for other legal relationships. However, the disturbance in such sense is far from decisive in rejecting the '*lex causae* approach'. Article 6(2) AGR on the disappearance of natural person enables the Japanese court to declare that a person is deemed dead only for such a particular relationship as marriage, when the person in question is neither of Japanese nationality nor domiciled in Japan. It is submitted that JPIL undoubtedly can live with the disturbance of a certain internal harmony, as far as the main interests of the persons involved are localized in a particular foreign country.

71. It seems that, whereas the *lex fori* method is basically preferable, the *lex causae* one may be more appropriate when no Japanese choice-of-law rules are capable of referring to the law relevant to the interests of the persons involved.[57]

§3. Substance and Procedure

72. Whereas substance is governed by the *lex causae*, procedure is governed by the *lex fori*. Particularly inspired by Article 25 (1) of the draft for the Belgian Civil Code made by *François Laurent* in 1882, Article 13 (1) of the *Former Horei* provided that matters of procedure should be governed by the law of the country of the court before which legal proceedings were taken. However, the legislator of the *Horei* took this principle as self-evident. Since 1898, there has been no explicit provision expressing it in JPIL.

73. When particular procedural rules are originally designed to accommodate themselves to the substantive institution peculiar to the *lex fori*, the foreign *lex causae* which knows no such institution would not be applicable without assimilation. For example, in the Japanese court practice, a spouse must petition for the conciliation proceedings at the family court, even though the foreign law applicable to divorce requires the party to proceed directly to divorce litigation.[58] Apart from such procedural rules, the rationale of the principle that procedure should be governed by the *lex fori* seems to lie in the practical consideration that local judges should not be obliged to conduct the proceeding in accordance with foreign procedural rules unfamiliar to them. Convenience being decisive, it follows that a foreign law should be applied when it can be applied without causing much inconvenience. It does not entail, however, that the clear demarcation line between substance and procedure can always be drawn. For example, a Japanese court at the first instance held

57. Yokoyama, 83; Kidana, 138–139.
58. *See*, para. 294 *infra*.

that, whereas the questions of heads of damages were substantive in tort actions, those of quantification of damages should be dealt with as procedural matters. In contrast, the appellate court *in casu* classified both questions into substantive matters, preferring the recourse to the *ordre public* in order to avoid the application of Argentine law as the *lex loci delicti* which would limit damages to extremely lesser sum in the eyes of the court.[59] It should be noted in relation to this case that, whereas the traffic accident took place in Argentine, the both parties were habitually resident in Japan. If Article 20 AGR, an exception clause, had been already in force, no one would have hesitated to apply Japanese law to both questions as a *lex causae*.[60]

§4. *Renvoi*

74. Since the enactment of the *Horei* in 1898, JPIL accepted the *renvoi* in the form of *renvoi au premier degré*. In the middle of the twentieth century, the *renvoi* was, *de lege ferenda,* criticized by academic writers with such catchwords as vicious circle or international table tennis. However, in the 1970s, voices were raised against such legislative criticism because it turned out to produce nothing constructive, *de lege lata*.[61] Indeed, the court continued to accept the reference back to Japanese law. In 1989 when the *Horei* was revised and in 2006 when the AGR was enacted, it were the judges who urged the Legislative Councils to retain the *renvoi* clause in spite of the proposal calling for its abrogation.[62]

75. Since the enactment of the *Horei*, the *renvoi* has meant the reference back to Japanese substantive law and has been restricted to matters governed by the *lex patriae,* namely, matters of personal status, family, and succession.[63] The current provision (Article 41 AGR) also reads as follows: '[i]f a person's national law is designated and that law refers back to Japanese law, Japanese law shall apply'.

76. The *renvoi* laid down by this provision is obviously a tool to make the administration of justice easier.[64] As mentioned above, the *renvoi* clause was retained at the strong urging of judges. What they particularly bore in mind in doing so was the difficult or puzzling problem which they would otherwise face in applying the law of the DPRK. Under the DPRK PIL, which was enacted and came into

59. Judgment of the Fukuoka High Court, 10 Feb. 2009, 53 *J.A.I.L.* 596 (2010).
60. *See*, Commentary I (Nishitani), 459.
61. *See*, Ikehara, 212.
62. *See*, Koide, 371–372.
63. Article 43 provides that the choice-of-law rules contained in the AGR do not apply to maintenance obligations arising from a family relationship, parentage, marriage, or affinity nor to the form of testamentary dispositions. The rejection of the *renvoi* in these law fields reflects the related two Hague Conventions according to which the 'internal law' is referred to. In addition, the reference back to Japanese law is only allowed, when the foreign law is referred to as a *lex patriae* of a natural person, namely, as a personal law. Otherwise, the foreign substantive law should be applied. It is also the case where a party's *lex patriae* happens to be the law which the parties chose as a law governing the contract, the tort or the matrimonial property regime.
64. *See*, Yokoyama, 71.

force on 6 September 1995, the connecting factor of the personal law is, in principle, nationality. There are, however, exceptions to the mandatory use of nationality as a determining connecting factor. Opting for a system of scission for succession, the DPRK PIL refers to the *lex situs* with respect to the succession of immovable property (Article 45 thereof). It may safely be said that this very provision drove the judges who were the members of the Legislative Council in charge of the enactment of the AGR to call for the survival of the *renvoi* clause. How could a Japanese court be expected to apply the substantive law of the DPRK under whose constitutional law the ownership of land cannot be inherited, when a portion of the land situated in Tokyo is a part of the inheritable estate of the deceased Korean? The application of Japanese law appeared to be the only feasible solution. It is true that, without accepting the reference back from DPRK law, Japanese judges might be able to apply Japanese law on the basis of the following reasoning: the sphere of application of the substantive law rules which are inextricably interwoven with the state's exclusive ownership of land are presumably limited to the boundary of the territory of the DPRK; inevitably, there is lacuna in the DPRK succession law as regards a portion of land situated in foreign countries including Japan; and the Japanese judge should apply his own law to fill the gap. But, judges do not like to engage in such subtle interpretation of a foreign law, which might remind us of the unilateralist's approach or the *désistement* theory. They needed a black-letter rule, which explicitly enables them to apply Japanese law, namely, the *renvoi* clause.

77. What we said about the DPRK is true with the People's Republic of China. The current Chinese choice-of-law rule on succession adopts the system of scission.[65] China's substantive rules on succession can also be understood only against the legal background that land is exclusively owned by the state or by the collective organizations. When the deceased Chinese's immovable property is situated in Japan, the application of Japanese law would undoubtedly facilitate the administration of justice.

78. It is worthy of noting that, even though the pragmatic idea underlies the acceptance of the renvoi in such an egoistic form, it has chance to enhance the international harmony of decisions to some extent. During discussions about the *renvoi*, the Legislative Council of 1989 appeared to pay little attention to the fact that it was uncertain whether the Chinese choice-of-law rules admitted the *renvoi*, too. In other words, their central concern was the easier administration of justice rather than the international harmony of decisions. Whatever role they expected the *renvoi* clause to play, it turns out to be capable of enhancing the harmony in relation to China, because Article 9 of the current Chinese PIL explicitly rejects the *renvoi*. So do Article 20 of the Peruvian Private International Law and Article 16 of the Brazilian Private International Law.[66] It follows that the unilateral acceptance of the *renvoi* on the Japanese side may promote the international harmony of decisions between

65. Article 31 of Chinese PIL.

66. Peru and Brazil have been the major countries whose nationals have been domiciled in Japan for a prolonged period of time as migrant workers.

these legal systems and the Japanese one. The same might be true with Hong Kong, because the common law *renvoi* doctrine does not seem to prevail there.[67]

79. Articles 29(1) AGR on acknowledgement and 31 (1) AGR on adoption are interpreted to exclude the *renvoi* in favour of the best interest of the child. When the *lex patriae* of the adopted child requires the consent for adoption by the third persons, institutions, and authorities, the relevant substantive law rules should be applied (Article 31 (1) AGR). For the purpose of ensuring the best interests of the adopted child, the relevant substantive law rules mandatorily applied under the *lex patriae* of the child have to be respected by Japanese judges. The exclusion of *renvoi* in favour of the best interests of the child holds true with the case where the *lex patriae* of the child born out of wedlock requires the consent to be given to an alleged father's voluntary acknowledgement by the relevant persons (Article 29 (1) AGR).

80. The *Horei* contained certain choice-of-law rules whose connecting factors were husband-oriented. In 1989, the legislator revised those choice-of-law rules so as to make them conformable to the principle of gender equality. This was achieved by substituting the husband's nationality with a cascade of connecting criteria common to the spouses, starting with the nationality which both spouses share. In connection with the spouses' *lex patriae*, the concern arose that, when the reference back from the *lex patriae* is accepted, Japanese judges might still be obliged to take into account a husband-oriented foreign choice-of-law rule. Such concerns drove the legislator to enact a provision designed to refuse accepting, in all cases, the reference back to Japanese law from the national law which the spouses share. A particular foreign choice-of-law rule which the legislator bore in mind at that time was Article 7(7) of the Introductory Law to the Civil Code of Brazil, which regards the domicile (*domicilio*) of the head of family as that of the other spouse. That Japanese provision which requires the court to apply invariably the substantive rules of the same national law of the spouses has remained unaltered in the AGR. The second part of Article 41 AGR sets out that the *renvoi* clause shall not apply to a case where the person's national law is to apply in accordance with Articles 25–27, namely, the choice-of-law rules relating to the personal effects of marriage, the matrimonial property regime, and the divorce.[68]

---

67. *See*, Graeme Johnston, *The Conflict of Laws in Hong Kong* 42 (2nd ed., Thomson Reuters 2012). Furthermore, it is submitted that the *renvoi* might make a useful addition of connecting factors to those which the legislator unsatisfactorily provided. The private international law of the ROK, in principle, admits the *renvoi*. This does not necessarily entail, however, that the acceptance of the *renvoi* on both sides of the Strait will necessarily result in the disharmony of decisions. The ROK private international law excludes the *renvoi* when the party avail himself or herself of a choice of law (Art. 9 of its PIL). Consequently, when a Korean testator chooses Japanese law pursuant to Art. 49 of the ROK PIL which allows the testator to choose either the law of his or her habitual residence at the time of choice or the *lex situs* with respect to the inheritance of immovable property, the respect of his or her choice of Japanese law by Japanese judges does not seem to disturb the international harmony of decisions.
68. It is submitted, however, that the acceptance of the *renvoi* does not run counter to the principle of gender equality when the relevant foreign choice-of-law rules are considered consistent with that principle. The total rejection of the *renvoi* from the same national law of the spouses certainly goes

81. The *lex patriae* referred to by a choice-of-law rule notably on such matters as divorce and adoption may adopt the jurisdictional approach to solve these matters. When Japanese courts find themselves seen as jurisdictionally competent either concurrently or exclusively in the eyes of the *lex patriae*, they tend to regard such jurisdictional grounds as adoptee's or adopter's domicile as bilateral connecting criteria in the sense of choice-of-law rules, with the result that they have often applied Japanese law with recourse to the *renvoi* clause. The academic writers criticized those judgments accepting the 'hidden' *renvoi* as distorting the *lex patriae's* rules on jurisdiction. Despite such criticism, however, the courts did not change their attitude towards the hidden *renvoi*. As one of the academic writers rightfully pointed out, it seems that the hidden *renvoi* is falsely thought of as the *renvoi* in the sense of Article 41 AGR.[69] According to this view, the Japanese court should not apply Japanese law pursuant to that *renvoi* clause but the substantive law rules of the *lex patriae*.[70] In adopting the jurisdictional approach, state laws of the US seem to intend to have their own courts unilaterally apply their own substantive law rules. Whereas they might be interested in whether foreign decrees on divorce or adoption deserve recognition in their states, they appear to be indifferent to what substantive law rules were applied by foreign courts. It seems that, in such indifference to the coordination of legal systems in terms of choice-of-law rules, we may detect a lacuna to be filled with Japanese law. It should be added that the number of cases explainable in terms of the hidden *renvoi* has steadily decreased for the last three decades. This seems due to the fact that the 1989 version of the *Horei* adopts the common habitual residence of the spouses for the dissolution of the mixed marriage and the nationality of the adoptive parent for adoption as the connecting criteria, which have turned out to refer to Japanese law in most cases.

§5. General Conflict Rules/Special Conflict Rule

82. The primary and general choice-of-law rules are contained in the AGR. Other choice-of-law rules exceptionally apply according to the maxim of *lex specialis derogate legi generali*. For example, Article 77(2) of the Cheques Act, which adopts the *renvoi au second degré* in relation to a person's capacity to bind himself by a cheque, takes priority over Article 41 AGR.

---

too far. Consequently, the Legislative Council of 2006 agreed, during the discussions for proposing the current AGR, that the provision which, if literally read, would entirely reject the renvoi from the same national law of the spouses, might be interpreted restrictively, namely, in such a way that, only in so far as a foreign choice-of-law rule is inconsistent with that principle, the reference back to Japanese law would be rejected. It follows that, if the current Brazilian choice-of-law rules relating to family matters are interpreted in line with that principle, it would result in accepting the *renvoi* on the Japanese side. *See also*, Commentary II (Kitazawa), 323.

69. *See*, Ikehara, 217.

70. *See*, Commentary II (Kitazawa), 331.

§6. ASSIMILATION

83. Every bilateral choice-of-law rule designates the most appropriate legal system for each category indicated by each rule. Even when two or more legal systems are called on to resolve one and the same dispute, such combination of diverse legal systems normally works well. However, one cannot always expect substantive rules of different origins to apply in a coherent way.

84. It is true that some choice-of-law rules of the AGR are designed to avoid incoherent applications of diverse rules. Article 20 AGR on tort aims to avoid the problem of assimilation which the concurrent liabilities may entail, by means of aligning the law applicable to tort with the law applicable to contractual obligations. According to Article 31 AGR on adoption, the *lex patriae* of the adopter at the time of the adoption governs its legal effects as well as its valid establishment. Otherwise, an *adoption simple* established under a law might turn into an *adoption plénière* under another law.

85. Classification might help organizing some coordination between substantive law rules belonging to different legal systems. For example, the *lex successionis* applies on condition that, under the *lex loci delicti*, a victim's right to claim damages is inheritable. A Taiwanese person, whose relative was killed by a plane clash in Japan, claimed damages against a Taiwanese airline as the deceased's heir. The *lex successionis* is Taiwanese law under which the compensation of the victim's lost life should be claimed by his family members based on their own rights, not through inheritance of the right of the deceased. In contrast, according to Japanese law, the *lex loci delicti*, the victim's right to claim all the loss can be inherited by his heir. A Japanese judgment applied Japanese law as the *lex loci delicti* in determining whether the victim's right to claim damages for his lost life is inheritable.[71]

86. Article 31 AGR contains no choice-of-law rule specifically dealing with the situation where a married couple adopts the same child. The legislator seems to have stood upon the assumption that, in such a situation, the two adoptions, the one between the adoptive father and the child and the other between the adoptive mother and the same child, would be established at the same time. This idea of double adoption causes no difficulty, as far as the husband and the wife are of the same nationality. However, when they are a mixed couple, it is likely to lead to the assimilation problem difficult to be resolved: for example, whereas the *lex patriae* of a spouse only knows the *adoption plénière,* the *adoption simple* is the solely permissible form of adoption under the other's *lex patriae*. The legislator was aware of this problem, but left the solution to the development of case law.

87. The assimilation problem, which was a most controversial among academic writers in the 1960s and 1970s, was how the court should assimilate foreign divorce

71. Judgment of the Nagoya District Court, 26 Dec. 2003, *Hanji* 1854-63.

laws with the 'conciliation first' rule under Japanese law applicable as the *lex fori*.[72] Even when the divorce conciliation is successful, it is hardly the result of the court's 'faithful application' of a foreign law, when the foreign law does not know the divorce by agreement but only the judicial divorce. One possible form of coordination between such foreign divorce law and the forum's law of procedure would be that, placing priority on the faithful application of such foreign law and at the expense of the 'conciliation first' rule, the court should allow a spouse to make a direct petition for the judicial divorce. However, whereas Japanese courts have always been mindful of uncertainty about such conciliation being recognized in foreign countries involved, they have not given up the application of the 'conciliation first' rule.[73]

88. It is hardly possible to formulate the general terms as to show the assimilation should be made. Experience tells that the distorted application of substantive law rules seems more likely to take place when they are foreign laws.

§7. Ordre Public (Public Policy)

89. Article 42 AGR allows Japanese courts to refuse the application of the governing foreign law, when its application yields a result contrary to the Japanese *ordre public*.

90. The *ordre public* exception may only be used when the three conditions are met. First, the application of a governing foreign law to an individual case must be found unacceptable in the eyes of Japanese law. The Japanese court does not pass judgment upon the abstract content of the foreign law itself. For example, a couple of 18 years of age may celebrate their marriage in Japan under their *lex patriae* which allows the 'child marriage'. Second, such an intolerable result must be brought about by fundamental difference between the governing foreign law and Japanese law. In other words, the mere difference between the two does not trigger the application of the *ordre public*, even though they yield the diametrically opposite results.[74] Third, there must be a certain links between the case and the forum (*Inlandsbeziehung*). How closely a case should be connected with the forum for the exclusion of foreign law seems to depend upon how universally accepted is the value which would be endangered by the application of the foreign law. The more universal the value in question is estimated, the less the link with the forum is required. For example, although Japanese family registrars are not empowered to make an enquiry into elements of individual circumstances which connect the fiancés with the forum, they were allowed to celebrate the marriage between a South

72. Under Japanese law, when a couple fails to reach an agreement on their divorce, they are required to make a petition to the family court for divorce conciliation prior to litigation. *See*, Minamikata, 85.

73. *See*, para. 294 *infra*.

74. Judgment of the Supreme Court, 27 Jun. 1975, *Kagetsu* 28-4-83. Japanese authors had tendency not to refer to this requirement for the operation of the *ordre public*. They may have tried to allot the role of a general exception clause to the *ordre public*.

African man and a Japanese woman, disregarding the law of South Africa which forbade interracial marriages.[75] In contrast, the more local the value is, the more the link with the forum is required. For example, in most of the cases where the Japanese courts excluded the application of Philippine law, which prohibits divorce, the elements of them seem to be almost identical: a Japanese wife habitually resident in Japan petitioned for divorce from a Philippine husband also habitually resident there.

91. When the application of the governing foreign law turns out to be intolerable from the viewpoint of Japanese law, its application is excluded. This is what Article 42 AGR sets out. The exclusion inevitably results from the overriding conclusion that a judge has reached in relation to an individual case in the eyes of Japanese law: for example, since the conclusion of 'X and Y shall be divorced' is inconsistent with that of 'X and Y cannot be divorced' and the former conclusion overrides the latter, the foreign law whose hypothetical application leads to the latter is excluded.

92. If the marriage of X and Y is void simply on account of difference of religion under the governing foreign law and the nullity of the marriage of X and Y leads to the operation of the exception of *ordre public*, the court will apply the governing foreign law to the exclusion of its particular substantive law rule laying down impediments founded on difference of religion.[76] However, the simple exclusion does not necessarily provide a judge with practically adequate solution of a case on its own.

93. One may ask a question as to what law a judge should apply to a case in which X, a Philippine wife, petitions for divorce from Y, a Philippine husband, when the judge has excluded Philippine law as a law applicable to the case. When the judge is asked to respond to a divorce petition in the form of either acceptance or rejection, most of academic authors are of the opinion that the exclusion of a foreign law leaves no gap to be filled with a law other than Japanese law. Since the overriding individual and concrete norm to the effect that X and Y should get divorced in accordance with the standards of Japanese law entailed the exclusion of Philippine law, no other alternative but to apply Japanese law would be left for the judge.[77]

94. A judge is not always asked to respond to an application or a petition in the form of either acceptance or rejection. He is sometimes called for to take a more positive measure. As far as such a measure is concerned, there arises a gap to be filled with some legal system. Suppose that, while the governing foreign law automatically grants the right of custody for the child to the father on divorce, X, the mother, petitioned for being a custodian because Y, the father in the concrete case,

---

75. Circular No. 1320 dated 17 Nov. 1973 issued by the Ministry of Justice.
76. The judgment of the Tokyo District Court, 29 Mar. 1991, 35 *J.A.I.L.* 184 (1992) excluded the rules of religious marriage impediments of Egyptian Law.
77. *See*, Ikehara, 262.

is not in a position to exercise his right properly. The overriding concrete norm which leads to the exclusion of the governing foreign law is that Y should not be a sole custodian of the child. It does not go so far as to require that X be a sole custodian. The question remains unanswered whether the child should be placed under the sole custody of X or under the joint custody of X and Y. Even if the overriding concrete norm derives from the standards of Japanese law, it does not follow that the above question should be necessarily answered by Japanese law. The judge might search newly for a law applicable to some adequate measure in order to fill a gap. The AGR has no provision such as Article 16 (2) of 'Reform of the Italian System of Private International Law', according to which, given the inapplicability of foreign law on the ground of *ordre public*, the law to be applied is that which is referred to by another connecting factor in cascade provided for the same matter. The recourse to a subsidiary law pursuant to a choice-of-law rule with a range of connecting criteria in cascade may be conceivable, *de lege lata,* for JPIL, too. It should be noted that, if a gap arises only in relation to cases where courts have to take some positive measure, it would be Article 32 AGR that may provide such a subsidiary connecting criterion.[78] There is a judgment of the Tokyo District Court to that effect, indeed.[79] It applied Japanese law as law of the child's habitual residence rather than as the *lex fori*, after having excluded the application of the child's *lex patriae,* Korean law, which automatically conferred upon the father the parental authority on divorce. However, we doubt that the search for another law on the basis of the subsidiary connecting criterion is practically significant in so far as JP is concerned. The requirement of the *Inlandsbeziehung* seems to make such search for the subsidiary law less compelling. In connection with the legal relationships between parents and child, the exception of *ordre public* is unlikely to come into operation without the child's habitual residence in the forum country. Under JPIL, the *lex fori* is most likely to be the law of the country of the habitual residence of the child and, therefore, suitable for filling the vacuum.[80]

---

78. In contrast, the search for a law on the basis of another connecting factor seems to be superfluous in certain situations. For example, when a Japanese court should apply Philippine law as the same national law of the spouses in the divorce proceedings but find its application intolerable in that case, it is very likely that the court has already come to the conclusion that the spouses should get divorced. This conclusion would remain unchanged, whatever law may be chosen on the basis of another connecting factor. In such a case, to look for a law on the basis of another criterion, e.g., the common habitual residence of the spouses seems to mean nothing more than to seek a law that may endorse the conclusion that the court has reached beforehand. *See*, Jun Yokoyama, *Reform of Japanese Private International Law and Public Policy*, in *Private Law in the International Arena* 851, 861 (Jürgen Basedow, Isaak Meier, Anton K. Schnyder, Talia Einhorn & Daniel Girsberger eds., T.M.C. Asser Press 2000).
79. Judgment, 28 Nov. 1990, 35 *J.A.I.L.*167 (1992).
80. Yokoyama, 102–103.

§8. Overriding Mandatory Rules

95. Unlike Chinese and Korean PIL, the AGR has no explicit provision relating to overriding mandatory rules.[81] It is simply because the legislator of the AGR found it difficult to explain to the Members of Diet convincingly the outer limits of this category of rules.[82]

96. Undoubtedly, certain mandatory rules, which may affect legal relationships between private parties, basically remain outside of the coordination between legal systems. There are the mandatory rules whose legislative purposes require them to apply to situations which, according to ordinary choice-of-law rules, are not subject to the *lex fori.* Their application is not determined by the ordinary (bilateral) choice-of-law rules but by their proper (unilateral) choice-of-law rules. For example, even when Article 32 AGR designates a foreign law as a child's *lex patriae*, the relevant rules as contained in the Child Welfare Act apply mandatorily,[83] as far as the case falls under the implicit ambit of the Act, namely, a child's residence in Japan.[84] Another example is Article 61 of the Labour Standards Act which prohibits an employer from having a person under 18 years of age work between the hours of 10 p.m. and 5 a.m.[85] When the case falls under the implicit ambit of the Act, namely, an employee's habitual workplace in Japan, the Act necessarily applies, irrespective of the *lex contractus* chosen by the parties (Article 7 of the AGR) or determined by Article 12 AGR which specifically deals with the employment contract. The spatial ambits of overriding mandatory rules are not necessarily territorial.[86] They may have even personal criteria. Article 18 (1) of the Unfair Competition Prevention Act, which prohibits bribery of foreign public officers in connection with commercial transactions, applies to Japanese businessmen wherever they tried to commit bribery.[87] Pursuant to that provision, Japanese courts will prohibit a Japanese businessman from performing contractual obligations, as far as the performance corresponds to the 'wrongful benefitting' set out by the said provision.

97. Japanese courts, in principle, do not coordinate with foreign legal systems in the form of applying their overriding mandatory rules. However, certain legal relevance has been given to them as data to be evaluated within the framework of the *lex causae.* A judgment took into account foreign overriding mandatory rules as facts which tainted a contract with immorality under the *lex contractus*. An American entered into an insurance contract with a Japanese insurance company to cover the transport by sea of his Persian carpets from Japan to California. The carpets

81. Article 4 of Chinese PIL and Art. 7 of Korean PIL.
82. *See*, Koide, 88.
83. Act No. 164 of 12 Dec. 1947.
84. For example, pursuant to Art. 27 of the said Act, a prefectural government shall take a measure necessary to protect a child, placing a child under a foster family or a child welfare institution.
85. Act No. 49 of 7 Apr. 1947.
86. Judgment of the Supreme Court, 12 Dec. 2017, 61 *J.Y.B.I.L.* 399 (2018) states that the provisions of the Japanese Anti-Monopoly Act should apply to cartel agreements concluded outside Japan, as far as they disturb the free competition economic order of Japan
87. Act No. 47 of 9 May 1993.

were lost on the way to California and the owner claimed damages under the insurance contract governed by Japanese law. The defendant insurance company alleged that the importation of any goods of Iranian origin into the US was prohibited under the Iranian Transactions and Sanctions Regulations of the US and that such contract was contrary to the *bonnes moeurs* in the sense of Article 90 of the Japanese Civil Code applicable to the contract.[88]

§9. Evasion of the Law

98. Evasion of the law has been understood to mean a party's fraudulent manipulation of a connecting factor with his intent to avoid the application of one law and to obtain the result of the application of another law more favourable to him. It seems that the doctrine of evasion of law has hardly developed in Japan.[89] It is fairly safe to say that there is no court practice which, in the name of evasion of law or with recourse to abuse, has applied the law that would apply if evasion had not occurred. The main reason of such negative attitude towards the doctrine of evasion of law is mainly due to the belief that it must be difficult to prove a party's intent to manipulate the relevant connecting factor in question. Furthermore, it is feared that to question always whether a person's activities leading to the alteration of a connecting factor are legitimate and genuine might entail legal uncertainty in the application of choice-of-law rules.[90]

§10. Reference to the Law of State with Multiple Legal Orders

99. Article 38 (3) AGR envisages the situation where the connecting factor 'nationality' leads to a law of state consisting of more than one law districts. If such a state has an internal choice-of-law rule designating which district's law applies to a person in question as a personal law, the court should apply the law of the district pursuant to that internal choice-of-law rule.[91] In the absence of such internal rule, the court is called on to have recourse to the connecting factor of 'the closest connection' in identifying the law district from the viewpoint of JPIL. For example, US has been believed to have no internal choice-of-law rules designed to identify such a law district. This is also the case with China. Although the said provision specifies no factors which the court should take into consideration in applying the 'closest connection' test, to search, in the first place, a person's habitual residence in a law district would ensure consistency with Paragraphs 1 and 2 of the said article which,

88. Judgment of the Tokyo District Court, 13 May 1998, *Hanji* 1676-129. However, the appellate court overturned it, stating that, unlike drugs and weapons, illegality under US law would not lead to immorality under Japanese law (Judgment of the Tokyo High Court, 9 Feb. 2000, *Hanji* 1749-157).
89. Article 10 of the Former *Horei* contained a provision inspired by the doctrine of the *fraude à la loi* in relation to the form of juridical act.
90. *See*, Ikehara, 286.
91. It should be noted that the case at hand is not entirely left to such an internal rule. The provision refers to such a rule only for the purpose of identifying a personal law within the state.

with explicit reference to a person's habitual residence, deals with a person with multiple foreign nationalities and a stateless person, respectively.

100. The court applies the rules as mentioned above to each person.[92] This is the case when the *lex patriae* common to the spouses should be determined. If a wife is most closely connected with New York (or Hong Kong) and her husband is so with California (Macao), the spouses have no same *lex patriae*. When both of them are habitually resident in Japan, Japanese law will apply to, for example, their divorce.

101. Taiwan is not 'foreign' in the eyes of China (the People's Republic of China).[93] For Taiwan (the Republic of China), the Mainland China is simply the 'Mainland Area.'[94] Then, a puzzling question is raised for Japanese judges. Which law is the *lex patriae* of a so-called Chinese, when China and Taiwan, both, claim that he or she is their own national? The debate arose about this question in the middle of the twentieth century within the Japanese academic circles.[95] The two approaches to take to it were proposed: the one that regards the so-called Chinese as holding the dual nationality;[96] the other that localizes such a person in one of the two law districts on the assumption that the Mainland China and Taiwan form a single state.[97] Most of decisions rendered by Japanese courts have adopted either of the two approaches. To whichever approach authors and judges might give preference, they have shared the following two points under the *Horei*: the pre-existing choice-of-law rules on multiple nationalities and on composite legal system do not apply to the question, because the nineteenth century legislator was unaware of the current situation in which the Mainland China and Taiwan are involved; and the only feasible way to take is to have recourse to the criterion of 'the closest connection' in each case, particularly attaching great importance to the choice of law by a person in question.[98] It should be added that Japanese courts were more frequently called on to tackle the same kind of problem in the same way in relation to Korean people whose number was much more than that of Chinese people in Japan.

102. It appears that, while drafting the current AGR, the Legislative Council did not want to choose legislatively either of the two approaches as mentioned above.[99] Demographic changes which have been occurring in Japan since the 1990s seemed

92. Cf. Tadashi Kanzaki, *Determination of the Nationals of Two Persons with Nationality of the Same Non-unified State*, 57 *J.Y.B.I.L.* 415 et seq. (2014).
93. *See*, Art. 5 of the Regulation on the Problems of Jurisdiction of Foreign-Related Civil and Commercial Litigation, promulgated by the Supreme People's Court of the PRC, in force since 1 Mar. 2002.
94. *See*, Art. 1 of the Taiwanese Act Governing Relations between Peoples of the Taiwan Area and the Mainland Area, in force since 31 Jul. 1991.
95. For the current situation of debates, *see*, Yayohi Sato, *Law Applicable to Personal Status of Korean and Chinese Nationals Before Japanese Courts*, 55 *J.Y.B.I.L.* 323 et seq. (2012).
96. Ikehara, 149–150.
97. Tameike, 192.
98. Most frequently, a Chinese is a member of either of the private organizations which support China and Taiwan. Thus, the objective factor of a person's membership seemed to serve preventing the fraudulent choice of law.
99. Koide, 377.

to lead to their wait-and-see attitude. Whatever causes may be attributed to the legislative silence, they left the court to identify the *lex patriae* of Chinese and Korean. It is submitted that, under the current AGR, Article 38 (1) on multiple nationalities should apply to that problem. Article 38 (3) which addresses the territorially composite legal system potentially capable of enacting the internal choice-of-law rules seems irrelevant to the relation between the Mainland China and Taiwan.

103. Article 40 (1) AGR deals with the situation where the connecting factor 'nationality' leads to a law of a state consisting of personal laws varying with categories of persons. If there are internal rules in force in such a state capable of identifying which personal law applies, the court should apply the relevant personal law pursuant to such rules, and, in the absence of such rules, the personal law with which the person has the closest connection. The said provision analogically applies to the case where the connecting factors of 'habitual residence' and 'the place where the spouses are most closely connected with' refers to such a state's law, because the connecting factors, spatial in nature, are not capable of identifying a personal category.

104. These explicit rules are newly made in line with its predecessor, namely, Article 7 of the Act on the Law Applicable to Maintenance Obligations incorporating the Hague Convention of 2 October 1973 on the Law Applicable to Maintenance Obligations. Although the Legislative Council was aware of the necessity of such rules in the field of personal law in general, it is not that they fully explored legal problems which might arise, when a Japanese choice-of-law rule designates laws of such Asian countries as Indonesia and Malaysia. It seems, however, that, not only under the *Horei* but also under the AGR, Japanese courts have seldom faced difficult problems in applying the law of the state consisting of different personal laws. In India, for example, the Hindu Marriage Act 1955 and the Parsi Marriage and Divorce Act 1936 regulate the marriage between two Hindus and that between two Parsis, respectively.[100] Whereas, at first glance, it looks as if two personal laws competed each other, each personal law, in reality, regulates the legal relationships between the members belonging to the same religion. It follows, in most of cases, that the court can identify a particular personal law without difficulty, when all the persons concerned belong to the same personal group. Even though the members of two or more different personal groups are involved in a legal relationship such as marriage, it does not necessarily bring about the conflict of laws. The legal systems consisting of personal laws varying according to categories of persons seem to make arrangements to accommodate different personal laws in a coherent way, e.g., by means of giving priority to a particular (dominant) personal law over the other personal laws[101] or by means of filling the gap with creating special substantive law rules.[102] These arrangements seem similar to those based on

100. Paras Diwan & Peeyushi Diwan, *Private International Law, Indian and English* 246–248 (4th ed., Deep & Deep Publications 1998).
101. Maurits S. Berger, *Conflicts Law and Public Policy in Egyptian Family Law: Islamic Law Through the Backdoor* 50 Am. J. Comp. L. 555, 561 (2002).
102. *See*, an Indian judgment, *Sarla Mudgal v. Union of India* (AIR 1995 SC 1531).

such an axiom as *lex specialis derogate legi generali* which may play a role of determining into which scope of the two codes transactions between the merchant and the non-merchant may fall, the commercial code or the civil code.

105. It is not that all the mixed legal relationships may be satisfactorily resolved with the help of the rule similar to such an axiom. When two or more personal laws stand on an equal footing with each other within the one legal system, or are to be so treated, the legislator may find it more adequate to have recourse to the 'closest connection' test as provided in Article 40 (1). However, there has been no case in which Japanese courts had to have recourse to that provision.

Part II. Conflict of Law Rules

Chapter 1. Persons

§1. Natural Persons

I. Legal Capacity

106. The question whether a natural person has legal capacity is governed by the *lex patriae* of the person. Whereas there is no provision to this effect in the AGR, it has been accepted for long. The legislative silence is mainly due to the fact that, albeit purely academic, there have been some controversies in relation to the questions regarding the beginning and the end of the legal capacity. With regard to the former question (namely, the capacity of *nasciturus*), the majority of academic writers take it for inseparable from the *lex successionis*, in other words, take it for practically useless to search the law applicable to the legal capacity in general. According to them, the *lex successionis* should be also applicable to the latter question (the *commorientes*).[103]

107. JPIL adopts the jurisdictional approach for the declaration of disappearance of a person.[104] Article 6(1) AGR provides the general jurisdiction, namely, the jurisdiction for the declaration of disappearance whose effect may be asserted in relation to all the legal relationships in which the person concerned is involved. The jurisdiction may be founded either when the person was domiciled in Japan or was of Japanese nationality at the last time that he or she was known to be alive. In absence of the general jurisdiction, Japanese courts may also entertain the special jurisdiction for the declaration of disappearance whose effect is limited only to the specific legal relationships. According to Article 6(2) AGR, they may have jurisdiction to declare the disappearance of a person with regard to the legal relationships in which his or her property situated in Japan is involved. In addition, the special jurisdiction may also be attributed to Japanese courts in relation to a certain legal relationships of the missing person as set out by the said provision, namely, those which are either governed by Japanese law or have a certain connection with Japan

103. For example, Tameike, 256–257.
104. When any person who has left his domicile or residence did not appoint an administrator of his or her property, the family court may exercise jurisdiction over the administration of such property situated in Japan (Articles 3-2 APFM).

under such individual circumstances of a case as shown by the nature of legal relationship or by the parties' domicile or nationality. Article 6(1) and (2) AGR applies, by analogy, to the revocation of the declaration of disappearance made by the court.

108. Once a Japanese court exercised jurisdiction to declare the disappearance of a person, it should take care of the revocation of the declaration, too. Article 3-3 APFM now provides that a Japanese court may assume jurisdiction over the revocation, when a Japanese court issued an adjudication declaring the person's disappearance. This provision adds that the Japanese court may assume jurisdiction over the revocation on the basis of the same grounds as provided in Article 6 (1) AGR, in case that a foreign court issued an adjudication capable of having effects in Japan.

109. As far as their jurisdiction is founded, whether general or special, Japanese courts always apply Japanese law.[105] The validity and the effect of the declaration of disappearance are governed by Japanese law. It follows that, at the request of any interested person, the family court may declare a person dead, in principle, when it is not clear whether the missing person is dead or alive for the period of seven years.[106] The declaration produces the effect that the person concerned is deemed to have died upon the elapse of that period of time. It should be noted that, under the Japanese substantive law, a missing person is not presumed but deemed to be dead with the declaration of disappearance. The reappearance of a missing person does not automatically cease the effect of the declaration unless and until the family court revokes the declaration.

110. It is worth noting that JPIL is said to distinguish the effect of the declaration of disappearance from its consequences which it will have upon the legal relationships in which the person is involved: e.g., the question as to whether the death of a husband entails the dissolution of marriage or to the opening of succession is governed by the law applicable to divorce or to succession, respectively.

111. Article 4(1) AGR provides that the capacity to act is governed by the *lex patriae* of the person concerned. In contrast to Article 5 AGR which deals with opening the measures for the protection of persons who are mentally not in a position to protect their interests, Article 4 deals with matters relating to a person whose capacity is restricted *ex lege.* The provision typically regulates e.g., who is a minor or whether or not a contract into which a minor enters without his legal representative's consent is voidable.[107] The principle of 'once mature, always mature' implicitly underlies the provision. It is worth adding that overriding mandatory rules

105. While there is no room for them to make declaration of disappearance according to a foreign law, the declaration of analogous nature made by foreign courts may be recognized, if the conditions of recognition, particularly, the jurisdictional ground, are met pursuant to the rule as set out in Art. 118 CCP.
106. Article 30 of the Civil Code.
107. On the other hand, the question who is his legal representative is governed by Art. 32 or by Art. 35.

such as Article 61 of the Labour Standards Act are necessarily applicable where the minor habitually carries out his work in Japan.[108]

112. The application of the *lex patriae* of a person concerned is conditioned by the security of transaction. Article 4(2) AGR provides that a person whose capacity is restricted under his *lex patriae* is deemed to have the capacity to act when he would have the capacity pursuant to the *lex loci actus* and when all the parties thereof are in the same *locus* at the time of the act. It should be noted that, whereas this provision is reminiscent of the *Lizardi* decision, it comes into operation irrespective of whether the other party was aware of or ought to have been aware of the restricted capacity of the person concerned under his *lex patriae.* This is due to the legislator's concern that it would be extremely difficult to identify the relevant factors capable of distinguishing the *bona fide* party from the *mala fide* one in this context, with the result that the relevancy of factors itself is likely to cause another issue to be resolved.

113. However, this provision which puts priority upon the security of transaction in domestic situations is neither applicable to juridical acts relating to family relationships and succession nor to juridical acts involving immovable property situated in a country different from the *locus actus* (Article 4(3) AGR).

II. Name

114. The AGR contains no choice-of-law rule on the name of a natural person. However, it seems undisputed that it is governed by the *lex patriae* of the person concerned.[109]

115. Until the middle of the twentieth century, both the prevailing view and the administrative practice preferred the *lex causae* governing the family relationship to the *lex patriae* of a person in relation to the question as to whether the change of name takes place when the person concerned enters into new family relationships, for example, through adoption, marriage, and divorce. Such preference of characterization seems to have reflected the Japanese household institution called '*ie*' endorsed by the Civil Code in the pre-war times. In contrast to the nuclear or conjugal family, the Japanese household was regarded as something like a corporate entity which could perpetuate itself through generations beyond the life span of any single member of the entity. The name was not conceived as identifying an individual but as denominating such a corporate entity. For example, once a woman who had originally belonged to a household whose lineal name was *Toyota* became a member of her husband's household *Honda* on their marriage, it automatically entailed her acquisition of the name of the household *Honda.* As far as a husband was Japanese, the application of the *lex causae* determined by the husband-oriented

108. It reads: [an] employer shall not have a person under 18 years of age work between the hours of 10 p.m.–5 a.m.
109. Cf. Commentary II (Kitazawa), 180–183.

choice-of-law rule led to the application of Japanese law in a mixed marriage, with the result that a woman of foreign nationality entered into a Japanese household and, consequently, bore the name of the husband's household.

116. At present, the majority of authors and the practice are of opinion that all the changes of name should be governed by the *lex patriae* of each person, irrespective of how the *lex causae* governing the family relationship regulates it. This shift is mainly explainable by the fact that the household institution was abolished immediately after the end of the Second World War. Furthermore, if the change of name on marriage were classified into the personal effects of marriage in the sense of Article 25 AGR, the applicable law might be eventually determined by the connecting criterion of the country with which the spouses have the closest connection. Such criterion appears to be hardly apposite to a person's name to be fixed with certainty.[110]

III. Nationality/Habitual Residence/Domicile

117. The acquisition and loss of Japanese nationality is regulated by the Nationality Act.[111]

IV. Stateless Persons and Refugees

118. Stateless persons have no *lex patriae*. Article 38(2) AGR provides the application of the law of their habitual residence. The domiciliary law in the sense of Article 12 of the Convention Relating to the Status of Refugees of 1951 seems to be regarded as the law of his or her habitual residence.

V. Transsexuals

119. The Act on Special Cases in Handling Gender for People with Gender Identity Disorder enables people with gender identity disorder to change their gender to be inscribed in the family registration book.[112] Whereas the Act contains no rule on jurisdiction and applicable law, Japanese courts whose jurisdiction is based upon a Japanese petitioner's domicile in Japan will undoubtedly apply Japanese law. It remains to be seen to what extent the jurisdiction extends to other petitioners and on what conditions foreign decrees ordering the change of gender should be recognized.

110. Yokoyama, 108–109; Tameike, 444.
111. Act No. 147 of 4 May 1950.
112. Act No. 111 of 25 May 2003.

§2. LEGAL PERSONS

I. Incorporated Organizations

120. There is no black-letter rule designed to determine the *lex societatis*. Nor is there a judgment of the Supreme Court that has decided on the proper law of the company. However, it is almost unanimously agreed in the court practice and among academic writers that JPIL has followed the 'incorporation' theory.[113] The entity established pursuant to the law of the country of incorporation has legal capacity under that law.

121. Under the Japanese substantive law, even when an entity is qualified as foreign, namely, incorporated under a foreign law, the entity is subject to some Japanese mandatory rules. According to Article 36 of the Civil Code, with the exception of any state, any administrative division of any state and any commercial corporation, no establishment of a foreign legal person shall be recognized unless it is approved pursuant to the provisions of a law or a treaty. Such cautious attitude towards the foreign legal person underlying this provision seems to have probably been inspired by the French and Belgian idea in the middle of the nineteenth century that the recognition of foreign corporations should be granted by the public organs on the basis of reciprocity. In addition, one of the drafters of the Civil Code seems to have had the wariness towards the activities of the Christian Church in Japan. The idea underlying Article 36 of the Civil Code is obviously outdated. Such denial of legal capacity would work even against the interests of Japanese persons, e.g., as creditors. Although the terms of the provision remain intact since its enactment in the late nineteenth century, experience tells us that it is undoubtedly obsolete. It should be noted that Article 36 of the Civil Code does not deny the legal capacity of 'any commercial corporation' incorporated under a foreign law. The reason why the legislator of the Civil Code made an exception for foreign companies seems to be due to the fact that transactions between Japanese merchants and foreign companies had been an everyday occurrence even during the period of the treaty port system.

122. Under the incorporation theory, it is supposed to be irrelevant where a company incorporated under a foreign law has the principal place of business. However, companies incorporated under foreign laws are subject to the mandatory rules as provided in the Companies Act enacted in 2005, in particular, Article 821(1) of the Act which deals with the pro-forma foreign company. According to this provision, a foreign company that has its head office in Japan or whose main purpose is to conduct business in Japan may not carry out transactions continuously in Japan. The predecessor of this provision was Article 482 of the Commercial Code, which is said to have been made, modelled upon Article 230 (4) of the Italian Commercial Code of 1882. Article 482 of the Japanese Commercial Code provided as follows: '[a] company that has its head office in Japan or whose main purpose is to conduct

113. *See*, Dai Yokomizo, *International Company Law in Japan*, in Basedow/Baum/Nishitani, 175 et seq.

business in Japan is subject to the same regulations to which a company established under Japanese law is subject, even when the company was established under a foreign law'. Since 'the same regulations' in the sense of that provision was interpreted to include the Japanese rules on the establishment of a company, it followed that such a *pro-forma* foreign company had to re-establish itself under Japanese law to acquire newly the legal capacity. This result shows nothing other than one of the intrinsic flaws of the 'real seat' theory. The current rule as provided in Article 821(1) accepts that, whereas, as mentioned above, it cannot carry out transactions continuously in Japan, such a pro-forma foreign company keeps its legal personality.[114]

II. Unincorporated Organizations

123. Organizations whose establishments do not need any form of registration are said to be subject to the law of the country where their central management is operated.

III. Scope of the *Lex Societatis*

124. The *lex societatis* governs, in particular, the subject matters which need to be uniformly regulated under the particular legal system: the organization's legal capacity, the formation, and the dissolution. So are the representative powers of the organs and the membership. The capacity to enter transactions is governed by the *lex societatis.* When the law puts limitations on legal capacity of a certain organization, Article 4(2) AGR is said to apply analogically for the protection of those persons who have entered transactions with the organization.[115]

125. The question whether the organization has the capacity to act as a party to judicial proceedings is governed by the *lex fori.* However, as far as Japanese law is the *lex fori*, Article 28 CCP refers to the legal capacity of an organization in determining that question. Consequently, it depends on the *lex societatis.*

IV. Liability

126. The liability for obligations of an organization with its own asset is governed by the *lex societatis.* So is the liability of the organization's officers. The

114. Paragraph 1 of Art. 821 is followed by para. 2 which reads as follows: '[a] person who has carried out transactions in violation of the provisions of the preceding paragraph shall be liable, jointly and severally with the foreign company, to perform obligations that have arisen from such transactions to the counterparty'.

115. *See*, Commentary I (Yokomizo), 162–163.

question as to whether one may pierce the corporate veil is governed by the law applicable to each *lex causae*, for example, the law applicable to contractual obligation or tort.[116]

V. Relocation

127. Relocation of the actual centre of administration entails no change of applicable law. A limited liability company remains as such irrespective of where the central management is carried out.

VI. Cross-Border Transformation

128. It is said that the requirements for and the effects of an international merger are to be determined under the law applicable to each *lex societatis*. Such distributive application is likely to lead to an accumulation of the applicable laws. It should be mentioned that the drafters of the Company Act of 2005 denied the possibility of mergers between Japanese companies and foreign companies.

116. Judgment of the Tokyo High Court, 30 Jan. 2002, 45 *J.A.I.L.* 183 (2002); Judgment of the Tokyo District Court, 28 Sept. 2001, *Hanta* 1140-227.

Chapter 2. Obligations

§1. Contractual Obligations

I. Party Autonomy

129. Since the enactment of the *Horei* in 1898, JPIL has allowed parties to a contract to choose the law which would govern their contract (party autonomy). At present, Article 7 AGR expresses this principle. The party autonomy enables parties to ascertain their rights and duties before disputes arise and to predict the outcomes when any dispute arises. The very fact that almost all the countries, more or less, honour the parties' choice of law would strengthen such prediction. The range of laws which parties may choose is not limited to those which have a certain link with the contract.[117]

130. The choice of law by the parties should be allowed not only in international situations but also in purely domestic or foreign ones. Even in such situations whose elements are all connected with one single country, the parties may have legitimate interests in choosing a law other than the law of such a country.

131. Article 7 AGR sets out that the law eligible to be chosen by the parties must be a state law. The legislator intentionally denies the possibility for the parties to choose as the applicable law a non-state body of law such as the UNIDROIT Principles of International Commercial Contracts, the Lando Principles of European Contract Law or the *lex mercatoria.* A contractual reference to such non-state body of law may be taken only as a method of incorporating a term or terms of the contract governed by an applicable state law. The legislator found it extremely difficult to find criteria capable of determining whether a particular non-state law is likely to deserve acceptance by the international community as adequately as state laws.[118]

132. While Article 7 AGR does not expressly state anything about splitting the applicable law (*dépeçage*), the legislative silence does not preclude parties from choosing the law applicable only to the part of the contract.[119]

133. The said choice-of-law rule does not preclude the court from accepting the implicit choice of law by the parities when they are found to have had the real intention to choose a law applicable to the contract.[120] The Legislative Council seemed to agree that, where the parties had no real intention to do so, the court should apply

117. *See*, Yuko Nishitani, *Party Autonomy and Its Restrictions by Mandatory Rules* in Basedow/Baum/Nishitani, 77 et seq. or the overview of the case law in relation to transactions within the East Asia, *see*, Yuko Okano, *Japanese Court Cases Involving East Asian Citizens and Corporations Law Applicable to International Transactions with Chinese, Taiwanese, and Korean Parties Before Japanese Courts*, 57 *J.Y.B.I.L.* 243 et seq. (2014).

118. Koide, 96.

119. Koide, 90–91.

120. Judgment of the Tokyo District Court, 28 Jan. 2015, 59 *J.Y.B.I.L.* 497 (2016) inferred English law from the agreed place of arbitration and the agreed canons of interpretation.

the law objectively determined pursuant to Article 8 AGR. While Article 7 AGR does not set out anything about what circumstances may allow the court to find such a real implicit intention, the range of such circumstances seems to be limited to some extent. First, according to Article 9 AGR as mentioned below, the parties who made no explicit choice of law may choose a law at any time after the conclusion of the contract.[121] The question as to whether they, although implicitly, made a real choice of law at the time of conclusion of the contract is raised only when they are not willing to make such a subsequent choice of law for some reason or other. Given that the parties failed to make such a subsequent choice of law, the court seems likely to be cautious in imputing the determination of applicable law to the real intention of the parties ascertained at the time of the conclusion of the contract. Second, under the Japanese international civil procedure, the place of performance as a jurisdictional ground is determinable by the law governing the contractual obligation when and only when the governing law was explicitly or implicitly chosen by the parties. In other words, the place of performance cannot be a ground of jurisdiction when it can be determined only by reference to the governing law objectively determined pursuant to Article 8 AGR. It is not only because the parties' predictability about the jurisdiction of Japanese courts should be ensured but also because the court should not be engaged in examining circumstances of a case at the outset of proceedings in order to search the country with which a contract is most closely connected pursuant to the said choice-of-law rule. It follows that the Japanese courts will assume jurisdiction on the ground of the place of performance when they may infer the parties' implicit choice of law without fully examining the merits of a case.[122]

134. Article 9 AGR provides that the parties may make a choice of law governing their contract at any time after the conclusion of the contract. They may vary the law which they previously chose as a law governing the contract and may make the choice of law to replace the law to which the contract would be otherwise subject under Article 8 AGR. The subsequent choice of law may also be made after the time of the filing of an action. It is true that the subsequent choice of law made, for example, immediately before the conclusion of oral pleadings would run counter to the procedural efficiency. This inevitable consequence, however, would be compensated for by what is brought by the application of the *lex fori* which the parties are most likely to agree pursuant to Article 9 AGR. It should be added that Japanese courts are allowed to infer the implicit choice of law by the parties from their exchange of pleading during the litigation, as far as their intention to choose a law is found real.

135. JPIL which allows parties to choose a law applicable to their contract should also regulate the validity of the choice of law itself. However, the AGR has no black-letter rule about it. Under the *Horei*, academic writers suggested the solution by the application of the unwritten substantive law rules on the level of PIL whose contents coincided with those of such rules as deceit or duress contained in

121. *See*, para. 135 *infra*.
122. *See*, para. 380 *infra*.

the Japanese Civil Code. It remains to be seen whether the suggested solution will keep persuasive under the AGR, account being taken of the fact that Articles 7 and 9 of the AGR were enacted, strongly inspired by the Rome Convention on the Law Applicable to Contractual Obligations.[123]

136. Article 8 AGR deals with the situation where the parties have made neither express nor implicit choice of the law governing their contract. The provision enunciates the principle of the closest connection in combination with the presumptive rules for the contracts relating to immovable property and for the other contracts.

137. Article 7 of the *Horei* provided the application of the *lex loci contractus* in the last resort, when the parties made no choice of law. In adopting the *lex loci contractus*, the legislator presumably bore in mind transactions which were likely to take place in Japan at the turn of the century from the nineteenth to the twentieth. Most of the contracts made between Japanese and foreign merchants seem to have been concluded *inter praesentes* in such a port town as Yokohama at least immediately after the abolishment of the treaty port system. In the course of the last century, Japanese courts tended not to fall back upon such inflexible connecting factor, when the parties did not explicitly choose a law governing their contract. Whenever they found the *lex loci contractus* inappropriate under circumstances of a case, they tended to apply another law under the pretext that the parties were found to choose it implicitly. To honour the implicit choice of law by the parties did not run counter to the terms of Article 7 of the *Horei*. It may safely be said, however, that, what Japanese courts often did, in reality, was not to search for the parties' real intention but to impute to their presumed intention the application of the law with which the contract was found to have objectively its closest connection under circumstances of a case. Such a search for the imputed intention tended to be regarded as an excusable manoeuver to escape from the rigid application of the *lex loci contractus*.[124] This is the background against which the Legislative Council was attracted by the formula of the closest connection with the contract.[125]

138. Article 8(1) AGR provides the application of the law of the country with which the contract was most closely connected at the time of its conclusion. This provision plays a double role. First, it enables the court to identify the law governing the contract without recourse to the presumptive rule as contained in the second paragraph of the said article, whenever the notion of characteristic performance is helpless for the presumption. Second, it allows the court to disregard the presumption as laid down by the second and the third paragraphs of the said provision, when it appears from circumstances that the contract is more closely connected with another country.[126]

123. Koide, 92.
124. Koide, 105.
125. This does not preclude the court from searching the law implicitly but really chosen by the parties. A judgment of the Tokyo District Court, 28 Jan. 2015, 59 *J.Y.B.I.L.* 497 (2016) inferred English law from the agreed place of arbitration and the agreed canons of interpretation.
126. Yokoyama, 173–174.

139. As mentioned above, Japanese courts tried to identify the law of the country with which the contract had the closest connection, under the pretext of searching for the inferred or imputed intention of the parties.[127] Whereas this flexible method was undoubtedly preferable to the rigid application of the *lex loci contractus*, the court practice revealed its own drawback: it is hardly predictable to what circumstances of a case the courts will give importance in identifying the governing law. One feared that this aspect not only would prevent the parties from entering into a settlement in and out of court but also would give foreign litigants a suspicion that Japanese courts might arbitrarily pick up circumstances leading to the application of Japanese law. These backgrounds militated in favour of adopting the presumptive rule as contained in Article 8(2) AGR. What is more important is that the laws, which, under the *Horei*, Japanese courts applied as governing laws in the absence of the explicit choice of law by the parties seem to have coincided almost with the laws which would be identified with the help of the characteristic performance. Consequently, the presumption based on characteristic performance seemed unlikely to cause serious change of the pre-existing court practice.

140. It is true that the notion of the characteristic performance was unfamiliar to JPIL. This unfamiliarity caused some apprehension among Japanese business circles during discussions of the Legislative Council, because their standard form contracts were formulated on the basis of Japanese law. Japanese law undoubtedly enabled them to promote their business and to comply more easily with Japanese mandatory rules regulating the incidents of performance. However, it did not take a long time for them to realize that the presumptive rule would be highly likely to lead to the application of Japanese law, as far as their products are suited for multiple markets.[128]

141. Article 8(2) AGR neither says anything about what the characteristic performance means nor illustrates it by giving examples. The provisions of the Japanese Civil Code relating to typical contracts are expected to be helpful for identifying what performance characterizes a contract. The presumption on the basis of the characteristic performance does not apply to the contract whose subject matter is related to immovable property. According to Article 8(3), AGR such a contract is presumed to have the closest connection with the country where the immovable property is situated.

II. Form

142. With respect to the form of contract, the first paragraph of Article 10 AGR refers to the *lex causae*, the law governing the contract. This is only natural because the formal requirements of contract must be usually satisfied with, in combination with the substantive ones to be governed by the *lex causae*.

---

127. *See*, para. 138 *supra*.
128. Koide, 112.

143. As mentioned above, according to Article 9 AGR, the parties may at any time choose a law other than that which previously governed it. What repercussions does the choice of the new applicable law have upon the fate of the contract which was formally valid or invalid under the original applicable law? In response to this question, the blanketed sentence of Article 10 (1) AGR lays down that, when the parties alter the law applicable to the contract, the previously governing law remains applicable to its formal requirements. It follows that the contract which was formally valid under the original applicable law remains valid, even when it turns out to be invalid under the new applicable law. However, if it was formally invalid under the original applicable law, it cannot be validated by the choice of the new applicable law. It means that the vice under the original applicable law is not cured simply by means of the choice of the new applicable law. The law subsequently called upon to govern the substance of the contract is put outside the range of the alternatively applicable laws as mentioned below.

144. The second paragraph of the said Article expresses an alternative choice-of-law rule. Compliance with the substantive law rules either of the *lex contractus* or of the *lex loci actus* will suffice as regards the form of contract. The connecting factor of the *locus actus* itself may militate in favour of concluding valid contracts, because the parties can make easier access to legal information available in the place of concluding the contract. The addition of the *lex loci actus* to the *lex contractus* as a possible governing law is expected to further facilitate its validity. The alternative application of the two laws, which had been already adopted in 1898, was retained under the AGR. However, in contrast to the legislators of the *Horei*, the members of the Legislative Council of 2006 were aware that the protective effects inherent in the formal requirements might be weakened to the corresponding extent. Consequently, the legislator of the AGR made the special provisions with respect to the consumer contract (Article 11(4) and (5) AGR).[129]

145. When a person's declaration of intent is made to another in a different country, the *locus actus* is deemed to be the place where the declaration is made (Article 10 (3) AGR). However, this 'deemed locus' rule does not apply to contracts. When the parties' declarations of intent consist of the offer and the acceptance of contract, the place, where each declaration of intent is made, is qualified as the place of concluding the contract. It follows that compliance with either of the two laws is sufficient for the formal validity of a contract, in addition to the *lex contractus* (Article 10 (4) AGR).

III. Validity and Formation

146. The formation of contract, namely, issues relating to 'offer' and 'acceptance' are governed by the *lex contractus* which would govern the contract if it were valid. The AGR contains no black-letter rule corresponding to Article 10 (2) of the Regulation (EC) No. 593/2008 of the European Parliament and of the Council of 17

129. *See*, para. 169 *infra*.

June 2008 on the law applicable to contractual obligations (Rome I) which deals with inaction or action by one party in the context of the formation of contract. The putative *lex contractus* also applies to questions relating to reality of consent such as mistake and fraud. The putative *lex contractus* also governs the validity of contract, issues relating to the effects of a statutory prohibition or of infringements of the public policy (*ordre public interne*).

IV. Performance

147. The *lex contractus* governs the conditions necessary for each party to discharge himself of his obligation, in particular: the conditions relating to the standard of care with which an obligation must be performed; to the place and time of performance; and the identification of a performing person.

148. The *lex loci solutionis* may be taken into account as regards rules concerning public holidays, business hours prevailing in fact in the place of performance. These rules affecting the manner of performance may not be applied but taken into account within the framework of the *lex contractus*. For example, when one of those rules hindered a buyer in his payment, the principle of good faith in the sense of the *lex contractus* applies to questions what steps the buyer should take then, and whether and how the seller should cooperate with the buyer. However, whereas authors tend to affirm the application of a single *lex contractus* to all aspects of performance, it remains to be seen how Article 403 of the Japanese Civil Code, which allows a debtor to discharge his debt expressed in a foreign currency by means of tendering the Japanese currency, is applicable. It is submitted that the *quantum* of money to be tendered is the matter governed by the *lex contractus* rather than the *lex loci solutionis.*[130]

V. Breach of Contractual Obligations (Including Damages)

149. What event triggers a breach of contractual obligations is the matter to be governed by the *lex contractus*. So are consequences of breach of obligations, for example, damages. Under JPIL, both the assessment and the quantification of damages are classified into questions of the substance, not the procedure to be governed by the *lex fori*.

VI. Rescission

150. The question whether a party has a right to rescind the contract is governed by the *lex contractus*. The formal validity of the declaration of rescission as a unilateral act is subject to the provisions as laid down in Article 10 (1)–(3) AGR.[131]

130. *See*, Yokoyama, 189. Cf. Commentary I (Morishita), 660–665.
131. *See* paras 143–146 *supra*.

VII. Representation

151. With regard to the representation of minors and incapacitated adults, the AGR contains the choice-of-law rules.[132] For the other forms of representation, the development of choice-of-law rules is left to case law,[133] whereas the powers of representation by the organizational body are undoubtedly governed by the *lex societatis.*[134]

152. With regard to the purely consensual or voluntary representation, it is undisputed that the internal relationship between the principal and the agent should be governed by the *lex contractus,* typically, the mandate contract made between the two. However, there were several views as regards the law applicable to the external relationship between the principal and the third party. The majority of authors are of opinion that the law of the country where the agent acts should govern the question of whether or not the principal is bound vis-à-vis third parties by the acts of the agent.[135] It seems that those views in favour of the connecting factor of the country where the agent acts is probably inspired by the Hague Convention of 14 March 1978 on the Law Applicable to Agency. If this observation is correct, they would not exclude the place of the agent's business establishment as a connecting criterion. It should be noted that the majority of authors implicitly assume that an agent to act on behalf of a principal always discloses the principal to a third party. The Legislative Council had no sufficient time in examining whether the place of the agent's acting would accommodate the doctrine of undisclosed principal.[136]

VIII. Interpretation

153. Interpretation of a contract is governed by the *lex contractus.* That law provides the canons of construction. Whereas this does not preclude the court from referring to the law other than the *lex contractus* or trade usages in clarifying the meanings of particular contractual terms, the *lex contractus* determines to what extent and how the terms whose meanings have been clarified should be incorporated in the contract.

132. *See* paras 339–342 *infra.*
133. Whereas the continuing powers of attorney for an incapacitated adult may derive from a mandate contract made in advance, the powers of attorney known under some legal systems are under the strict supervision of the court for the protection of adult, for example, the Japanese Act on Voluntary Guardianship Contract (Act No. 150 of 8 Dec. 1999). It remains to be seen whether the *lex contractus* or the *lex fori* is applicable to the powers of attorney.
134. For the representation of the legal person, *see* para. 125 *supra.*
135. *See*, Commentary I (Sakurada), 337–339.
136. *See*, Koide, 399–401.

IX. Third Parties and Multiparty Agreements

154. The AGR contains no black-letter rule specifically dealing with the multiparty agreements. With regard to the rights of the third party, Article 9 AGR, which allows the parties to make a choice of law governing their contract at any time after the conclusion of the contract, adds that such subsequent choice of law should not adversely affect the rights of third parties. For example, a third party in the context of a contract for the benefit of a third party is entitled to assert his or her rights pre-existing under the previous *lex contractus* against the parties to such contract. So is a surety against the creditor and debtor on the ground of the law governing the contract of suretyship.[137]

X. Assignments and Subrogation

155. Article 23 AGR, which replaced Article 12 of the *Horei*, regulates only effects of assignment of a claim against a debtor or other third parties.[138] Whereas those effects were governed by the domiciliary law of the debtor pursuant to Article 12 of the *Horei*, those effects are governed by the law governing the assigned claim in accordance with current Article 23 AGR. The connecting criterion adopted by the former, namely, the debtor's domicile, presumably derived from the French case law in the late nineteenth century against the background that the substantive law rules on assignment of claim as contained in the Japanese Civil Code were modelled upon the corresponding rules of the French Civil Code. The legislator of the *Horei* appears to have stood on the assumption that, as far as the debtor was in a position to be readily aware of the assignment, his domicile should be regarded as the most important among the places which are foreseeable by the interested persons such as assignees or creditors of assignors. Under the current Japanese substantive law rules, however, a certain type of assignments may be filed in the public register so that the debtor has not been regarded any longer as such an important informational source of assignments as he used to be.[139] Against the background of such a development of the domestic substantive law rules and supported by the Japanese financial institutions, the Legislative Council decided to displace the law of the debtor's domicile in favour of the law governing the assigned claim with regard to those effects.

156. During discussions of the Legislative Council, some experts of PIL advanced a proposal to adopt the connecting factor of the assignor's habitual residence for the effects of assignment against the third parties other than the debtor. They argued that their proposed connecting factor would facilitate the assignment of future receivables and the bulk assignments, whereas such facilitation would be

137. *See*, Koide, 121–122.
138. *See*, Aki Kitazawa, *Law Applicable to the Assignment of Receivables in Japan*, in Basedow/Baum/Nishitani, 137 et seq.
139. Act on Special Provisions, etc., of the Civil Code Concerning the Perfection Requirements for the Assignment of Movables and Claims (Act No. 104 of 12 Jun. 1998) enables corporate assignors to make registration of assignment of future monetary claims.

difficult to achieve with the recourse to the law governing each assigned claim. However, the members of the Legislative Council from Japanese banks strongly opposed to this proposal, insisting upon necessity of checking the law applicable to each claim. It seems that Article 23 AGR turned out to reflect such cautious attitude taken by a group of Japanese banks towards the cross-border assignments.[140]

157. Article 23 AGR contains a choice-of-law rule which only deals with effects of assignment of a claim against a debtor or other third parties. The provision does not say anything about the other choice-of-law problems related to the assignment. Whereas it is undisputedly accepted that the underlying contract of the assignment concluded between the assignor and the assignee should govern the obligations which cause the transfer of the claim, it remains to be seen which law should govern the property aspect of assignment between the assignor and the assignee. Whereas some opine that the law of the contact underlying the assignment also governs such property aspects of an assignment *inter partes*, the majority of academic writers seem to be in favour of the application of the law of the assigned claim to those aspects, too.[141]

158. The AGR contains no black-letter rule concerning legal subrogation, either. It seemed hardly disputed during discussions of the Legislative Council that, when the insurer had the duty to satisfy the insured under the indemnity insurance contract, the insurer's right to assume the rights of the insured against another should be governed by the law applicable to the insurance contract. However, legal phenomena which may be understood under the term 'legal subrogation' seem to be varied in terms of interests involved or grounds which justify such subrogation. For example, when a tortfeasor destroyed an object which a debtor has the duty to deliver to a creditor under their sales contract, the creditor probably may take over the debtor's claims for damages against the tortfeasor. In such a case, one may wonder whether the law applicable to the sales contract should govern the subrogation as does the law applicable to the insurance contract. Time did not allow the Legislative Council to elaborate a choice-of-law rule capable of embracing various forms of legal subrogation.[142]

§2. Particular Contracts

I. Sales Contract

159. Since 1 October 2009, Japan has been a party to the United Nations Convention on Contracts for the International Sale of Goods of 1980 (CISG). She did not declare the reservation of Articles 95 of CISG, which allows a reservation state not to be bound by Article 1(1)(b) thereof.

140. *See*, Koide, 275.
141. *See*, Koide, 274.
142. *See*, Koide, 299.

160. There is no choice-of-law rule specifically dealing with sales contracts. Articles 7–9 AGR determine the *lex contractus* of a contract for sale. When the *lex contractus* has not been chosen in accordance with Articles 7 and 9, the presumptive rule of characteristic performance applies (Article 8(2)). It follows that the contract for the sale of goods is presumably governed by the law of the country where the seller has his habitual residence.[143] For example, when an original equipment manufacturer of Taiwan produces and delivers their products to a Japanese company under the Japanese company's brand name and only for the Japanese market, the presumption in Article 8(2) would point to Taiwanese law. However, if the rationale of the presumptive rule is that the obligations of the seller are more complex than those of the buyer, circumstances may rebut such presumption.

161. The presumption on the basis of the characteristic performance does not apply to the contract whose subject matter is related to immovable property. According to Article 8(3), such a contract is presumed to have the closest connection with the country where the immovable property is situated. Obviously, this provision covers only the obligatory effects of the contract. This presumption is also rebuttable. For example, a sale contract made between a Japanese real estate agent and a customer in relation to a holiday home in Hawaii may not be governed by Hawaiian law but by Japanese law, when the agent targeted Japanese corporate customers.

II. Service Contract

162. There is no specific choice-of-law rule that, in the absence of the choice of law by the parties, determines the law applicable to service contracts. Pursuant to Article 8(1) and (2) AGR, the court should search the law of the country with which the contract is most closely connected, with the help of the notion of characteristic performance. It follows that a contract for the provision of service is governed by the law of the country where the service provider has his habitual residence unless there is another country with which the contract is more closely connected.

III. Consumer Contracts

163. The general choice-of-law rules on contract as contained in Articles 7, 8, and 10(2) and (4) AGR may prejudice the interests of the consumer. First, the party autonomy expressed by Article 7 enables a business to choose the law of its own home country which is usually not familiar to consumers, even if it does not intend to deprive consumers of a certain protection. Second, the presumption on the basis of characteristic performance is likely to result in the application of the law unfamiliar to the consumer who pays for goods or services. Third, while promoting the formal validity of transactions, the alternative choice-of-law rules as contained in

143. Judgment of Kobe District Court, 21 Jan. 2016 60 *J.Y.B.I.L.*520 (2017) (related to fuel supply contract).

Article 10(2) and (4) may deprive consumers of the protection supplied by mandatory rules of their habitual residence. Taking into account these three aspects disadvantageous to consumers, Article 11 lays down the special choice-of-law rules working in favour of consumers. The combination of this provision with Article 3-4(1) CCP allows a consumer to seek remedy under the law and at the court of the country to which the consumer is most accessible.[144]

164. All contracts concluded between the 'consumer' and the 'business entity' fall under Article 11 AGR. In line with Article 2 of the Japanese Consumer Contract Act,[145] the former is defined as a natural person who does not become a party to a contract as a business or for the purpose of business and the latter as a legal person, an association or a natural person who becomes a party to a contract as a business or for the purpose of business. The object of contract is entirely irrelevant to its application.

165. According to Article 11(1) AGR, when the law chosen by the parties is a law other than the law of the country where the consumer is habitually resident, the court should apply a certain mandatory rules of that country to issues relating to the substantive validity and the effects of the contract, on the following conditions: (1) the consumer himself specifies the relevant mandatory rules; and (2) he expresses his intent to assert their application towards the business entity. It should be noted that the mandatory rules covered by the provision are not understood to mean the overriding mandatory ones but the substantive rules which cannot be derogated from by agreement, such as rules on error in communication. For example, when a consumer habitually resident in Japan incorrectly transmitted his declaration of intent to make an offer or an acceptance for an electronic consumer contract with a business entity, the consumer may assert the invalidity of the contract pursuant to Article 3 of the Japanese Act on Special Provisions to the Civil Code Concerning Electronic Consumer Contracts and Electronic Acceptance Notice.[146]

166. Article 11 AGR stands upon the assumption that it is the consumer who decides which law will bring the result better to him. Unless he refers to the substantive effects of contract pursuant to the specific mandatory rule of his habitual residence, Japanese courts will apply the *lex contractus* chosen by the parties. During discussions of the Legislative Council, such a preferential approach as provided in Article 5(2) of the Rome Convention and Article 6(2) of the Regulation (EC) No. 593/2008 of the European Parliament and of the Council of 17 June 2008 on the law applicable to contractual obligations (Rome I) faced strong opposition from the

144. For the consumer collective redress, *see*, Dai Yokomizo, 'Consumer Collective Redress and Japanese Conflict of Laws', 61 *J.Y.B.I.L.* 189 et seq. (2018).
145. Act No. 61 of 12 May 2000.
146. Act No. 95 of 29 Jun. 2001. This provision does not apply to the situation where the business entity has taken measures to confirm the consumer's intent to make an offer or to accept the offer by electromagnetic means on the visual browser or where the consumer declares expressly his intent to the business entity that there is no need for such confirmation measures.

judge members who feared it difficult to compare such mandatory rules with the substantive rules of the law chosen by the parties.[147]

167. In the absence of choice, Japanese courts always apply the law of the country where the consumer is habitually resident without recourse to the principle of the closest connection coupled with the presumptive rule as laid down in Article 8 AGR (Article 11(2) AGR).

168. When the law chosen by the parties is a law other than the law of the country where the consumer is habitually resident, the same preferential approach as taken by Article 11(1) AGR is adopted with regard to the formal validity of consumer contract. According to Article 11(3) AGR, the specific mandatory rules which the consumer expresses his intent to invoke against the business entity should apply to issues otherwise governed by the laws referred to by the choice-of-law rules as laid down in Article 10(1), (2), and (4) AGR. Furthermore, when the chosen law coincides with the law of the country where the consumer is habitually resident, Japanese judges should honour the consumer's preference, disregarding the *lex loci actus* (Article 11(4) AGR). According to Article 11(5) AGR, in the absence of the parties' choice, the law of the country where the consumer is habitually resident always applies.

169. It is not that all natural persons who fall under 'consumers' as defined in Article 11(1) AGR are entitled to the protection as mentioned above. Article 11(6) AGR sets out the four scenarios in which consumer contracts should be treated like business-to-business contracts. When contracts fall into one of such scenarios, the general rules on contracts as contained in Articles 7–10 AGR should be applied. First, the two scenarios as set out by Article 11(6)(iii) and (iv) AGR are based on the idea of appearance. When the business entity could not be expected to be aware of the place of the consumer's habitual residence on the reasonable ground, or when the business entity misconceived on the reasonable ground that the other party was not a consumer, priority is given to the good faith and reasonable expectation of the business entity rather than the consumer protection. The relevant time in both situations is the time when a contract was concluded. Second, the 'active consumers' are not entitled to the protection as provided by Article 11(1)–(5) AGR. According to Article 11(6)(i) and (ii) AGR, the following consumers are regarded as 'active': those who headed out for the place of the business entity's establishment where either all the elements of the conclusion of the contract or of the performance of the contract took place. Japanese tourists, in principle, cannot buy shoes in Milano nor enjoy themselves in a European theme park, carrying their suitcases crammed with the Japanese mandatory rules on consumer protection. However, they can rely on those mandatory rules, when the consumers headed out for the place of the business entity's establishment as a result of the business entity's 'solicitation' for them to do so (Article 11(6)(i) and (ii) AGR). The promotion e-mail sent to a consumer undoubtedly falls under the concept of solicitation in the sense of the said

147. *See*, Koide, 142–143. Such comparison does not seem to cause much trouble to the consumer, for example, in Judgment of the Tokyo District Court, 17 Jan. 2017, 61 *J.Y.B.I.L.* 412 (2018).

provisos. It remains to be seen what activities of the business entity may fall within the notion of solicitation, particularly with regard to the website which gives information to potential consumers all over the world. It should be added that the said provisos contain no terms such as 'target' or 'direct'.

IV. Employment Contracts

170. Under the *Horei*, Japanese judges usually applied the law chosen by the parties for individual employment contracts.[148] It was constantly observed, however, that there were judgments which affirmed the application of some Japanese substantive law rules, for example, relating to dismissal as if the courts had been unaware of the choice-of-law problems involved. Such judgments seem to have been explained and endorsed by Japanese experts of labour law who tended to regard those rules as overriding mandatory rules whose sphere of application was delimited by the employee's habitual workplace in Japan. This tendency is probably due to the fact that Japanese substantive law rules on individual employment contract developed out of the case law in connection with the Labour Standard Act which provides penal and administrative sanctions as well as private law effects.[149] The Labour Contract Act which aimed at restating such case law came to make more discernible the category of mandatory rules which cannot be derogated from by means of an agreement but are not of overriding mandatory nature.[150] It seems that Japanese mandatory rules which Article 12 AGR refers to are likely to be the rules as set out by that Act.

171. Article 12 AGR, in principle, allows an employee to rely on mandatory rules of the law of the country where the employee habitually carries out his work. In combination with Article 3-4(2) CCP, Article 12 AGB enables an employee working in Japan to seek effective remedy under Japanese law and at the court of Japan which is most accessible to him. Article 11 AGR (consumer contracts) and Article 12 AGR (employment contracts) share the basic idea, namely, the protection of the weaker parties from the viewpoint of inequality of bargaining power. However, there is some difference between the two. The contract of employment creates a lasting relationship between the parties and brings the employee within the organizational framework of the business entity. Furthermore, to facilitate the contract of employment is not necessarily unbeneficial to the employee. In view of these elements being involved in the contract of employment, the legislator adopted the choice-of-law rules different from those contained in Article 11 AGR. As a matter of fact, it seems that consumers frequently lack the actual and implicit intents to choose the law, because most of them seem to be unaware of even the possibility of choice of law. In contrast, Japanese courts do not seem to hesitate to find the implicit choice of law, when a contract of employment was entered into on the basis of the

148. Most of cases were related to whether the termination of employment contract was effective and whether the employee was entitled to receiving wages.
149. Law No.49 of 7 Apr. 1947.
150. Act No. 128 of 5 Dec. 2007.

collective bargaining agreement which is subject to the law other than that of the country where the employee habitually works. Furthermore, it is likely that the both parties do not want the governing law to change each time that the employee's habitual workplace shifts from one country to another.

172. Article 12(1) AGR adopts such a preferential approach as provided by Article 11(1) AGR on consumer contracts, as mentioned below.[151] However, there is difference between the two provisions. Whereas the law whose mandatory rules may be invoked by the consumer is always that of the consumer's habitual residence at the time of the conclusion, the law whose mandatory rules may be invoked by the employee is not fastened on that of the place where he habitually carried out his work at a particular time. The law applicable in the absence of choice of law is the law of the country which the contract of employment is most closely connected with, although such place is presumed to be that where an employee carries out his work (Article 12(2) AGR).

173. When the law chosen by the parties is a law other than the law of the country where the employee habitually carries out his work, the specific mandatory rules of the latter which the employee expresses his intent to invoke against the employer should apply to issues governed by those rules.[152] For example, when, pursuant to a foreign law chosen by the parties, an employer terminates a contract of employment, an employee who habitually carries out his work in Japan may assert that the dismissal lacks any reasonable ground in the sense of Article 16 of the Japanese Labour Contract Act.[153] Cherry-picking both the *lex contractus* and the law of his workplace is justifiable from the viewpoint of the *favor laboratoris*. Among other things, it is the employer who directed the employee to work in a country whose law does not coincide with the *lex contractus*.

174. As mentioned above, in the absence of choice, the applicable law is the law of the country which the contract of employment is most closely connected with. Such a place is presumed to be that where the employee habitually carries out his work in the performance of the contract. When there is no identifiable place of work, the presumably applicable law is that of the country of business establishment through which the employee was engaged.

175. Unlike consumer contracts, Article 12 AGR contains no special choice-of-law rule as regards the formal validity of the contract of employment. The general rules as provided by Article 10 (1) to (4) AGR apply to the problem. The alternative application of the *lex contractus* and the *lex loci actus* was thought to be not inconsistent with the idea of *favor laboratoris* underlying the provision laid down in Article 12 AGR.

---

151. *See*, para. 174 *infra*.

152. For example, judgment of the Tokyo District Court, 26 Sept. 2016, 60 *J.Y.B.I.L.*526 (2017) applied Japanese law as the most closely connected with the employment contact, although the parties chose English law.

153. It reads that, if a dismissal lacks objectively reasonable grounds and is not considered to be appropriate in general societal terms, it is treated as an abuse of rights and is invalid.

176. It should be added that, alongside with such mandatory rules applicable by means of Article 12 AGR, there are overriding mandatory rules which Japanese courts should, ex officio, apply to the contract of employment irrespective of the governing law and of the employee's invocation, as far as he carries out his work in Japan. For example, Article 7 of the Labour Union Act which prohibits an employer to dismiss an employee by reason of his having tried to join or organize a labour union should be treated as of overriding mandatory nature.[154] So is Article 58 of the Labour Standards Act which enables the administrative authorities to terminate a contract of employment if they find it disadvantageous to the minor employee.

V. Contracts of Carriage

177. The AGR contains no choice-of-law rules specifically dealing with contracts of carriage, whether they may be concerned with persons or goods. It follows that the *lex contractus* is determined by Articles 7 to 10 AGR, subject to Article 11 AGR on consumer contracts.

A. *Carriage of Persons*

178. Unlike Article 5 Rome I, there is no special choice-of-law rules to accommodate the protection of weaker parties. The party autonomy is not spatially restricted as regards the carriage of persons, regardless of the means of transportation.[155] In the absence of choice by the parties, the country of the carrier's habitual residence is presumed to be the country of the closest connection (Article 8 AGR). As far as one of the parties is a consumer, the choice-of-law rules as expressed in Article 11 AGR applies to the contract for carriage of person, too.

B. *Carriage of Goods*

179. The AGR contains no choice-of-law rule for a contract for the carriage of goods, either. Thus, the party autonomy applies to the fullest extent, regardless of the means of transportation.[156] In the absence of choice, the principle of the closest connection determines the *lex contractus*, coupled with the presumptive rule based on the characteristic performance. The rule would mostly lead to the application of the law of the country of habitual residence of the carrier. Whereas the presumption can be rebutted in each individual case, the habitual residence of the carrier does

154. Act No. 174 of 1 Jun. 1949.
155. Japan is a contracting party of the Convention for the Unification of Certain Rules for International Carriage by Air (the Montreal Convention).
156. Japan is a contracting party of the Protocol to Amend the International Convention for the Unification of Certain Rules of Law Relating to Bills of Lading (the Visby Rules).

not need to be strengthened by factors such as the place of receipt or delivery or the habitual residence of the consignor. However, Article 11 AGR on consumer contracts remains applicable.

VI. Insurance Contracts

180. The AGR contains no specific choice-of-law rules dealing with insurance contracts. They are not treated differently from other contracts. As a consequence, the party autonomy applies here, too. The scale of choice is not restricted by the size of the insured risk. In the absence of choice, the principle of the closest connection determines the *lex contractus*, coupled with the presumptive rule based on the characteristic performance. The rule would mostly lead to the application of the law of the country of habitual residence of the insurer, though rebuttable in each individual case. The consumer may always rely on Article 11 AGR.

VII. IP Contracts

181. There have not been many cases in which the applicable law to the contract concerned with the transfer or licensing of intellectual property rights are at issue.[157] It is undisputed, however, that, whereas the questions relating to the transfer of the intellectual property rights as such are governed by the law governing such rights, namely, the *lex loci protectionis*, the contract out of which the obligation of such transfer arises is governed by the *lex contractus* determinable with the same choice-of-law rules as other contracts such as sales contracts.[158] Thus, the principle of party autonomy applies here, too. In the absence of the parties' choice of law, the presumptive rule based upon the characteristic performance applies. It follows that the contract which simply aims at the transfer or licensing of an intellectual property is presumed to be most closely connected with the law of the country in which the transferor or the licensor has his habitual residence. However, patent licence agreements or trade mark agreements have been often included in distribution or franchise contracts only as clauses of them. The main obligations arising out of those contracts are usually for the distributed parties to distribute the goods or for the licensees to develop the franchised businesses. Authors suggest to search which side of the contracting parties assume the main duties in individual contracts rather than to indiscriminately apply the presumptive rule of characteristic performance to all contracts concerning intellectual property rights.[159]

157. R Kojima, R Shimanami & M Nagata, *Applicable Law to Exploitation of Intellectual Property Rights in the Transparency Proposal*, in *Intellectual Property in the Global Arena* 179, 218 (Jürgen Basedow, Toshiyuki Kono & Axel Metzger eds).

158. Judgment of the Tokyo High Court, 13 May 2001, *Hanji* 1797-111.

159. For a variety of views, *see*, R Kojima, R Shimanami & M Nagata, *supra* 221–221.

A. *Licence Agreement*

182. *See*, paragraph 182 *supra*.

B. *Trade Mark Agreement*

183. *See*, paragraph 182 *supra*.

C. *Other*

184. *See*, paragraph 182 *supra*.

VIII. Hybrid Contracts

185. Though apparently single, the complexity of a contract may motivate the parties to choose different laws to different parts of the contract, but they may choose one single *lex contractus* to govern the whole contract. However, when the parties of a complex contract fail to choose one single *lex contractus*, one may face the question how a single characteristic performance can be identified, when both parties effect more than the payment of money. There seems neither case law nor scholarly writings suggesting some general solutions, e.g., in relation to leasing, factoring and so on. All that can be said is that the presumptive rule based on the characteristic performance becomes more easily rebuttable or that the test of characteristic performance straightforwardly cannot be applied.

A. *Leasing*

186. The law applicable to the leasing contract is governed by the choice-of-law rules expressed in Articles 7 to 9 AGR. When a lessor and a lessee fail to choose the *lex contractus*, judges are likely to fall back on the principle of the closest connection with the help of the presumptive rule based on the characteristic performance. As a consequence, in the absence of choice, the law of the country of the lessor's habitual residence would have more chance to apply as the law of the country most closely connected with the contract.

B. *Factoring*

187. The law applicable to the factoring contract is also governed by the choice-of-law rule as set out in Articles AGR. When a supplier and a factor fail to choose the *lex contractus*, judges are likely, here again, to fall back on the principle of the closest connection with the help of the presumptive rule based on the characteristic performance. As a consequence, in the absence of choice, the law of the country of the factor's habitual residence would have more chance to apply as the law of the country most closely connected with the contract.

C. *Franchise*

188. The law applicable to the franchise contract is governed by the choice-of-law rule as set out in Articles 7 to 9 AGR. When a franchisor and a franchisee fail to choose the *lex contractus*, the principle of the closest connection applies coupled with the presumptive rule based on the characteristic performance. Under JPIL, there is no choice-of-law rule working in favour of the law of the country of the franchisee's habitual residence. As a consequence, in the absence of choice, the country of the franchisor's habitual residence is presumed to be most closely connected with the contract.

D. *Publishing Contract*

189. In the publishing contract, the author normally undertakes to write and deliver the manuscript and to grant a licence to copy the work to the publisher in exchange for a royalty. The author's performance is, however, counterbalanced by that of the publisher who publishes and distributes the work. One would hesitate to say that the author is considered to perform the characteristic obligation simply because, without manuscripts, there would be no distribution. The obligations on both sides are vital to the contract. It is submitted that judges should have direct recourse to the test of the closest connection without help of the notion of characteristic performance.

E. *Other*

190. The joint venture contract seems to belong to the type of contract whose applicable law, in the absence of choice, is most likely to be determined without recourse to the test of characteristic performance.

IX. Negotiable Instruments

A. *Bills of Exchange*

191. The Bills of Exchange Act which was enacted in 1932, modelled upon the 1930 Geneva Convention Providing a Uniform Law for Bills of Exchange and Promissory Notes, is the main source of substantive rules relating to the bills of exchange.[160] The Act, at the same time, reproduces a certain choice-of-law rules set out in the 1930 Convention for the Settlement of Certain Conflict of Laws in Connection with Bills of Exchange and Promissory Notes. As a result, the Act (Articles 88–90) contains the choice-of-law rules basically adopting the principle of *lex loci actus* (Articles 2–4 of the Convention).

B. Cheques

192. The Cheques Act was also modelled upon the 1931 Geneva Convention Providing a Uniform Law for Cheques and the 1931 Geneva Convention for the Settlement of Certain Conflict of Laws in Connection with Cheques.[161] Consequently, the choice-of-law rules contained in the Act (Articles 77 and 80) tend to use the place of payment as a connecting factor.

C. Letters of Credit

193. Letters of credit generally incorporate the Uniform Customs and Practice for Documentary Credits ('UCP'). The law governing the contract in which the UCP is incorporated is undoubtedly determined by Articles 7 to 9 AGR. Those provisions determine the law applicable to the following distinct relationships: that between the (usually) buyer and the issuing bank, that between the issuing bank and the corresponding bank, that between the corresponding bank and the (usually) seller, and that between the seller and the issuing bank. To date, it is in connection with the last relationship that the Japanese court has determined the governing law in the absence of the choice of law by the parties. Whereas fully aware of the primary role played by the issuing bank, the court regarded the agreed place of payment as more important in the particular case and held that the parties implicitly chose the law of that place.[162] It should be noted that this judgment had been rendered before the AGR came into force. If the same case should arise under the AGR, the Japanese court might apply the law of the agreed place of payment as the law of the closest connection with the contract between the seller and the issuing bank in the sense of Article 8(1) AGR, rebutting the presumption in favour of the law of the issuing bank's habitual residence.

X. Agency Contracts

194. The external relationship between the principal and the third party is, in principle, governed by the law of the contract where the agent acted.[163] Unless a

160. Act No. 20 of 15 Jul. 1932.
161. Act No. 57 of 29 Jul. 1933.
162. Judgment of the Tokyo District Court, 27 Sept. 2003, *Kinyu Homu* 1706-40. The judgment was approved by the judgment of the Tokyo High Court, 30 Mar. 2004, 48 *J.A.I.L.*184 (2005).
163. *See*, para. 153 *supra.*

contract is classified into the consumer or the employment contract in the sense of Article 11 or 12 AGR, the choice-of-law rules as set out in Articles 7 to 9 AGR are applicable to the contractual relationship between the principal and the agent. As a consequence, to the extent that the *lex contractus* was not chosen by the parties, the choice-of-law rules as contained in Article 8 AGR will apply. The presumptive rule based on the characteristic performance will lead to the application of the law of the place where the agent as service provider is habitually resident. Under JPIL, there is no rule aimed at protecting commercial agents vis-à-vis their principals, for example, in the event of rescission of contract.

§3. Non-contractual Obligations

I. Party Autonomy

195. According to Article 21 AGR, the parties to a tort may agree the law applicable to obligations arising out of the tort after the event giving rise to the damage occurred. The law explicitly or implicitly chosen by the parties governs the non-contractual obligations which, in the absence of choice, would be governed by one of the laws objectively applicable pursuant to the preceding choice-of-law rules as contained in Articles 17 to 20 AGR.[164] There is no restriction in terms of the type of torts and the spatial range of choice. This *post factum* choice of law is also available for unjust enrichment as well as *negotiorum gestio* to the same extent (Article 16 AGR).[165] This extension of the party autonomy to all types of non-contractual obligations is welcome, because it would enhance the parties' legitimate expectations as to the applicable law.[166]

196. The both provisions as set out in Articles 16 and 21 AGR allow the parties to choose the applicable law only after the event giving rise to the damage occurred. The protection to be given to the weaker party underlies this temporal restriction.[167] However, this restriction on the party autonomy does not entirely deprive the *ex-ante* agreement of significance. If there was a pre-existing contractual relationship governed by the law chosen by the parties, all types of non-contractual obligations are likely to be governed by the same law through the channel of the escape clause as contained in Articles 15 and 20 AGR. To that extent, the *ex-ante* agreement may be honoured by Japanese courts.

164. It is said that, although the *Horei* had no black-letter rule allowing the party autonomy in tort, the parties, in the maritime practice, agreed the law applicable to disputes after collisions of their vessels.
165. Articles 16 and 21 AGR have no black-letter rule designed to regulate the question as to the validity of an agreement on the choice of law itself. It still remains to be seen which law should govern the question.
166. The persons who have succeeded to the parties' rights and obligations are undoubtedly included in the 'parties' in the sense of the said provisions.
167. JPIL stands on the assumption that the weaker party is not necessarily the consumer or the employee.

197. The third party, typically the insurer, whose rights are prejudiced by the law subsequently chosen by the parties may assert the application of the law which would be applicable in the absence of the choice of law. For example, Japanese courts will approve a third party's allegation that the non-contractual obligations have extinguished after the elapse of prescription period laid down by the *lex loci damni*, even when, under the law subsequently chosen by the parties, those obligations are still before the expiry of the period. It seems that the choice of law by the parties is not deactivated between them, but that it does not operate to the detriment of the third party's rights.[168]

II. Objective Connection

198. Article 11 (1) of the *Horei* adopted the same connecting factor, namely, the country where the event giving rise to the obligations took place, for all the non-contractual obligations arising out of *negotiorum gestio*, unjust enrichment and tort. The current provision dealing with both *negotiorum gestio* and unjust enrichment remain unaltered since 1898 (Article 14 AGR), whereas it is coupled with the escape clause expressing the principle of the closest connection (Article 15 AGR).

III. Law of Torts

199. The connecting factor of the *locus delicti* was disintegrated into the two, when the AGR was enacted: the *locus damni* and the place of action (Article 17 AGR). The former may be displaced by the latter, when it is established that no reasonable men normally could foresee that the harmful event would occur in the alleged *locus damni*. Furthermore, the two provisions for product liability and defamation were added (Articles 18 and 19 AGR). They are the *leges specialis* in relation to the choice-of-law rules as set out in Article 17 AGR. The laws designated by those choice-of-law rules on tort may be displaced by the law having the closer connection with the case (Article 20 AGR). Regrettably, the legislator of the AGR decided to maintain the double actionability rule for all kinds of torts which had been inspired by an English case law of the late nineteenth century (Article 22 AGR).

A. Lex Loci Delicti

200. As mentioned above, the connecting factor of the *locus delicti* was disintegrated into the two: the *locus damni* and the place of action (Article 17 AGR). Whereas, as mentioned below, the former may be displaced by the latter, the *lex loci damni* is, in principle, applicable to obligations arising out of tort. This connecting

168. *See*, Toshiyuki Kono, *Critical and Comparative Analysis of the Rome II Regulation on Applicable Laws to Non-contractual Obligations and the New Private International Law in Japan*, in Basedow/Baum/Nishitani, 221, 240 .

factor was adopted on the ground that the place where the result of the harmful event occurred may be, under normal situations, foreseen by the person liable as well as the person sustaining damage, and that it seems to be more faithful to the compensatory aspect of substantive laws on tort. The *locus damni* is understood as the place where the injury was sustained or where the property was damaged. Its indirect consequences which derive from such injury or damage are immaterial to determination of the *locus damni*. Otherwise, the choice-of-law rule would designate the law of the place which may be beyond the tortfeasor's legitimate expectations. If, for example, a Japanese tourist was injured by a Chinese tourist at a ski slope situated in British Columbia, the *locus damni* is British Columbia. The economic consequences which flew from the victim's hospitalization in Japan are irrelevant to the determination of the *locus*.

201. The Legislative Council was aware, at the same time, that, even if the indirect consequences were immaterial, there might still remain certain types of situations where the *locus damni* is likely to run counter to the tortfeasor's foreseeability about the link between his act and the country in which the direct consequences occurred. Such concern, first, brought them to adopt such a 'but for' test rule as contained in Article 18 AGR for product liability, probably on the implicit presupposition that Japanese manufacturers are likely to be tortfeasors. Then, the *lex generalis* was thought necessary to be synchronized with the *lex specialis* on product liability. The general choice-of-law rule as enunciated in Article 17 AGR came to be coupled with the clause designed to ensure the tortfeasor's foreseeability about the causal link between a tortfeasor's act and the *locus damni*. According to the second sentence of Article 17 AGR, the *lex loci damni* may be displaced in favour of the law of the place where the tortfeasor acted, when it is established that no reasonable men normally could foresee that the harmful event would occur in the alleged *locus damni*. Suppose that an earthquake with a massive scale directly hit an area of country A. The building owned by Y collapsed because of Y's failure to make it quake-proof in spite of repeated warnings by the local authority of the country A. A Japanese tourist who happened to take lunch in a restaurant within that building was dead on that occasion. Where his death was broadcast in Japan to the distress of his father X, which law should Japanese courts apply to determine the defendant Y's liability for the claimant X's psychiatric harm? Even though the *locus damni* is Japan, the law of the country A should be applicable as the law of the place where the person liable acted, when the nervous shock sustained in Japan does not bear the test of foreseeability about the causal link. It should be stressed that, in applying the second sentence of Article 17, Japanese courts are required to refer not to a particular tortfeasor's foreseeability but to reasonable men's. The legislator found it inappropriate for an individual tortfeasor's subjective element to be decisive in choosing one of the limbs of the *lex loci delicti*.

202. However, a particular tortfeasor's and a particular victim's foreseeability in individual circumstances should be taken into account within the framework of the escape clause as contained in Article 20 AGR. Suppose that a tortfeasor sent a letter from country A to country B where a victim is habitually resident. The victim, who was about to leave for a business trip to country C, did not open it at home but only after he reached a hotel situated in country C and immediately sustained the nervous shock because of its content. Neither the law of C which is the *locus damni* nor the law of A where the tortfeasor acted seems to be appropriate in terms of both parties' foreseeability. The application of the law of country B is most likely to satisfy it. In such a case where the two limbs of the *lex loci delicti commissi* are incapable of designating the law foreseeable to the parties, Japanese courts will have recourse to the escape clause of Article 20 AGR.

203. Article 18 AGR is a provision for product liability. It is the *lex specialis* in relation to Article 17 AGR. The requirements which trigger the application of the choice-of-law rule contained in Article 18 AGR are three. Unless all of them are met, the law applicable to liability for damages is determined by the general rule as set out by Article 17 AGR. First, the choice-of-law rule as contained in Article 18 AGR covers the 'product'. While the 'product' appears to reflect the concept of 'product' as referred to in Article 2(1) of the Japanese Product Liability Act,[169] it is understood as meaning broader range of products, probably as broad as those as set out in Article 2a) of the Hague Convention of 2 October 1973 on the Law Applicable to Products Liability. Second, the persons claimed to be liable must be the 'producers, etc.'. The concept of 'producers, etc.', as set out in Article 18 encompasses the following persons: manufacturers, processors, exporters, or importers of the product in the course of trade and other persons in the commercial chain of preparation or distribution of the product. The said provision appears to juxtapose the 'manufacturers, etc.', as referred to in Article 2(3) of the Japanese Product Liability Act with the 'persons' set out by Article 3 of the Hague Convention of 2 October 1973. Third, in addition to the group of persons claimed to be liable and to the category of objects, Article 18 AGR requires that damage be caused by a 'defective' product. A product seems to be regarded as defective, not only when the product as such does not meet the standard of safety, but also, e.g., when adequate or appropriate information failed to be given, e.g., about its method of use. When all these requirements are met, the law applicable to liability is determined by the law of the country where a product was delivered to the person sustaining damage.[170] The place of delivery seems to be understood as meaning the place where, whatever the title to it may be, the product was legally placed at a person's disposal, which does not necessarily coincide with the place of acquisition of physical possession.[171] The place of delivery was adopted as the connecting factor, because it seems likely to coincide with the place of marketing which is, in principle, foreseeable to producers as well as other potentially liable persons, or with the place of the habitual residence of the victim. The law of the country of delivery may be displaced by the law of the country where a producer has the principal place of business (or, in its absence, the habitual residence). The displacement is conditioned by the tortfeasor's foreseeability. However, the foreseeability clause as contained in Article 18

169. Act No. 40 of 1 Jul. 1994.
170. The connecting factor of the place of delivery would implicitly define the category of persons sustaining damage. Persons such as children or employees who are taken care of by another person to whom a defective product was supplied would fall under the category of persons covered by Art. 18 AGR.
171. This connecting factor covers the case of downloading of a software product through the internet.

requires that reasonable traders in general could not foresee the delivery of the product in the alleged country of delivery. A particular tortfeasor's foreseeability in individual circumstances of a case should be taken into account within the framework of the escape clause as contained in Article 20 AGR.

204. Article 19 AGR contains a choice-of-law rule for defamation. It is the other *lex specialis* in relation to Article 17 AGR. There were a few cases relating to defamation in which Japanese media was involved. In light of the likelihood that defamation actions will be raised in Japanese courts in the future and the inadequacy of the *locus damni* as a connecting factor for defamation, the Legislative Council decided to make a specific choice-of-law rule for that matter. The defamation in the sense of Article 19 AGR covers only the violation of a person's reputation or business creditability. The Legislative Council did not intend to extend the material scope of the provision to personality rights in general. Consequently, wrongful interference with other personality rights than a person's reputation or business creditability is regulated by the general choice-of-law rule on tort (Article 17 AGR) in combination with the escape clause (Article 20 AGR). According to Article 19 AGR, defamation claims are governed by the law of the country in which the victim is habitually resident or has the principal place of business. The recourse to the *locus damni* in the context of defamation was thought to entail that two or more laws may be applied on a distributive basis, which seemed to be hardly practicable. Unlike the product liability, the place of acting was rejected even in the subsidiary connecting factor, because the place of publication, in particular, may be subject to the tortfeasor's manipulation. It should be added in this context that the Japanese media industry has hardly operated their business on the worldwide scale.[172] In any event, the reputation or the business creditability which was or will be compromised was thought to be usually localized within the social environment in which the victim is habitually resident. The law applicable determined by Article 19 AGR may be displaced, here again, in favour of the law determined by Article 20 AGR.

205. Article 20 AGR is an escape clause which enables the court to displace the laws applicable pursuant to Articles 17 to 19 AGR in favour of the law of another country with which the tort is manifestly more closely connected. The provision exemplarily refers to the habitual residence of the parties in the same country as a circumstance which the court should take account of in applying the manifestly closer connection test.[173] This is most welcome. Japanese courts constantly have dealt with tort cases which arose out of traffic or sport accidents taking place abroad but between tourists or businessmen habitually resident in Japan.[174] In such cases, Japanese law is more likely to meet the legitimate expectations of the parties than the law of the foreign country where they stayed temporarily. It should be added

172. *See*, Koide, 227.
173. It should be stressed that, under the AGR, the common habitual residence has not so much weight as to displace automatically the law identified in one of the preceding provisions but only indicates one of possible bases for the displacement.
174. For example, Judgment of the Chiba District Court, 24 Jul. 1997, *Hanji* 1639-86.

that Japanese insurers, with whom persons claimed to be liable entered into contracts of liability insurance, are usually prepared to pay insurance money under Japanese law. Article 20 AGR also exemplarily refers to the situation where the conduct of a person claimed to be liable consists of the breach of obligations arising out of the pre-existing contract between the parties. It follows that, when the conduct of the defendant falls short of the standard set by the law applicable to the contractual relationship of the parties, the *lex contractus* may also govern the tort claim. For example, the law applicable to a deposit contract will be also applied to a tort claim, when the depositary negligently gave damage to the deposited thing. The determination of the law applicable to tort on such an 'accessory basis' is welcome. First, the standard set by the law applicable to the contract is likely to be more satisfactory in terms of the parties' expectations. Second, the accessory determination of the applicable law is capable of avoiding difficult problems of assimilation which the concurrent liabilities might entail.

206. It is worthy of repeating that the situation to which Article 20 AGR refers to as scenarios of accessory determination of applicable law is only illustrative. The displacement would be justified in light of the parties' expectations, even when the defendant's liability does not exactly derive from conducts falling short of contractual standards. Whether or not a particular duty to care is voluntarily assumed does not seem to be always decisive in determining whether a particular law is more foreseeable than another. Furthermore, the pre-existing relationships between the parties are not limited to the contractual one. The laws governing other relationships such as marriage or parenthood may be applied on the accessory basis.[175]

207. It should be stressed here that the special *ordre public* clause as expressed in Article 22 AGR puts the cap of Japanese substantive law rules on the existence and extent of liability provided by foreign applicable laws. Whereas the special *ordre public* clause, which, as mentioned earlier, originally derived from the English case law,[176] the scope of application of Article 22 AGR, unlike the Part III of the Private International Law (Miscellaneous Provisions) Act 1995, is not limited to defamation claims. This Japanese double actionability rule should be undoubtedly criticized, because, if it is literally interpreted, the *lex fori* may intervene even when a foreign law is designated as the law of the closest connection (Article 20 AGR) or was chosen by the parties (Article 21 AGR).[177]

175. Article 3-3 PSLA confers jurisdiction upon a Japanese divorce court over a claim concerning compensation for damages arising from the facts which constitute the divorce ground.
176. *Phillips v. Eyre* (1870) L. R. 6 Q.B. 1.
177. The members of business circle, whose views were hardly negligible in relation to tort, strongly proposed the survival of this double actionability rule at the very last stage of discussions of the Legislative Council. *See*, Koide, 259. In the present author's view, academic writers are expected to interpret the scope of application of Art. 22 as narrowly as possible.

B. Scope of Application

208. The choice-of-law rules as set out in Articles 17–21 AGR are understood to govern the following issues: grounds and extent of liability;[178] existence, nature, and extent of damages; preventive measures; transfer of claims for damages, including the inheritance of the victim's right to compensation for non-pecuniary loss; persons entitled to compensation; liability for acts of another person such as vicarious liability; and causes extinguishing obligations, particularly prescription.

C. Damages (Compensation)

209. Not only the heads of damages but also the assessment of damages should be governed by the law applicable to tort, not by the *lex fori*. This is the governing view of academic writers and the general attitude of the court.[179] In quantifying the loss of anticipated interests of the victim in accordance with the law applicable to tort, Japanese law *in casu*, the Supreme Court took account of all the actual circumstances surrounding the victim in the countries where he has been and will be habitually resident.[180]

D. Insurance and Social Security Law

210. There is neither provision nor case law addressing the question whether the liability of an insurer to an injured party is classified into tortious or contractual matters. It seems, however, that the question would be governed by the *lex contractus* between the insurer and the insured. Except the vehicle liability insurance, the current Japanese insurance law does not allow the person having suffered damage to bring his claim directly against the insurer.[181] It presupposes that the liability insurance is for the benefit of the insured, not the third party victim. The victim is protected to the extent that he is entitled to the preferential right (*privilège*) to secure payment in situations where the insured is subject to bankruptcy, winding up, or other similar proceedings. In view of such Japanese substantive insurance law, it is hardly conceivable that the relationship between the insurer and the injured person is classified into one of tortious matters. Therefore, a choice-of-law provision equivalent to Article 18 of the Regulation (EC) No. 864/2007 of the European Parliament and of the Council of 11 July 2007 on the law applicable to non-contractual obligations (Rome II) seems unlikely to be enacted in the near future.

178. The rules of safety and conduct such as traffic law rules prevailing at the place of the event may be taken into account as data, when judges are called for to determine whether or not, for example, the driver claimed to be liable was negligent under the law of the place where both parties are habitually resident.

179. *See*, para. 74 *supra*.

180. Judgment of the Supreme Court, 28 Jan. 1997, *Minshu* 51-1-78.

181. Act No. 56 of 1 Apr. 2008.

IV. Unfair Competition

211. Defamation in the business context is governed by the law designated by Article 19 AGR, i.e., the law of the place where the victim's principal establishment is situated or the place where he is habitually resident. Other issues as set out in Article 2 of the Unfair Competition Prevention Act[182] are understood to be governed by the general choice-of-law rules as laid down by Articles 17 and Articles 20 to 22 AGR. This view seems to be conformable to the assumption that the substantive law provisions of the said Act has been regarded as the *lex specialis* in relation to those on tort contained in the Civil Code.[183] In discussions of the Legislative Council, the enactment of a choice-of-law rule specifically dealing with the unfair competition was proposed. However, the suggested connecting factor, the market, was hardly convincing, partly because the proposal did not seem to succeed in specifying whose interests are likely to be protected by such connecting factor and principally because of the paucity of judgments on the unfair competition in the international context.[184] As a result, the Council found the enactment of such choice-of-law rule still premature and decided to leave the matter to the development of case law.

V. *Negotiorum Gestio*

212. Article 14 AGR contains a choice-of-law rule on *negotiorum gestio*. It provides that obligations arising out of an act performed without due authority in connection with the affairs of another person are governed by the law of the place where the event giving rise to the obligations took place. The terms of the choice-of-law rule remains unaltered since 1898. In contrast to Article 11 of the *Horei*, the law applicable pursuant to that choice-of-law rule may be displaced in favour of the law determined with the closest connection test as enunciated in Article 15 AGR. Furthermore, the parties may choose a law applicable to the obligations after the event occurred.

213. It appears that there was no authoritative judgment that clarified what was meant by 'the event giving rise to the obligations' under Article 11 of the *Horei*, when the country where the intervener's unauthorized act was performed does not

182. The Act was originally enacted in 1934 for the purpose of implementing the 1883 Paris Convention for the Protection of Intellectual Property. The comprehensive reform was made in 1993 (Act No. 47 of 19 May 1993).

183. Cf. Commentary I (Nishitani), 450.

184. To the present author's knowledge, there were the following three cases at the time of the enactment of the AGR: Judgment of the Tokyo District Court, 24 Sept. 1991, *Hanji* 1429-24 (infringement of know-how); Judgment of the Tokyo District Court, 16 Oct. 2003, *Hanji* 1874-23 (unjustified requests towards customers); Judgment of Osaka District Court, 9 Nov. 2004, *Hanji* 1897-103 (passing off). It is observed that the number of international cases tends to increase in relation to the application of the Act. However, some judgments applied it as a *lex loci delicti*, whereas others did it as if they were unaware of foreign elements involved. Besides, none of them was mindful of whether the alleged act of unfair competition was related to the interests of a specific competitor or the collective interests of the market.

coincide with that where the direct consequences of such act occurred. The majority of academic writers seem to have been in favour of the application of the law of the place where the direct consequences of the intervener's unauthorized act took place.[185] For example, when, having learnt that the winter house owned by a New Yorker had been damaged by a storm in Honolulu, the owner of the neighbouring house resident in Tokyo made necessary arrangements to repair leaks in the roofs of his neighbour's house, he may claim for the reimbursement of expenses to the New Yorker under Hawaiian law. However, in view of scarcity of cases, which will be also likely under the AGR, the legislator did not dare to elaborate a choice-of-law rule dealing with such a situation. It is noteworthy that, whereas the *negotiorum gestio* cases, which are most likely to take place in international situations, seem to be related to the salvage, the maritime practice shows that disputes have been resolved on the basis of contracts entered into immediately before each assistance.

214. Article 15 AGR is an escape clause according to which, where it is clear from all the circumstances of the case that the obligation arising out of the *negotiorum gestio* is more closely connected with a country other than that indicated in Article 14 AGR, the law of that other country shall apply. For the sake of exemplarily indicating such circumstances, Article 15 refers to the common habitual residence of the parties and the contractual relationship in connection with which an act was performed without due authority. In the hypothetical episode as mentioned above, if the principal is not resident in New York but in Japan, Japanese law is likely to apply to a claim for the reimbursement in lieu of Hawaiian law. Where an agent enters into a contract with a third person beyond the authority granted by the principal, the law applicable to the agency contract may have a stronger claim to govern their reciprocal obligations arising out of the agent's unauthorized act.

215. Article 16 AGR allows the parties to choose the law applicable to the *negotiorum gestio*. The provision contains the two restrictions: the parties may choose the law only after the relevant event took place; and they cannot assert the chosen law against the third parties, when that law prejudices the rights of the third parties.

VI. Unjust Enrichment

216. Articles 14 to 16 AGR also contain the choice-of-law rules as regards unjust enrichment. According to Article 14 AGR whose content remains unaltered since 1898, obligations arising out of unjust enrichment are governed by the law of the place where the event giving rise to the obligations took place. That law may be displaced in favour of the law applicable under the escape clause as set out in Article 15 AGR. Further, the law applicable pursuant to either Article 14 AGR or Article 15 AGR is superseded by the law which the parties choose after the relevant event occurs.

---

185. *See*, Commentary I (Kitazawa), 391.

217. Subject to Articles 15 and 16 AGR, Japanese courts will apply the law of the country where the relevant event took place. When some enrichment takes place by operation of law under the rules of the *lex rei sitae*, e.g., rules on accession, the connecting factor as enunciated in Article 14 would coincide with the *situs*. However, the legislator did not specify where is the place in which the event giving rise to obligations arising out of the unjust enrichment took place, when a person disadvantaged acted in the country other than that where a person enriched received or enjoyed economic benefits. It remains to be seen how this connecting factor will be determined in varied types of situations. As far as Article 14 is as it stands, much seems to be left for Article 15 AGR.

218. Article 15 AGR is an escape clause according to which, where it is clear from all the circumstances of the case that the obligation arising out of the unjust enrichment is more closely connected with a country other than that indicated in Article 14, the law of that other country shall apply. Article 15 exemplarily refers to the contractual relationship between the parties, namely, the party disadvantaged and the party enriched. As a result, laws governing contracts will be applicable to claims to reverse enrichments in connection with contracts which turned out to be either void or avoided. The said provision also refers to the common habitual residence of the parties as one of the circumstances capable of indicating the country more closely connected.

219. According to Article 16 AGR, the parties may choose a law applicable to the unjust enrichment on the same condition as mentioned above with respect to the *negotiorum gestio*.

VII. *Culpa in Contrahendo*

220. Under the Japanese substantive law, contractual parties may be liable on account of an act or an omission taking place during the period of negotiations prior to concluding contracts. Without using the notion of *culpa in contrahendo*, the Supreme Court founded this liability upon the idea of good faith and fair dealings in 1984.[186] Whereas it is debated whether the notion of *culpa in contrahendo* originated in Germany has been implanted in Japan or whether such pre-contractual liabilities may be explained in terms of contract or tort, academic writers of private law have usually referred to the four typical scenarios: (1) the void or voidable contract; (2) the unjustified breaking-off of negotiations; (3) the misrepresentation, and; (4) the physical injury that occurs on the occasion of negotiations.

221. The AGR contains no choice-of-law rules specifically dealing with the *culpa in contrahendo*. The legislative silence seems to be due to the paucity of relevant cases and, above all, to the fact that the contours of the category of *culpa in contrahendo* could hardly be drawn. If, under the current PIL, it should be assumed that the contractual obligations as envisaged by Articles 7 to 9 AGR are only the

186. *See*, Oda, *supra*, 154–155.

obligations freely and voluntarily assumed by the parties, it would follow that the pre-contractual liabilities in the above-mentioned scenarios should be governed by Articles 17 to 21 AGR on tort. The personal injury suffered by a customer who slipped on a piece of banana on the floor in a department store would be entitled to have compensation pursuant to the *lex loci delicti* (scenario 4). When a contract turned out to be void on the ground of the rule of *impossibilium nulla obligatio*, the pre-contractual liability can hardly dissociate itself from the concluded contract. It follows that, pursuant to Article 20 AGR, the *lex contractus* is likely to govern such liability as the law more closely connected than the *lex loci delicti* (scenario 1). The accessory application of the *lex contractus* also seems appropriate to the liability arising in the context of the scenario 3, for example, when a party failed to disclose essential facts to the other party before concluding their contract. Furthermore, the application of the *lex contractus* can be talked about in the scenario 2. Suppose that a party primarily claims for compensation on the ground of the other's failure to perform his contractual obligations but, alternatively, anticipating that the court might find the alleged contract inexistent, the same party claims for compensation on the ground of the unjustified breaking-off of negotiations. When a party makes such primary and secondary claims before the court on the alternative basis, the parities may have reached the mature stage of negotiations, mature enough for the court to be able to identify the plausible *lex contractus*. However, this may not be always the case.[187] It remains to be seen how the Japanese court will deal with situations where such *lex contractus in negotio* cannot be identified. It should be noted that Article 20 AGR does not require the court to apply the *lex contractus in negotio* in cascade hierarchy but to take it into account as one of circumstances that indicate the law of the place more closely connected with the case than the *lex loci delicti.*

187. The judgment of the Tokyo District Court, 30 Jul. 1985, 29 *J.A.I.L.* 255 (1986) (related to breaking-off of negotiations aimed at joint venture arrangement between a Malaysian entrepreneur and a Japanese company over lumber products situated in Indonesia) applied the law of the place of the negotiations as the *lex loci delicti*.

Chapter 3. Property

§1. *Lex Rei Sitae*

222. Article 13 AGR contains the two choice-of-law rules. The first paragraph reads as follows: the existence and the effects of property rights are governed by the law of the country in which the property is situated. This choice-of-law rule is followed by the rule according to which the acquisition and the loss of such rights are governed by the law of the country in which the property is situated at the time when all the requirements triggering the acquisition or the loss are perfected. The distinction between movable and immovable property is irrelevant to the application of those choice-of-law rules.[188]

223. The principle of the *lex rei sitae* seems to be justified by the four reasons. First, property rights, in nature, affect the interests of the third parties such as creditors and purchasers who intend to acquire those rights. It entails that one has to adopt the connecting factor as manifest as possible to everyone who cares to know about the property rights. Second, the principle of *numerus clausus* would not allow such rights over things situated in a country to be created under the law of another country, in the interests of clarity and legal certainty. Third, although the Japanese court has no exclusive jurisdiction over immovable property situated in Japan, the *situs* rule is likely to lead to the application of the *lex fori* as regards immovable property. This will also facilitate the works of registrars and of execution officers. Fourth, land is a state's natural resource whose availability is linked with the state's economic and political interests. For example, Article 17 of the Mining Act prohibits foreign nationals to hold the mining rights, unless otherwise provided for in the treaty concerned.[189] The *lex rei sitae* rule allows such substantive law rules to apply without recourse to the notion of overriding mandatory rules. The sphere of application allotted by the choice-of-law rule referring to the *lex rei sitae* coincides with the scope of operation required by such overriding mandatory rules.[190]

224. The *lex rei sitae* also governs the formalities of transactions which directly create, transfer or extinguish property rights. Unlike contracts underlying such transactions, the principle of *locus regit actum* does not apply to such transactions of proprietary nature (Article 10 (5) AGR).

225. The connecting factor of the *situs* is hardly appropriate for ships and aircraft. Their *situs* at a particular time might not be ascertained or can be so only fortuitously. It has been often said that, as far as the things destined to move across borders are concerned, the *situs* should be replaced by the place of registration. The place of registration was agreeable to the members of the Legislative Council as regards aircraft. Whereas the AGR contains no explicit choice-of-law rule dealing

188. For the critical overview of the judgments relating to the *lex rei sitae* rule, *see*, Naoe Fujisawa, *Conflict of Laws in Matters Concerning Property*, 53 J.Y.B.I.L. 490 et seq. (2010).
189. Act No. 289 of 20 Dec. 1950.
190. *See*, Yokoyama, 151–152.

with rights in rem of the aircraft, the court will undoubtedly apply the law of the country where an aircraft was registered. By contrast, the place of registration of the ship appeared to be dubious as a connecting factor. Experience told the members of the Legislative Council that ships were sometimes registered in more than one country and that places of registration might have almost nothing to do with their ownerships and managements. They could not reach the conclusion as to what issues the law of the place of registration should adequately govern.[191] Everything was left to the development of case law.[192]

§2. MOVEABLE PROPERTY

226. As mentioned above, the *lex rei sitae* determines what the *iura* in rem are (Article 13 (1) AGR).[193] If the *situs* changes from one country to another, the content of the *ius* may also change. When the current *lex rei sitae* does not know the same type of right as created under the previous *lex rei sitae*, the previous right turns into the right different but most similar under the current *lex rei sitae*. It also determines whether the ownership of a certain movable property is inalienable.

227. According to 13(2) AGR, the *lex rei sitae* determines whether a property right over a particular object comes into existence, or passes to another person, or is extinguished. Once the requirements for the acquisition of a *ius* in rem was satisfied pursuant to the law of a country during the period of the object being situated in that country, the acquired right remains in force elsewhere, too. In contrast, when the acquisition of a *ius* in rem was not perfected under the law of a country, the defect is not cured simply by the transport of the object to another country. It is irrelevant whether, if hypothetically applied, the new *lex rei sitae* would regard the acquisition as having been perfected. On the other hand, it is possible that the new *lex rei sitae* takes account of a certain facts having taken place in the previous *situs*. For example, if a possessor brought an object to Japan before the period of limitation required by a foreign *lex rei sitae* was completed, the elapse of time having taken place in the foreign country may be taken into account under Japanese substantive law rule on the acquisition of ownership by the possessor in good faith.

---

191. *See*, Koide, 423, 426.
192. A car registered in Germany which had been stolen in Italy was imported to Japan through the UAE. In subrogation of the original car owner, a German insurance company raised the action of vindication against the bona fide purchaser of the stolen car. The Supreme Court faced the question which law should be applied, the *lex originis* (German law) or the *lex rei sitae* (Japanese law). The Court applied Japanese law on the assumption that, given that one is allowed to drive a registered car in Japan, unregistered cars are as good as antiques (Judgment of the Supreme Court, 29 Oct. 2002, 46 *J.A.I.L.* 175 (2003)).
193. It also applies to the problem whether the tenants' claim against the landowner for the use of real property may turn into the *ius* in rem when the claim is registered in the public register.

I. Collateral

228. In Japan, the practically important exception to the rule of *lex rei sitae* concerns maritime liens. Most of the authors used to be of opinion that the law of the flag should govern maritime liens on condition that they also exist under the *lex contractus*. However, it is said that, in the majority of cases on maritime law, either the law of the actual *situs* or the *lex fori* has applied to maritime liens disregarding the *lex contractus*.[194] However, this solution has been criticized because the application of such laws might run counter to legitimate expectations of ship owners and other persons involved.

II. Goods in Transitu

229. There has been no Japanese authoritative judgment on transfer of goods *in transitu*. It is academically conceivable that goods whose *situs* is unknown or only fortuitously ascertainable at a particular moment are transferred from one party to another. Authors tend to propose that the law of the place of their final destination should apply to such situations. However, the current commercial practice tells us that such imaginative situation would hardly happen.[195]

III. Cultural Property

230. The *lex rei sitae* governs almost the whole range of questions concerned with proprietary rights, namely, how they are acquired, exercised, transferred, or lost (Article 13 AGR). It follows that the *lex rei sitae* is applicable to questions about the transfer of the ownership over a cultural property, including the question whether the principle of *nemo dat quod no habet* applies to the cultural property. As a consequence, for example, when an art object which a foreign state regards as *res extra commercium* was stolen and brought into Japan, it becomes the *res in commercio* whose fate depends on the current *lex rei sitae*, Japanese law.

231. Japan is a party of the Convention on the Means of Prohibiting and Preventing the Illicit Import, Export, and Transfer of Ownership of Cultural Property 1970. The Act implementing the Convention allows the victim of theft to claim for the *rei vindicatio* from the bona fide purchaser within a total period of ten years from the time of the theft, extending the normal period of two years as set out in Article 193 of the Civil Code (Article 6 of the Act).[196] However, the Act contains no choice-of-law rule designed to facilitate the prevention of illicit transactions over cultural properties.

---

194. Commentary I (Takeshita), 383–384. *See*, Judgment of the Fukuoka District Court, 4 Dec. 2015, 60 *J.Y.B.I.L.*517 (2017) and Judgment of the Kobe District Court, 21 Jan. 2016, 60 *J.Y.B.I.L.*520 (2017).
195. *See*, Koide, 166.
196. Act No. 81 of 3 Jul. 2002.

§3. IMMOVABLE PROPERTY

232. The *lex rei sitae* applies to real rights on immovables as well as movables (Article 13 AGR). To the present author's knowledge, there has been no Japanese judgment that doubted the scope of application of the *situs* rule with regard to rights on immovable property, whether they may be related to ownership or limited real rights such as mortgage. There is no case concerning immissions nor easements due to the geographical situation where Japan is located. Most of the authors are also silent about those problems.

I. Mortgage

233. *See,* paragraph 233 *supra.*

II. Immissions

234. *See*, paragraph 233 *supra.*

III. Easements

235. *See*, paragraph 233 *supra.*

§4. SECURITIES

236. As far as tangible property is concerned, the *lex rei sitae*, in principle, governs the creation of a security right, its effectiveness against a third party and its priority against competing claimants (Article 13 AGR). When the tangible property is represented by negotiable document of title such as a bill of lading, the *situs* is not determined in terms of the actual property but the document.

237. The Act on Special Provisions, etc., of the Civil Code Concerning the Perfection Requirements for the Assignment of Movables and Claims introduced a digitally organized filing system with which legal persons may perfect the assignment of movables by way of security in movables.[197] Article 3 of the Act equates a registration of assignment of movables in the file with the physical delivery of the movables as set forth in Article 178 of the Civil Code.[198] It should be noted that this provision seems to presuppose that Japanese law is applicable as the *lex rei sitae* and that it appears not to cover the situation where assets are located in more than one country.

197. Act No.104 of 12 Jun. 1998.

198. Article 178 of the Civil Code reads as follows: the transfers of real rights concerning movables may not be asserted against third party, unless the movables are delivered.

238. With regard to a right to payment of a monetary obligation, Article 23 AGR applies to its creation, its effectiveness against a third party and its priority against competing claimants. All the issues are governed by the law applicable to each monetary obligation. The Act on Special Provisions, etc., of the Civil Code Concerning the Perfection Requirements for the Assignment of Movables and Claims also enables financial institutions to perfect the assignment of receivables including future ones when a registration of assignment is made in a claim assignment registration file with regard to the assignment of the claim. According to Article 4 of the Act, the registration is assimilated to the notice to all third parties other than the debtor of the claim in the sense of Article 467 of the Civil Code.[199] The Act appears to presuppose that Japanese law is applicable to each monetary obligation to be assigned even when a bulky assignment is involved.

§5. TRUST

239. In 1922, the Trust Act,[200] combined with the Trust Business Act which purported to regulate trust companies,[201] was enacted, modelled upon the Indian Trust Act 1882 and the California Civil Code 1872. Therefore, it is not surprising that the Japanese delegation at the fifteenth session of the Hague Conference wanted the Japanese institution to be encompassed by the future convention, namely, the Hague Convention of 1 July 1985 on the Law Applicable to Trusts and on their Recognition.[202] Whereas the above-mentioned foreign pieces of legislation seemed to deal with family trusts as their main paradigm, the Japanese trust business after the Second World War curiously developed under the said Trust Act, centring around commercial trusts such as pension trusts, loan trusts, or asset securitization. For the purpose of meeting the developments of such financial environments and promoting the wider utilization of trust in the family context, the Trust Act whose provisions had been only broad-brushed was finally revised in 2006.[203]

240. That revision of the Trust Act went on almost simultaneously as that of PIL. The Legislative Council in charge of the latter work was fully mindful of the progress of the revision of the Trust Act, but could not foresee definitely how the said Act would be revised. Even if the Legislative Council of PIL could have foreseen it, it would probably have put forward no proposal about choice-of-law rules on trust. First, there seemed no serious debate on trust among experts of PIL due to paucity of cases. Second, it was easy for the members of the Legislative Council of

199. Article 467 of the Civil Code reads as follows: the assignment of a nominative claim may not be asserted against the applicable obligor or any other third party, unless the assignor gives a notice thereof to the obligor or the obligor has acknowledged the same.
200. Act No. 62 of 21 Apr. 1922.
201. Act No. 65 of 21 Apr. 1922.
202. *See*, *Actes et documents de la Quinzième session 8 au 20 octobre 1984*, 375.
203. *See*, Lusina Ho & Rebecca Lee, *Reception of the Trust in Asia: An Historical Perspective*, in *Trust Law in Asian Civil Law Jurisdictions: A Comparative Analysis* 10 et seq., (Lusina Ho & Rebecca Lee eds., Cambridge University Press 2013).

PIL to imagine what a formidable task they would carry out in addressing the problem of the trust. There are a variety of borderlines to be drawn between the trust and other institutions such as succession, guardianship, legal person, and property. Furthermore, it had to be decided which provisions of the Trust Business Act[204] revised in 2004 should be classified into overriding mandatory rules. As a result, the matter was left to the development of case law.[205]

§6. Expropriation

241. There has been only one case concerning effects of an expropriation by a foreign state, in which it was disputed whether the Iranian nationalization order issued in 1951 was valid so as to legitimatize a Japanese oil company's title to the extracted oil originally owned by the dispossessed Anglo-Iranian Oil Company. The Tokyo High Court affirmed the Japanese company's ownership, applying Iranian law as the *lex rei sitae,* without examining whether or not the expropriation decree was in conformity with international law.[206] The majority of experts seems to be of opinion that the court should have 'recognized' the Iranian order because it expressed a norm as individual as a divorce decree rendered by a foreign court.[207]

204. Act No. 154 of 3 Dec. 2004.
205. *See*, Koide, 413–416.
206. Judgment of the Tokyo High Court, 11 Sept. 1953, *Kosai Minshu* 6-11-702.
207. *See*, Yokoyama, 159.

Chapter 4. Intangible Property Rights

§1. Rights of Personality

I. Applicable Law

242. The AGR contains no specific choice-of-law rules for 'rights of personality' in general such as Articles 33 and 139 of the Swiss Private International Law and Article 24 of the Italian Private International Law. The legislative silence is due to the fact that no member of the Legislative Council was confident of defining the boundary of the category of 'rights of personality'.[208] The explicit provision relating to such rights is only Article 19 AGR on defamation. That provision covers defamation cases whose victims are not only natural but also legal persons. It is still not clear whether the choice-of-law rule as set out in that provision will encompass such types of tort as violation of privacy and disclosure of confidential data. It is likely that judges will have recourse to Article 17 AGR (tort in general) with the help of the escape clause of Article 20 AGR.

II. Remedies

243. The law designated by one of those choice-of-law rules will govern the remedies, for example, whether the victim is entitled to the right of reply or equivalent measures and prohibitory injunctions against publishers. It should be noted that the double actionability rule puts the cap of the *lex fori* on the kinds of remedy available under foreign applicable laws (Article 22 (2) AGR).

§2. Patents

244. The AGR and the Japanese Patent Act[209] contain no specific choice-law-rules dealing with patents.[210]

I. Creation

245. It is undisputed among academic writers that the creation of patent rights is governed by the *lex loci protectionis*, namely, the law of the country where the application was brought for its governmental agency and where they were granted

208. *See*, Koide, 224.
209. Act No. 121 of 1959.
210. For the development of the Japanese choice-of-law rules on intellectual property in general, *see*, Shoichi Kidana, *Private International Law Principles on Intellectual Property Recent Development of Court Precedents in Japan and Current Characteristics*, 52 *J.Y.B.I.L.* 454 et seq. (2009).

by it. Referring to Article 4(2) of the Paris Convention for the Protection of Industrial Property, a judgment of the Supreme Court affirmed that the national patent rights were created on a country-by-country basis.[211]

II. Protection

246. According to the above judgment of the Supreme Court, the *lex loci protectionis*, namely, the law of the country under which a patent right was created also governs issues relating to effects of the patent right. Whereas the Court did not explain fully what the effects of a patent right meant, it seems to include the content of exclusive rights and their duration.

III. Ownership and Transfer

247. First, it seems logical that the *lex loci protectionis* which governs the creation of the patent should be applicable to who is entitled to it. Another judgment of the Supreme Court approved the application of the *lex loci protectionis* with regard to the first ownership issue.[212] So is its transferability, namely, the question of whether the patent right can be transferred.

248. The second important question is the employee's invention. In the said judgment, the Court distinguished the questions relating to the transfer of patent rights as such from the contractual ones such as employees' compensation for inventions. It held that the *lex loci protectionis* would govern the question who was entitled to file a patent application. However, the Court allowed an employer and an employee to choose the law applicable to the employee's compensation in return for the employer's rights to obtain the patent rights of several countries. As a result, the Court reached the conclusion that Japanese law as the *lex contractus* implicitly chosen by the parties, including the provision of the Japanese Patent Act concerning the remuneration, should apply to the possibility of the employee's obtaining compensation. It is arguable, however, that the provisions should have been applied as the overriding mandatory rules irrespective of whether the *lex contractus* was Japanese, which seems more consistent with the idea underlying the Patent Act, as acknowledged by the Court, that to assure the employee's remuneration would serve as an impetus to their inventions eventually leading to the national industrial development.[213]

211. Judgment of the Supreme Court, 7 Jul. 1997, 41 *J.A.I.L.* 100 (1998): a German manufacturer of aluminium car wheels tried to prevent a Japanese purchaser from reselling the German patented wheels in Japan.

212. Judgment of the Supreme Court, 17 Oct. 2006, *Minshu* 60-8-2853.

213. *See*, Mari Nagata, *The Applicable Law in Patent Infringement*, 55 *J.Y.B.I.L.* 496 et seq. (2012); Toshiyuki Kono & Paulius Jurčys, '*General Report*', in *Kono*, 185.

IV. Infringement

249. There is no specific choice-of-law rule dealing with infringements of intellectual property rights. What seems to represent the current case law is a judgment of the Supreme Court known as the *Card Reader* case.[214] A Japanese who owned a patent of US, not of Japan, filed a suit against a Japanese company seeking three remedies: (1) an injunction against production and export of the products to the US; (2) destruction of the products; and (3) compensatory damages. The Court held as follows with regard to (1) and (2): the law of the country for which protection is sought is the law of the country where the patent was registered, the US law *in casu*; although the defendant's acts done in Japan are within the spatial reach of the US Patent Law, such extraterritorial reach of the protective measures is so incompatible with the fundamental idea of territoriality underlying the Japanese Patent Law as to be disregarded out of the *ordre public* consideration. However, the Court characterized the claim for compensation arising out of the infringement of the US patent right as tortious and took the US Patent Law for the *lex loci delicti*, but denied its application on account of the double actionability rule which requires that the act in question be the one which would be also regarded as a tort under Japanese Law.

250. One of the reasons why the AGR is silent on the applicable law to the infringements of patent rights derives from this judgment of the Supreme Court which had been rendered immediately before the legislative work of the AGR started.[215] Whereas the parallelism between the infringement of patent right and its protection seemed to militate in favour of the *lex loci protectionis*, one could not ignore the judgment expressing the approach of the *lex loci delicti*. It is submitted that Japanese courts will not continue to take the *lex loci delicti* approach under Article 17 AGR on tort, because they are not capable of identifying the *lex loci damni* without taking the *lex loci protectionis* at least for the starting point of searching the applicable law.

§3. Copyright

251. The AGR and the Japanese Copyright Act[216] contain no specific choice-law-rule dealing with copyrights, either. It is disputed whether Article 5(2) of the Berne Convention expresses a choice-of-law rule. Unlike patent rights and other rights subject to registration, the *lex loci protectionis* in the context of the copyright is understood to mean the law of the country where the copyright work is exploited.[217]

---

214. Judgment of the Supreme Court, 26 Sept. 2002, 46 *J.A.I.L.*168 (2003).
215. *See*, Koide, 229–230.
216. Act No. 48 of 6 May 1970.
217. Commentary I (Dougauchi), 636.

I. Creation

252. It seems that the creation of copyright should be governed by the *lex loci protectionis.*

II. Protection

253. It is arguable that issues relating to protection of copyrights are also governed by the *lex loci protectionis*, because the right of a certain exclusive nature was created under that law. Academic writers tend to regard moral rights as one aspect of a copyright to be governed by the *lex loci protectionis*, not as a personality right of the author to be governed by some other law determined in alignment with personality rights, e.g., privacy.[218]

III. Ownership and Transfer

254. There seems no Japanese judgment dealing with which law governs who the first owner of the copyright is. It seems to be accepted that the creation of the copyright being inextricably linked to the identification of the owner, the *lex loci protectionis* should govern the question to whom the copyright is granted. There seems no Japanese author advocating the *lex originis*.

255. The question whether the copyright is transferrable is also governed by the same law. A judgment of the Tokyo High Court distinguished the law applicable to the contract causing the transfer of the copyright from its transfer as such and applied the *lex contractus* to the former and the *lex loci protectionis* to the latter.[219] This approach has been followed by the subsequent court decisions.[220]

IV. Infringement

256. There is no Supreme Court judgment that dealt with copyright infringements. Inferior courts had tendency to separate claims for injunction from those for compensatory damages. Relying on Article 5(2) of the Berne Convention, they applied to the former question, Japanese law, as the country where protection was sought. However, they classified claims for compensatory damages into tort.[221]

---

218. Commentary I (Deguchi), 487–488.
219. Judgment, 28 May 2003, 47 *J.A.I.L.* 218 (2004).
220. For example, Judgment of the Intellectual Property High Court, 27 Mar. 2008, available at <http://www.courts go.jp/app/files/hanrei jp/pdf/229/036229_hanrei.pdf>.
221. Judgment of the Intellectual Property High Court, 24 Dec. 2008, *Minshu* 65-9-3363.

§4. TRADE MARKS

257. The AGR and the Trade Mark Act[222] contain no specific choice-law-rules dealing with trademarks. The *lex loci protectionis* in the trademark context seems to mean the law of the country in which the application for registration, for example, to the Japanese Patent Office has been filed.

I. Creation

258. It is undisputed among academic writers that the creation of trade marks is governed by the *lex loci protectionis*. However, unlike patent rights, the Supreme Court and inferior courts have had no opportunity to clarify their position that national trademarks might be created on a country-by-country basis.

II. Protection

259. The *lex loci protectionis* is also believed to govern the protection of trademark.

III. Ownership and Transfer

260. There is no judgment rendered by Japanese courts in relation to the ownership and transfer of the trademark.

IV. Infringement

261. The strong link between infringement and protection seems to require that the *lex loci protectionis* apply to issues of compensatory damages as well as injunction. It means that, when claims by a trademark holder are related to the infringements having occurred in several countries, the alleged infringements should be assessed on the basis of the law of each country. When the alleged infringements took place in relation to the trademarks registered in China, Taiwan, and Hong Kong, Japanese courts were expected to apply, separately, Chinese, Taiwanese, and Hong Kong law to each claim for damages arising out of infringement of each registered trademark. An inferior court indeed made such distributive application of Chinese, Taiwanese, and Hong Kong law, when the plaintiff claimed for the compensatory damages. It should be noted, however, that the court applied each law as the *lex loci damni* after regarding the claims as tortious.[223]

---

222. Act No. 127 of 13 Apr. 1959.
223. Judgment of the Tokyo District Court, 25 Mar. 2011, available at < http://www.courts.go.jp/app/files/hanrei_jp/564/081564_hanrei.pdf>.

§5. Industrial Designs

262. The AGR and the Japanese Design Act[224] contain no specific choice-of-law rules on industrial designs. There has been no case worthy of mentioning. The remarks made in relation to patents and trademarks presumably apply to registered designs.

224. Act No. 125 of 13 Apr. 1959.

Chapter 5. Family Law

§1. State Law – Religious Law

263. Religions such as *Shinto, Confucianism,* and *Buddhism* have had nothing to do with JPIL. If there is something indigenous whose elements have affected the applicable law in the field of family law, it is what we call the *ie*, the household system institutionalized by the Civil Code of 1898.

264. During the course of the seventeenth century, people living in Japan are said to have carried the image of society called 'a nation of family business' whatever they were engaged in *samurai* work, commerce, or farming. The *ie* was an institutional mechanism, a customarily accepted type of legal person.[225] The property belonging to the *ie* was neither conceived of as the sum total of the individual assets of the members of the *ie* nor as subject to the co-ownership. The property was the collective one to be passed on for their descendants to keep running their family business. Although we have some fear of misleading readers, it seems to resemble the *zadruga* in the Balkans whose legal personality was expressed by Article 984 of the Code of Property of Montenegro (1888).[226] Like corporation or association, the *ie* had a single representative, namely, the head of the household and its name to be inherited through generations. Whereas the traditional *ie* had such common characteristics, customs on *ie* had a variety of forms depending on regions and social classes. For example, in some regions, the household head held strong authority over status changes of household members such as marriage and adoption but, in other regions, his authority was weak. The primogeniture rule did not necessarily prevail in all regions and social classes.[227] Although reflective of such varied forms of the *ie,* the Civil Code made a new and standardized model of *ie*, the household system through which the state tried to intervene in the family relationships.[228] One could talk about 'family members' as far as they belong to a particular household

225. Hiroshi Watanabe, *A History of Japanese Political Thought 1600-1901* 61 et seq. (International House of Japan 2012).
226. The observation was already made in the 1930s by a Japanese expert of PIL. *See*, Koichi Yamaguchi, *Studies in Family law and International Family Law* (in Japanese) 65 (Ganshoudou 1943). For his work, *see*, Jun'ichi Akiba, *The Beginning and Development of Japanese Doctrine on the Private International Law Koichi Yamaguchi (1866-1945) and Iwataro Kubo (1897-1980)*, 56 *J.Y.B.I.L.* 196 (2013).
227. Kenji Mori, '*The Development of the Modern Koseki*', in David Chapman & Karl Jacob Krogness (eds), *supra*, 59.
228. Under the Civil Code, the collective character of the property belonging to the household was simply denied, because such character could not accommodate itself to the newly made system of public record of property. Individual members of a household could own their own properties. Alongside with individual members' rights, however, the pre-existing property of the household was concentrated in the hands of its (in principle, male) head as an individual whose position was inheritable pursuant to the primogeniture rule. *Valtazar Bogišić*, the author of the Code of Property of Montenegro (1888), is said to have met a Japanese official in Paris in 1878. Although *Bogišić* seems to have suggested that the family law should not be included in the future Japanese Civil Code, the Japanese legislator did not take the suggested course of action. Werner G. Zimmermann, *Valtazar Bogišić 1834-1908* 184–185 (Franz Steiner Verlag, 1962).

bearing the lineage name.[229] It is true that, for example, two individuals, a husband and a wife, could form a new relationship upon marriage. Under the household system, the marriage also meant that the changes of membership simultaneously occurred in the two households: on marriage, the wife loses her membership of the household of origin and becomes a new member of her husband's. Besides, the change of the membership was subject to the control of the household head. Consequently, when a female member of a household married a male member of another household, the both household heads' consents to the marriage were required. Furthermore, some of the effects of marriage were conceived as directly deriving from the wife's entry in her husband's household. Surnames, for example, were not attached to individuals nor to marital communities, but to households. On marriage, the wife was called by the same surname as her husband's, because she became a member of the husband's household.

265. The legislators of Japanese PIL in the late nineteenth century must have been perplexed with the question how the substantive law rules on the household, which looked peculiar to the Japanese Civil Code, should be applied, for example, to the marriage between a Japanese husband and a foreign wife whose personal law was not supposed to know such household system. It is true that they desired to enact the choice-of-law rules in line with the tendency prevailing in Western nations at that time. At the same time, they had to be mindful of mandatory nature of the Japanese household system, at least, with respect to the rules on the membership of the household and its control by the head. Fortunately, they could enact most of the choice-of-law rules without expressly declaring that those rules were of overriding mandatory nature. The distributive application of each party's *lex patriae* to the substantive validity of marriage ensured the Japanese household head's right to consent to the marriage of a member of his household just like (and in addition to) the parental consent for the marriage of the minor child, as far as a party was Japanese. Furthermore, the legislator adopted the bilateral choice-of-law rule referring to the husband's *lex patriae* as regards the personal effects of marriage. The husband's *lex patriae* enabled Japanese law to govern the question whether a wife of foreign nationality would enter the husband's household. However, such a choice-of-law rule does not always bring about the result compatible with the household system, because the Civil Code allowed the female member to hold the headship on the supposition that no male members were available within her household. Article 736 of the Civil Code of 1898 read as follows: '[a] husband who marries a wife holding the headship of her household enters that household and takes the headship in her place on marriage'. The legislators feared that, when a Japanese wife holding such headship got married to a foreign husband, his foreign *lex patriae* applicable to the effects of marriage would not trigger the application of the said Japanese substantive law provision. Consequently, they added to the said husband-oriented choice-of-law rule the following one that would prove to reveal the overriding mandatory

229. Intertwined with the Civil Code, the Family Register Act of 1898 gave a virtual idea of each actual household and its membership on the ledger compiled by household unit. To date, the Japanese civil status register has not been compiled on the basis of the individual but of the household consisting of the conjugal family.

nature of the household system: in case that a foreigner marries a female head of household, the effects of marriage shall be governed by Japanese law (Article 14 (2) of the *Horei* before amendment in 1947). Such fear, however, came to be unnecessary one year later, namely, when the Nationality Act of 1899 was enacted, because, pursuant to the Nationality Act, a foreign husband automatically obtained Japanese nationality on his marriage with a Japanese wife. Consequently, without the said Article 14 (2) of the *Horei*, the effects of marriage came to be always governed by Japanese law. Subsequently, that provision of the *Horei* was regarded as meaningless and, *de lege lata,* ignored by academic writers. The said Nationality Act enabled them to rank the substantive law rules on the household system along with mandatory but non-overriding other institutions of family law. Nevertheless, they seemed to be fully aware that the household system was of more mandatory nature than other family institutions. Although they tried to interpret the bilateral choice-of-law rules in abstract and neutral terms, their comments seemed to be always conformable with the household system. For example, how does marriage influence the woman's surname? Most writers classified the question into the 'personal effects of marriage' rather than the 'personal rights of the wife'. Such preference seems to have been interwoven with the idea that the household consisted of a group of persons with the same surname and that a wife became a member of the husband's household on marriage.

266. All the provisions on the household system were stripped from the Civil Code because of its patriarchal nature in 1947. Its abolishment, however, did not immediately lead to the radical review of authors' ideas of PIL prevailing during the pre-war times. It took some time for such ideas to be put under review.

§2. MARRIAGE

267. What is described in this section deals with the heterosexual marriage, except the part of 'Same-Sex Marriage' (III).

I. Engagement

268. The Japanese Civil Code contains no specific provision dealing with the engagement. It is only natural that the AGR has no choice-of-law rules on engagement. Some authors are of opinion that the choice-of-law rules on marriage should analogically apply to the questions surrounding the engagement.[230] According to this view, the choice-of-law rule as contained in Article 24 (1) AGR designates the law applicable to substantive conditions for engagement such as the required age, consent, impediments, and those rules of Article 24 (2) and (3) AGR refer to the law for the formal requirements, except the second sentence of Article 24 (3) which lays down the mandatory notification of marriage to the Japanese family registrar.

230. Tameike, 479–480.

It seems logical that the connecting criteria as set out in Article 25 on effects of marriage are valid for the effects of engagement such as consequences of breaking the engagement, in particular, returning the gifts.

II. Heterosexual Marriage

A. *Form*

269. The current choice-of-law rules contained in Article 24 (2) and (3) AGR seem to be understood more easily against the background of the Japanese substantive law rules on the formal validity of marriage. Under the Japanese substantive law, marriage notification to the local family registrar is necessary and sufficient for the marriage to be valid. Pursuant to Article 739 of the Japanese Civil Code, the marriage notification can be given by a document with the signatures of the parties and not less than two adult witnesses or given orally by these persons. In the family registration practice, the parties have been allowed to make their marriage notification even by post. Neither marriage ceremony nor solemnization other than such notification is required.

270. Article 24 (2) and (3) AGR is construed as encompassing all the matters relating to the external conduct necessary to the formation of a legally valid marriage. Article 24 (2) AGR provides that compliance with the form of *lex loci celebrationis* is sufficient for the formal validity of marriage. The provision enables the Japanese family registrar to register the marriage notification pursuant to the Japanese Family Registration Act. Where a marriage was entered into in a foreign country pursuant to its substantive law rules, it is also held valid in Japan as far as the form is concerned.

271. Until the revision of the *Horei* in 1989, compliance with the *lex loci celebrationis* was not only sufficient but also necessary. It seems that the legislator who enacted the *Horei* in 1898 regarded the form of marriage as relating to the *ordre public*. However, this explanation was hardly convincing to those who looked at the relevant provisions contained in the Japanese Civil Code which bear no religious elements nor are inspired by a postulate of *laïcité*. Consequently, academic writers, who were critical about the mandatory nature attributed to the principle of *lex loci celebrationis,* suggested that *de lege ferenda*, it should bear the nature as facultative as the general rule of *locus regit actum*. Besides, the mandatory nature of the *lex loci celebrationis* puzzled the Japanese family registrars. When a couple residing abroad sent, by post, a document notifying their marriage to a Japanese family registration office, could the registrars accept the document pursuant to Japanese law? In their practice, they were ready to accept it under Japanese law on the pretext that the place of destination, Japan, should be regarded as the *locus celebrationis*.

Whereas this practice, which enabled Japanese emigrants to celebrate their marriage pursuant to Japanese law, was hardly objectionable, it was admitted that the administrative interpretation of the term of *locus celebrationis* was absolutely tortious.[231]

272. Against these backgrounds, an amendment was made in 1989 to add the paragraph 3 which reads: '[n]otwithstanding the preceding paragraph, a marriage shall be valid regarding its form when it complies with the formal requirements under the *lex patriae* of either party'. This provision is principally designed to play a twofold role. First, it gives facultative nature to the rule of the *lex loci celebrationis* as laid down in paragraph 2. Second, it enables the family registrar to accept a document of marriage notification sent by post from a foreign country pursuant to Japanese law applicable as the *lex patriae* of a Japanese party.

273. Under the AGR, those provisions remain unaltered, together with what we call a 'Japanese clause' as mentioned below. They certainly help the parties to have their marriage recognized, when they fulfil the conditions provided by one of the following laws: the *lex loci celebrationis* or one of the *leges patriae* of the parties. A marriage may be validly celebrated in Japan in the religious form required by one of the *leges patriae* of the parties. The consular form of marriage is also recognized as complying with the *lex patriae* of a party. It seems that such an alternative choice-of-law rule as expressed in paragraphs 2 and 3 reflect the attitude religiously indifferent to the formal validity of marriage underlying the Japanese Civil Code.

274. However, this alternative choice-of-law rule is subject to the exception as contained in the second sentence of Article 24 (3) AGR. As far as one of the parties is a Japanese national, the couple cannot claim the validity of their marriage celebrated in Japan pursuant to a foreign law unless their marriage was notified to the Japanese family registrar. The form of marriage, which is valid in light of a *lex patriae* of the party, does not suffice to validate the marriage. This exception is explainable by the desire of the Ministry of Justice to have every change of status of Japanese national be reflected in the family registration book as accurately as possible. It is true that the necessary notification is to facilitate proof of the marriage, as far as a party is Japanese. Experience tells us, however, that it is likely to create an unexpected result for a mixed couple including a Japanese party. The marriage which was celebrated in Japan in accordance with the *lex patriae* of the party may turn out to be invalid under JPIL many years later, particularly when the problem of succession arises after the death of a spouse.[232] Besides, the Japanese clause applies to consular marriage. When a marriage between a Japanese and a foreigner is solemnized by or before a diplomatic or consular representative of the foreign state in Japan, the marriage is not valid unless and until the parties notify their marriage to the Japanese family registrar.

231. Yokoyama, 240–241.
232. *See*, para. 68 *supra*.

B. Substance

275. The choice-of-law rule on substantive validity of marriage is the one whose content remains unaltered since 1898. The current rule as now contained in Article 24 (1) AGR covers all the matters relating to the validity of marriage other than those falling into the category of formal validity: e.g., the consent of the parties to marriage, the marriageable age, the parental consent for marriage for minors, and consanguinity.

276. This choice-of-law rule is said to be of distributive application: each of the parties should comply with the conditions laid down by his or her own *lex patriae*, but not with those of the other party's *lex patriae*. As far as an impediment is construed obviously as unilateral, namely, as concerning only the party whose *lex patriae* provides the impediment, the system of distributive application is clearly distinguishable from that of cumulation. However, the former, sometimes, may be almost tantamount to that of cumulation. Certain impediments to valid marriage are classified as bilateral in the sense that they are designed to apply to both parties, for example, prohibition of polygamous marriage. How should one classify an impediment as unilateral or bilateral? A view was dominant according to which such classification should be the matter to be decided by the forum's private international law.[233] This view expressed around 1930 in Japan was greatly inspired by a German author's idea which had proposed the same approach primarily with regard to the old Hague *Convention du 12 juin 1902 pour régler les conflits de lois en matière de mariage*.[234] At present it seems to be fairly widely agreed that the distinction between the unilateral impediments and the bilateral ones should be made pursuant to constructions of each substantive law rule relating to the marriage impediment in question.[235]

III. Same-Sex Marriage

277. It has been said that Japan is comparably tolerant to same-sex issues.[236] It certainly does not belong to a group of countries which penalize sexual acts between persons of the same sex. It has been believed, however, that the Constitution and the Civil Code envisage only marriage between two persons of different sexes. Whereas some local authorities such as cities and wards have taken initiatives in recognizing the relationship between the couple of the same-sex, their measures do not purport to grant such relationship the same effects with those of a classic marriage between heterosexual couple but to assimilate it to a heterosexual couple of non-marital cohabitation as mentioned below.[237]

233. *See*, Commentary II (Uematsu), 12–16.
234. Otto Lenel & Hans Lewald, *supra*, 63.
235. *See*, Yokoyama, 237–238.
236. *See*, for example, Claire Maree, '*Sexual Citizenship at the Intersections of Patriarchy and Heteronormativity*', in David Chapman & Karl Jacob Krogness (eds), *supra*, 187.
237. *See*, paras 306–308 *infra*.

278. Japanese judges have never addressed choice-of-law problems relating to the validity and the effects of the same-sex marriage, probably due to the fact that neighbouring countries such as China and Korea do not know such institution, either. The Legislative Council had time to discuss how to deal with partnerships of the same-sex couple registered in foreign countries rather than the same-sex marriage as such,[238] but, in view of absence of cases, no member seems to have felt a specific choice-of-law rule on the subject urgently needed.[239] Among other things, given that such institution is unknown to the Japanese substantive law, a conceivable choice-of-law rule such as the *lex loci registrationis* would inevitably refer only to foreign laws. However, such a choice-of-law rule of outwardly unilateral character has been alien to Japanese PIL.

279. Whereas procreation is not believed to be an essential element of the institution of marriage provided by the Japanese Civil Code, it is also true that the idea of non-discrimination between heterosexual and same-sex couples is not enshrined in the Civil Code.[240] One wonders whether or not the same-sex marriage should fall into the category of marriage as set out in Articles 24–26 AGR. It seems still premature to discern the tendency of academic writers' opinions. It is submitted, however, that those provisions do not cover the same-sex marriage. Those choice-of-law rules seem to presuppose, *de lege lata*, that the legal status of the couple granted by the *lex patriae* or by the *leges patriae* pursuant to Article 24 (1) AGR is necessarily capable of unfolding its legal consequences wherever the couple is habitually resident. If a French couple of the same-sex celebrated their marriage in France, its legal effects would be governed by the same *lex patriae*, French law. There would be no problem for Japanese judges to apply the applicable law to its legal effects. In contrast, Japanese judges would be puzzled by the lack of relevant substantive law rules to apply, when a French man celebrated the marriage with a Japanese man in France and they are habitually resident in Japan. The Japanese Civil Code applicable as the law of the couple's habitual residence is believed to contain no provision dealing with the same-sex marriage. Whereas it is uncertain what the silence of the Civil Code implies, the choice-of-law rules contained in Articles 24–26 AGR do not envisage such a situation likely to puzzle judges in applying the law governing the effects of marriage. Article 33 AGR provides that family relationships or rights and obligations arising therefrom other than those provided for in Articles 24–32 shall be governed by the national law of the party concerned.[241] It is arguable that the same-sex marriage falls into the category of 'other family relationships' in the sense of that provision.[242]

238. They bore in mind something similar to but different from marriage, for example, the 'life partnership' of German law.

239. *See*, Koide, 324–325.

240. The Act on Special Cases in Handling Gender Status for Persons with Gender Identity Disorder (Act No. 111 of 16 Jul. 2003). Its Art. 3(1) allows a person with gender identity problems to alter his or her gender status, unless he or she is currently married. It means that, under the Japanese family registration system, only two persons of different sexes may qualify as husband and wife.

241. The choice-of-law rule is a reminiscent of Art. 6 of the Preliminary Provisions of the Italian Civil Code of 1865.

242. *See*, Tameike, 486–487.

A. Form

280. It seems likely that, instead of relying on the choice-of-law rule on the formal validity of marriage (Article 24 (2) and (3) AGR), Japanese judges might apply Article 34 AGR which provides the alternative application either of the *lex loci celebrationis* or one of the *leges patriae* of the parties in relation to family relationships provided for in Article 33 AGR. For example, when the two French nationals of the same sex celebrated their marriage at the French embassy or consular office in Japan in accordance with French law applicable as the same *lex patriae*, it would be regarded as valid as regards the form of marriage.

B. Substance

281. As mentioned above, the establishment and legal consequences of the same-sex marriage would be covered by the supplementary and default choice-of-law rule that family relationships or rights and obligations arising therefrom shall be governed by the *lex patriae* of the party concerned (Article 33 AGR). Where a couple of the same-sex shares the *lex patriae*, both the legal status and the legal effects flowing from it are governed by the same *lex patriae*. For example, the marriage of the French couple mentioned in the previous paragraph may be valid and unfold the consequences under French law. If one of the parties possesses the nationality of a state whose law does not allow the same-sex marriage, the couple cannot celebrate marriage. Where both of the two *leges patriae* allow such marriage but differ from each other as regards legal consequences stemming from the marriage, the minimum consequences granted commonly by both laws would be respected. Whereas one may doubt whether such cumulative application of the two laws will be desirable or even feasible, such solution seems inevitable *de lege lata.*

IV. Personal Effects of Marriage

282. From the enactment of the *Horei* to its revision in 1989, the personal effects of the heterosexual marriage were governed by the *lex patriae* of the husband. The current provision (Article 25 AGR) whose content remains unaltered since the revision arranges the three connecting criteria in cascade or in the shorter *Kegel*'s ladder consisting of the three steps. The provision contains the three choice-of-law rules: the personal effects of marriage are governed by the same *lex patriae* of the spouses; in the absence of such law, they are governed by the law of the same country in which both spouses have their habitual residence; in the absence of such law, they are governed by the law of the country with which the spouses are most closely connected. Articles 26 and 27 AGR lay down the analogical application of Article 25 AGR to matrimonial property regime and divorce, respectively.

283. All the connecting criteria as enlisted in Article 25 AGR are subject to mutability. Priority is given to nationality. The legislator preferred the term 'the same *lex patriae* of the spouses' to 'the law of their common nationality of the spouses', in trying to ensure the application of the *lex patriae* only when a *lex patriae* familiar to one spouse is, at the same time, that to the other. If a wife holding the nationality (A) shares a particular nationality (B) with the husband, it does not automatically follow that the law of the shared nationality (B) governs their matrimonial relationships. If the law indicated by the nationality (A) is the one that, because she is more familiar with it, would govern her personal status pursuant to Article 38 (1) AGR, their relationships are to be governed by the law designated by the second or the third connecting criterion as set out in Article 25 AGR. If both spouses are the nationals of the same state consisting of more than one law districts such as China, judges should, first, identify the territorial unit whose law should be qualified as a personal law of each spouse. For example, if one of the spouses is found habitually resident in Macao and the other in Hong Kong, it follows that the couple has no same *lex patriae*, with the result that Japanese judges might apply Japanese law as law of the country with which the spouses are most closely connected. In the absence of the same *lex patriae* of the spouses, the law of the country in which both spouses are habitually resident may apply, even when the spouses do not live together under one roof. What is relevant to the second connecting criterion is that they are habitually resident in the country where the same law is in force. For example, the matrimonial relationships are governed by French law, when one spouse is habitually resident in Paris and the other in Tahiti. In the absence of the law of the same habitual residence, the law of the country is applicable with which the spouses are most closely connected in individual cases. In the framework of searching such a country, judges are expected to take account of such circumstances as nationality or habitual residence previously shared by the spouses.

284. Until 1898 when the *Horei* was enacted, the choice-of-law rule on personal effects of marriage held the important position in JPIL. The connecting criterion of the husband's nationality not only served for matrimonial property regime and divorce but also for relationships between married parents and children. It may safely be said that the choice-of-law rule for personal effects of marriage expressed some collective idea of the family. However, since the revision of the *Horei*, such notion became almost alien to JPIL. The area to be encompassed by Article 25 AGR is confined to a narrow and unimportant one. The more important other questions are governed by the laws different from that designated by the said provision. For example, the question as to what name the spouses are to carry on marriage is governed by the *lex patriae* of an individual spouse. Maintenance obligations between the spouses have been governed by the law applicable under the Act on the Law Applicable to Maintenance Obligations since 1986. The question as to whether marriage gives full capacity to a minor spouse is to be governed by the law designated by the choice-of-law rule on capacity to act as laid down by Article 4 AGR. It is true that conjugal duties such as duty to cohabit undoubtedly fall into the category of the personal effects of marriage. However, those duties seem to be practically just the one side of the same coin whose reverse and more visible side is the ground of divorce. The question as to whether capacity of a married woman is reduced on marriage may also be governed by the law designated by Article 25 AGR. However, the application of a foreign substantive law rule to that effect will be, with all the likelihood, excluded by means of the *ordre public* clause.

V. Dissolution

A. Annulment

285. With respect to the formal validity of the heterosexual marriage, the law according to which a marriage was celebrated applies to the question of its annulment (Article 24 (2)(3) AGR). As regards the substantive requirements, when one of the parties fails to satisfy the requirements under his or her *lex patriae*, its effects are to be governed by that law. When both of the parties violated his and her *leges patriae*, the law whose sanction is stricter applies. For example, if the marriage is void under one of the laws and voidable under the other, the former law is applicable.[243]

B. Divorce

286. The state's indifference towards individuals' marital lives is discernible in the Japanese divorce law. Many matters are, in principle, left to the spouses' disposal. It should be noted that this tendency seems to be shared by Chinese and Korean law.[244] There are four types of divorces under Japanese law: divorce by agreement; divorce by conciliation at family court; divorce by adjudication of family court; and divorce by judicial decree. Most of divorces are done by notifying their divorce agreement to the Japanese family registrar who is only empowered to verify whether the necessary formalities are satisfied with. When a husband and a wife cannot reach an agreement, either party can petition for the conciliation proceedings at the family court. That petition is mandatory in the sense that the party cannot proceed directly to divorce litigation. This 'conciliation first' rule has mandatorily applied, irrespective of whether or not cases bear foreign elements. If the divorce conciliation is successful, the mediated agreement is regarded as having the same effect as the final and conclusive decree. Otherwise, the family court may issue an adjudication for divorce under certain circumstances. Either if the family court finds the issuance of such adjudication inappropriate or if the party unsatisfied

243. The Japanese courts have jurisdiction to annul a marriage, whether void or voidable, according to Article 3-2 PSLA.

244. As far as divorces between Japanese spouses are concerned, the statistics of 2008 shows that the divorce by agreement represents 87.2% of the total 232,362 divorces. It is noteworthy that, while the number of divorces between Japanese and foreign nationals is 18,774 (7.4% of the total divorces), 94.8% of this figure is represented by the divorce by agreement. *See*, Statistics and Information Department, Minister's Secretariat, Ministry of Health, Labour and Welfare, *Divorces Specified Report of Vital Statistics in FY 2009*.

with such an adjudication appeals within two weeks after the issuance of the adjudication, then the case moves into the judicial proceedings in which evidentiary hearings and oral arguments are to be carried out.[245]

287. The current Article 27 of the AGR provides, in its first sentence, that Article 25 AGR should be, by analogy, applied to divorce. Such connecting criteria as the same nationality or the same habitual residence as set out in Articles 25 and 27 AGR are expected to indicate the same country in both contexts. In contrast, 'the country with which the spouses are most closely connected' may be differently determined, according to whether or not the matrimonial life has been irretrievably broken down. For example, when each divorcing spouse is, respectively, resident in his and her home country at the time of petition for divorce, Japanese judges might eventually have no choice but to apply Japanese law, the *lex fori,* which is only common to both spouses.

288. According to the provision as expressed in the first sentence of Article 27 AGR, the law of the country with which the spouses are most closely connected should govern the divorce between a mixed couple who has no habitual residence in the same country. However, when one of the spouses is Japanese and has his or her habitual residence in Japan, the Japanese authority does not apply to the divorce of such a mixed couple the law indicated by such an open-ended clause but Japanese law (the second sentence of Article 27 AGR). The concern underlying the exception called the 'Japanese clause' lies in incompatibility between such an open-ended clause and the limited power of the family registrar. As mentioned above, under Japanese law, a husband and wife may dissolve their marriage by agreement. This is done by notification in writing of their divorce agreement to the family registrar. The registrar practically has no difficulty in finding whether the spouses, who are going to avail themselves of the form of divorce agreement under Japanese law, have Japanese nationality in common. So is the habitual residence in Japan, as far as a mixed couple has been lawfully resident in Japan, which the registrar may identify only by reference to the relevant public registry. Thus, the connecting factor of the common habitual residence was expected to cause, in principle, little difficulty for the registrar who needs to accept the divorce notification under Japanese law. Yet, the Ministry of Justice in charge of keeping the family registration book was perplexed by the open-ended connecting criterion, because, unlike judges, the family registrar is not empowered to make an enquiry into elements of individual matrimonial life, which may or may not eventually indicate that a couple is most closely connected with Japan. Consequently, the Ministry found it essential to formulate a rule that enables family registrars to identify easily the situation where Japanese law should be applied, instead of applying the open-ended clause.

289. It goes without saying that, though applicable on the basis of the combination of a spouse's Japanese nationality with his or her habitual residence in Japan, Japanese law is not necessarily appropriate in terms of proximity. According to the explanation of the Ministry, the rule in question can only be justified in light of the

245. Article 3-2 PSLA provides jurisdictional rules on divorce litigations.

limited power of the family registrar. We have to point out, however, that the rule goes further than compelled by necessity. First, it is not only registrars but also judges who may have recourse to the Japanese clause. Second, the reservation of Japanese law extends to the effects of divorce, in particular, the maintenance obligations between the divorced spouses (Article 4(1) of the Act on the Law Applicable to Maintenance Obligations). One would say that what is unjustifiable in light of necessity or proximity may be explained only by the desire to ensure the possibility and the effects of divorce available under Japanese law for a Japanese spouse habitually resident in Japan.

290. Article 27 AGR does not expressly specify the relevant time at which each connecting criterion should be determined. It implicitly means that the law applicable to divorce is mutable. Temporal changes of the connecting factors may lead to rendering a different law applicable from that which would have been applied before the change took place. For example, a change of a spouse's nationality or habitual residence, which has occurred before the oral proceedings are closed, may have such effect. When the divorcing spouses take advantage of the divorce by agreement, the time of their divorce notification to the family registrar is decisive. The mutability has much to commend itself, particularly, with respect to maintenance obligations between divorced spouses. Given that, pursuant to Article 4(1) of the Act on Law Applicable to Maintenance Obligations, the law applicable to the maintenance obligations and their revision is identical with the law applied to the divorce, the latter should be the law of the country with which the divorced spouses have the latest link.[246]

291. The law applicable to divorce governs the admissibility of divorce. Before 1989, as mentioned earlier, Japanese courts frequently rejected the application of Philippine law, which was applied as the *lex patriae* of the husband, on the ground of the *ordre public*.[247] Under the AGR, Philippine law is likely to apply only to divorce between Philippine spouses.

292. The law applicable to divorce governs the admissibility of the relief sought. Japanese law enables the spouses to dissolve their marriage merely by notifying their intent of divorce to the Japanese family registrar. When an applicable foreign law knows such extrajudicial divorce as Japanese law does, the spouses may also make the notification of divorce to Japanese family registrars pursuant to the foreign law. For example, they have accepted the notification of divorce agreement by Chinese spouses pursuant to Chinese law. However, it is always questionable whether such divorce by agreement will be regarded as valid under relevant foreign legal systems. For example, the Korean authority made it clear, in 2004, that recognition should not be accorded to the divorce by agreement done in Japan unless the Korean family court had confirmed the spouses' true intention to divorce beforehand. In general, whenever Japanese registrars have doubts as to the possibility of

246. *See*, Yokoyama, 261–262.
247. *See*, paras 91–94 *supra*.

recognition in relevant foreign countries, they usually advise the spouses to avail themselves of the conciliation proceedings at the Japanese family court.

293. Either when a couple cannot reach an agreement of divorce or when it is uncertain that their purely consensual dissolution as provided by Japanese law is regarded as valid by relevant foreign legal systems, either party is expected to petition for the conciliation of divorce to the family court. As mentioned above, divorcing parties are required to petition for a conciliation to the family court before raising a divorce action. It should be noted that, in the court practice, the 'conciliation first' rule has been regarded as mandatory, even when applicable foreign laws allow only the judicial divorce. The practice has been explained on the ground that procedural matters should be governed by the *lex fori*. However, although, under Japanese law, the conciliation made by the parties with intervention of the family court has the same effect as the final and conclusive decree, the fact remains that, being essentially based on the parties' will, the conciliation is not made on the basis of a constitutive decision which the court should make as a result of the application of law. Thus, whenever it is doubtful that recognition will be accorded to the conciliation in relevant foreign legal systems which, particularly, know only the divorce by judicial decree, the family court is expected to proceed to make an adjudication of divorce.[248] It should be noted that the grounds of divorce prescribed by the law designated by the choice-of-law rule are usually taken into consideration within the framework of the conciliation proceedings or the proceedings for the court adjudication of divorce.

294. The Japanese divorce law knows the grounds based on both fault and irretrievable breakdown. A spouse at fault is also allowed to claim for divorce under a certain condition. Against the background of such substantive law rules, some Japanese decrees excluded the application of the foreign law on the ground of the *ordre public*, when the applicable foreign law requires a certain period of separation to elapse before the divorce.[249]

295. The question to whom parental authority, rights of custody, and rights of contact are granted after the divorce is not governed by the law applicable to divorce but by the law designated by the choice-of-law rule on the parental relationships as provided in Article 32 AGR.[250]

§3. Matrimonial Property

296. What is described in this section deals with the heterosexual marriage.

---

248. *See*, Tameike, 467. The Japanese courts, now, have jurisdiction over divorce litigations pursuant to Article 3-2 PSLA.
249. For example, Decree of the Yokohama Family Court, 30 Oct. 1987, *Kagetsu* 40-10-53) (Italian divorce law requiring three years separation).
250. The divorce court may exercise jurisdiction over these matters pursuant to Article 3-4 PSLA. *See*, para. 410 *infra*.

297. As far as the objective connecting factors are concerned, Article 26 (1) AGR provides that Article 25 AGR on the personal effects of marriage should be, by analogy, applied to matrimonial property regime. Whereas the laws objectively applicable to both categories are designed to be, in most cases, identical, a question relating to the matrimonial property regime is governed by the law governing the personal effects of marriage only on the analogical basis. In drafting the provision, the Legislative Council of 1989 anticipated that the same connecting criterion of 'the country with which the spouses are most closely connected' might refer to different laws depending on the context in which a particular question would be placed: e.g., the situation of a spouse's immovable property may be likely to have more importance for the purpose of localizing a question relating to matrimonial property.

298. The applicable law determined pursuant to Article 26 (1) AGR is subject to mutability. The Legislative Council preferred not to subject the spouses' relationships to a legal system from which both of them have been detached long after the celebration of marriage. Unless the spouses agree otherwise as mentioned below, the law governing matrimonial property regime changes automatically with subsequent changes in nationality or habitual residence. The new governing law applies with no retrospective effects, because it was feared that such retroactive extension of the new applicable law might betray the expectations of the spouses. Consequently, at the time of the dissolution of marriage long after the date of the celebration of marriage, one has to examine, under which law and, therefore, under which matrimonial property regime the spouses acquired each property. It was thought that, although such *système des wagons* inevitably might make the liquidation complicated, it would not cause so much practical difficulty as one imagined.[251] Among other things, the *professio juris* was expected to enable the spouses to foresee their future planning.

I. Choice-of-Law Agreement

299. In order to counter-balance the effects of the mutability of the objectively applicable law, Article 26 (2) AGR allows the spouses to choose the law applicable to their matrimonial property regime. Once the spouses choose or change the governing law, which is allowed at any time, that law may apply to their matrimonial property regime until the dissolution of marriage. The *professio juris* plays a role of stabilizing their matrimonial property relationship regardless of any change of their nationality or habitual residence. Such choice of law will have no retrospective effects.

300. The range of laws which the spouses are entitled to choose is limited to the following ones: the law of one of their nationalities; one of the laws of the countries where they are habitually resident at the time of the choice; the law of the country

251. Yokoyama, 254.

where all or some of the immovable properties are situated. The choice of law should be made in writing, dated, and signed by both spouses.

301. The effects of the matrimonial property regime on the relationships between a spouse and a third party are also governed by the law applicable pursuant to Article 26 (1) and (2) AGR. However, the scope of application of the applicable foreign law is restricted, in relation to a certain domestic transaction, by the provision designed to protect the bona fide third party as contained in Article 26 (3) AGR. According to this provision, where the matrimonial property regime is governed by a foreign law, the spouses cannot assert their matrimonial property regime, whether statutory or contractual, against the third party who neither knew nor should have known of the foreign law applicable to that matrimonial property regime. This protection of the bona fide third party only applies, either when the legal transaction was entered into with the third party in Japan or when a particular property in question was situated in Japan. The bona fide third party in such a situation can rely on Japanese law.

302. In order for the spouses to assert their foreign matrimonial property regime against the third party even in such domestic situations, they may make a marriage contract into which the foreign matrimonial property regime is incorporated and, then, may enter the contract in the marriage property register (Article 26 (4) AGR). This provision aims to equate the foreign matrimonial property regime with terms of the marriage contract to be registered pursuant to Article 756 of the Japanese Civil Code.[252]

II. Relationship to Succession Law

303. The choice-of-law rules as set out in Article 26 AGR first applies to the question as to what property belongs to the deceased. Then, the law governing inheritance referred to by the choice-of-law rule as contained in Article 36 AGR applies to the fate of the deceased's property. Whereas JPIL does not arrange for the laws applicable to both areas of law to coordinate with each other, it seems to have brought about no difficult problems necessitating the technique of assimilation in the court practice.

§4. Registered Partnership – Partnership/Civil Unions

304. As mentioned above, the same-sex marriage seems to be governed by the law designated by the residual choice-of-law rule which covers the 'other family relationships' (Article 33 AGR). It is irrelevant whether it has been registered or not

252. Article 756 of the Japanese Civil Code reads: '[i]f a husband and wife have entered into a contract that departs from the statutory property system, the contract may not be asserted against the successor in title of the husband or wife, or a third party unless registered prior to notification of marriage'.

in a foreign country. With regard to the registered partnerships of the heterosexual couple, the *locus registrationis* is not qualified for a connecting factor as such. When a particular heterosexual partnership registered in a foreign country is characterized as the union capable of producing legal consequences as full as the classic marriage in light of JPIL, such union would be equated with the marriage. An administrative circular issued by the Ministry of Justice regards the dissolution of a partnership registered in the Netherlands by an Italian man and a Japanese woman as falling into the category of divorce in the sense of Article 27 AGR on the ground that the partnership in question appeared to be hardly distinguishable from the classic marriage as regards its requirements and effects.[253] It should be noted that Dutch law *in casu* was not applied as the *lex loci registrationis* but as the law of the country where that mixed couple was habitually resident under Article 27 AGR. By contrast, if the partnership in question is found the 'downgraded' one, namely, incapable of deploying legal effects on matrimonial property and succession, the couple would be put on the same footing with that of the extra-marital cohabitation as mentioned below. The fact of its being registered in a foreign country may serve as one of the evidential circumstances indicating that the couple deserves the protection as much as that of such extra-marital cohabitation.

§5. Extra-Marital Cohabitation

305. There has been no specific provision for the extra-marital cohabitation in the Civil Code since 1898. Without registering their marriage, no couple should expect any legal protection a husband and wife can enjoy. That was what the legislator of the Civil Code intended in the late nineteenth century. However, in the early days of the Civil Code, there were many people unaware of the necessity of the registration to validate their marriages. Consequently, a large number of couples, who considered themselves husbands and wives and who were reputed to be married in their local communities, did not register their unions in the family registration book. The Civil Code was certainly not a restatement of local customs having prevailed in Japan before its entering in force. Besides, under the Civil Code before 1947, a couple could not get married, when the household head did not allow a member of the household to do so. In a series of judgments since the 1910s, the judges who were sympathetic with cohabitees, whose partners arbitrarily broke their relationships, continued to protect the interests of those cohabitees. Such tendency culminated in the judgment of the Supreme Court which recognized that the cohabitation could be treated as a quasi-marriage.[254] The elapse of time since the enactment of the Civil Code and the abolishment of its household system, however, turns out not to have entirely oriented people in the direction the legislator of the late nineteenth century desired. At present, there are people who do not wish to notify their marriage to the family registrars: some do not want a state's involvement in their private lives; and some prefer the way of staying as singles on the family registration book to avoid the compulsory change of the name on marriage.

253. Circular No. 1320 of 26 Apr. 2004.
254. Judgment of the Supreme Court, 11 Apr. 1958, *Minshu* 12-5-789.

306. The current substantive law rules on non-marital cohabitation derives from the case law. The cohabitation to be legally protected requires the parties to see themselves as a husband and wife and to be reputed to be so in a community. As far as such subjective and objective requirements are satisfied, a certain prohibited degree of consanguinity, e.g., uncle and niece relationship, does not prevent the parties from being the parties of cohabitation. The cohabitation triggers legal consequences similar to the marriage in terms of marital obligation, property, and child maintenance. In addition, several Acts equate extra-marital cohabitees with married couples in light of their specific legislative purposes, for example, the Vehicle Accident Compensation Act,[255] the Industrial Accident Compensation Insurance Act (Workman's Compensation Act),[256] and the State Pension Act.[257] However, the legal consequences of cohabitation differ from those of marriage in such matters linked with the registration of marriage as surname, right to succession of the deceased's property,[258] and presumption of legitimacy.

307. The AGR contains no choice-of-law rule specifically dealing with non-marital cohabitation. However, a certain heterosexual union has been classified into a category of 'extra-marital cohabitation' under a set of choice-of-law rules, when the union in question cannot be seen as a marriage simply because of its lacking the formality of marriage. The choice-of-law rules (Articles 24–27 AGR) are said to apply, by analogy, to the establishment and its legal effects of extra-marital cohabitation. Experience tells that conflict of law problems have arisen between Japanese law and Korean law which also knows the extra-marital cohabitation known as '*sasilhon*' (de facto marriage).[259]

I. Dissolution

308. Article 27 AGR on divorce applies, by analogy, to the question whether the death of either party triggers the dissolution of the extra-marital cohabitation. The question whether the surviving cohabitee may have rights of successions should be governed by the *lex patriae* of the deceased (Article 36 AGR). In this context, it should be noted that Article 958 (3) of the Japanese Civil Code provides that, failing heirs, 'persons specially related to the deceased' are entitled to a whole or a part of the property of the latter.[260] It was disputed whether that provision should apply as part of the law applicable to succession or should apply as an operation of territorial sovereignty over *bona vacantia*. Since Korean law knew no institution corresponding to Article 958 (3) of the Japanese Civil Code, it was of practical importance which approach courts should take in the case of Japanese-Korean

255. Act No. 97 of 29 Jul. 1955.
256. Act No. 50 of 7 Apr. 1947.
257. Act No. 141 of 16 Apr. 1959.
258. The courts, however, may grant a certain payment to a surviving cohabitee on the ground of his or her contribution to the deceased cohabitee acquiring the assets. *See*, Minamikata, 100.
259. Yoshio Tameike, *'Naien'* in *Japanese Private International Law*, 22 *J.A.I.L.* 21, 22 (1978).
260. It should be stressed that, while the provision purports to protect the surviving cohabitee, it is effected to a limited extent, namely, only when there exist no heirs. *See*, *ibid.*, 37.

cohabitation: if the question should be governed by the *lex patriae* of the deceased, a Japanese surviving cohabitee would not be entitled to the property of a Korean deceased. However, in 1990, a provision which corresponded to the said Article of the Japanese Civil Code was added to the Korean Civil Code (Article 1057*bis*). As a result, the difference of the approach came to be less important.

309. Article 27 AGR should also apply, by analogy, to the question whether the cohabitation can be dissolved by facts corresponding to grounds of divorce. What law should govern the question whether either party's unjustifiable breaking off renders the other entitled to claiming for the solatium of the loss sustained as a consequence of the dissolution? In the context of Japanese substantive law, courts and writers tend to treat it in terms of tort. Reflective of this tendency, under the *Horei,* the courts tended to classify the question into the category of tort,[261] whereas the authors were of opinion that the law applicable to divorce should govern it.[262] Under the AGR, it is arguable that such difference of classification is of less importance than it was, because Article 20 AGR, namely the escape clause attached to the rule of the *lex loci delicti*, allows courts to apply the law of the place more closely connected with the case than the *locus delicti*, taking into consideration individual circumstances, including elements falling under the connecting criteria as set out in Article 27 AGR.

310. The question whether a cohabitee can claim the distribution of the other's property on the dissolution is said to pertain to the effects of the dissolution. It follows that Article 27 on divorce should, by analogy, apply to it.

II. Property

311. Article 26 AGR on matrimonial property is said to apply, by analogy, to the cohabitees' proprietary relationships. It follows that one of the laws referred to by that provision would be applicable to the question whether the cohabitees can enter into their property contracts. However, when Japanese law is applicable to such contract, the parties cannot avail themselves of the system of the registration of contract which enables them to assert their contracts against the third party, because the registration is available exclusively for the marital couple's contracts (Article 756 of the Civil Code).

312. The proprietary relationship between the cohabitees who do not enter into a property contract should be governed by one of the laws referred to by Article 26 AGR. The designated law governs the question whether the property acquired by a cohabitee in his or her name prior to or during the cohabitation constitutes his or her separate property. As mentioned earlier, in accordance with Article 26 (4) AGR, marital spouses can assert their matrimonial property regime subject to a foreign

261. Judgment of the Supreme Court, 27 Dec. 1961, *Kagetsu* 14-4-177.
262. *See*, Tameike, 484.

law, whether statutory or contractual, against the bona fide third party, by means of the registration.[263] It seems, however, that such registration system is not available for the extra-marital cohabitees.

§6. Maintenance Law

313. The Act on the Law Applicable to Maintenance Obligations, which incorporates the Hague Convention of 2 October 1973 on the Law Applicable to Maintenance Obligations, applies to maintenance obligations arising from family relationships.[264] Article 33 AGR embraces 'other family relationships' than those provided for in Articles 24–32. It is arguable that, given that the 'other family relationships' in the sense of Article 33 AGR are covered by the term of the 'family relationships' set forth in Article 1 of the Act, the Act applies to all the maintenance obligations.[265]

I. Spousal Maintenance

314. The spousal maintenance is governed by the choice-of-law rules laid down in the Act on the Law Applicable to Maintenance Obligations, not by the law applicable to the effects of marriage designated by Article 25 or 26 AGR. The maintenance obligations between the ex-spouses are governed by the law applicable to divorce (Article 4 of the said Act, Article 8 of the 1973 Hague Convention).

315. With regard to the same-sex marriage, it should be pointed out that, a creditor habitually resident in Japan is most likely to be able to obtain maintenance from a debtor under the law of their common foreign nationality (Article 2(1) of the Act, Article 5 of the Hague Convention), subject to the *ordre public* clause (Article 8(1) of the Act, Article 10 (1)). In addition, given that Japanese courts may have no jurisdiction to declare the dissolution of the same-sex marriage, the law applicable to the divorce would be limited to the one that a foreign court has applied to the dissolution (Article 4 of the Act, Article 8 of the Hague Convention).

---

263. *See*, paras. 302–303 *supra*.

264. To date, Japan has not ratified 'The Hague Convention of 23 November 2007 on the International Recovery of Child Support and Other Forms of Family Maintenance' and 'the Hague Protocol of 23 November 2007 on the Law Applicable to Maintenance Obligations'. *See*, Shinichiro Hayakawa, *International Aspects of Family Maintenance Law in Japan*, 52 *J.Y.B.I.L.* 413, 414–419 (2009).

265. In principle, a Japanese court may exercise jurisdiction over the maintenance obligation, when either a respondent maintenance debtor or a maintenance creditor is domiciled in Japan (Article 3-10 APFM).

II. Partnership Maintenance

316. What is mentioned at the preceding paragraph is likely to hold true with the partnership of the same-sex couple. In other words, a creditor is unlikely to obtain maintenance from a debtor under Japanese law applicable as the law of the creditor's habitual residence or as the *lex fori* (Article 2(1) of the Act, Articles 4(1) and 6 of the Hague Convention). If a partnership of the heterosexual couple registered in a foreign country can produce legal consequences, broadly speaking, as full as the classic marriage in light of JPIL, there is basically nothing to choose between the two unions with regard to their maintenance obligations. When a partnership of the heterosexual couple registered in a foreign country which can produce less consequences than the classic marriage in light of JPIL, their maintenance obligations would be treated like those of the non-marital cohabitees as mentioned below.

III. Maintenance of Cohabitees

317. When the cohabitees see themselves as a husband and wife and are reputed to be so in a community, their relationships between the extra-marital cohabitees may qualify as the 'family relationships' to be analogically covered by Articles 24 to 27 AGR. It follows that the said Act applies to their maintenance obligations.

§7. Child Law

I. Determination of Parenthood

318. The *Horei*, in its Article 17, connected the question of whether a child was legitimate with the *lex patriae* of the mother's husband at the time of the child's birth. The constitutionality of this father-oriented choice-of-law rule was doubted, which led to its revision in 1989. The revised choice-of-law rule which took the form of alternative one was designed to be neutral in terms of the gender equality and was inspired by the idea of *favor legitimitatis*.[266] It remains unaltered under the AGR. The current Article 28 (1) AGR provides that, where the child is legitimate by one of the *leges patriae* of the parents at the time of its birth, the child is regarded as legitimate.

319. This alternative choice-of-law rule does not militate in favour of legitimacy so much as it appears, because the time periods which are relevant to the presumption of legitimacy do not vary with legal systems in a marked way. What is more remarkable is the difference of substantive law rules relating to the rebuttal of presumption of legitimacy, namely, rules about who may challenge it during what period and by what procedure. In the phase of the presumption being rebutted, the alternative choice-of-law rule implies that, when the *leges patriae* of the parents confer legitimacy to a child, the child who wishes to challenge its legitimacy

266. The provision of the *Horei* was inspired by Art. 21 of the Austrian Private International Law.

has to do so under both laws. Experience tells that such application of both *leges patriae* of the parents tends to militate against the interests of the child who, seeking to elevate the biological tie with its true father to the legal one, tries to deny its legitimacy. It is regretted that the AGR has no black-letter choice-of-law rule inspired by the idea of *favor impugnationis.*[267]

320. Article 29 AGR contains the two sets of choice-of-law rules. The one is for the creation of non-marital parenthood by operation of law, in a way similar to that of marital parenthood. The other one is for the creation of such parenthood by acknowledgement or paternity action (Article 29 (1) AGR). The creation of non-marital parenthood by operation of law is governed only by the *lex patriae* of the alleged mother or father at the time of the birth.

321. Tortuous as Article 29 (1) and (2) AGR is in its wording, this provision expresses an alternative choice-of-law rule for the establishment of the paternity of non-marital child by acknowledgement or paternity action. In connection with the status of the child born out of wedlock vis-à-vis its father, it lists the following three potentially applicable laws: the *lex patriae* of the father at the time of the child's birth; his *lex patriae* at the time of the establishment; and the *lex patriae* of the child at the time of the establishment. It is enough, if the paternity is established by one of these *leges patriae*, whether by the father's voluntary acknowledgment or by judicial determination. The idea behind this provision is, obviously, to facilitate the establishment of the status of the child born out of wedlock. The Legislative Council which amended the former choice-of-law rule in 1989 did not hesitate to adopt this idea, having regard to the trends observed in the reforms or the codifications of private international law in the latter half of the twentieth century. We have to note that, at the same time, they bore in mind the situation where, before the revision of 1989, even the *ordre public* could not correct the result of the application of the foreign law, however intolerable it might be.[268] It should be added that Article 29 (1) and (2) provides, in the second sentence, that, if a child's *lex patriae* requires that the child or the third person give consent to the voluntary acknowledgment, such

267. *See*, Yokoyama, 271.

268. In a series of cases, Japanese children brought actions seeking the judicial determination of paternity. Their Korean fathers had been dead. The proceedings were, in most cases, commenced more than one year after the children had become aware of their fathers' deaths. Japanese law, the *lex patriae* of the children, allows a child to bring such an action, until a period of less than three years has elapsed from the date of the decease of the alleged father. On the other hand, Korean law, the *lex patriae* of the father, fixed a different time limit for such an action, namely, a period of one year after a child had learnt of the parent's death. Thus, whereas, according to Japanese law, the children could have successfully brought actions, their actions failed to satisfy the condition required by Korean law. The cumulative application of both *leges patriae* led to the impossibility of the judicial determination of paternity. The children sometimes called for the intervention of the *ordre public* in order to have the application of Korean law excluded but in vain. In one of such cases, the Supreme Court held that the application of the Korean provision was not contrary to the Japanese *ordre public*, stating that the difference between the two substantive law rules was merely technical and that the Japanese rule in question was not so mandatory not to allow such a slight derogation from it (Judgment of the Supreme Court, 27 Jun. 1975, *Kagetsu* 28-4-83).

requirements should be also fulfilled in addition to the *lex patriae* of the acknowledging person (cumulative application). Since it aims to establish the minimum safeguards for the best interests of the child, the *renvoi* from the *lex patriae* of the child to Japanese law is not put in operation.

322. Article 30 AGR also contains the alternative choice-of-law rule for legitimation. It lists the following three potentially applicable laws: the *lex patriae* of the father or the mother and the *lex patriae* of the child. The child obtains the status of legitimacy if the requirements of legitimation are satisfied by one of the three laws. The first two alternative limbs are justifiable by the fact that they are also adopted by Article 28 AGR for legitimacy. The *lex patriae* of the child which is one of the limbs for acknowledgment as laid down in Article 29 AGR was also adopted for legitimation, because the Legislative Council thought that the child should be legitimated when so treated under the *lex patriae* of the child according to which the father made acknowledgment. The relevant time at which each connecting factor should be determined is that when all the requirements provided by one of the *leges patriae* are met, namely, the time of the parents' marriage or that of the acknowledgement.

II. Custody and Contact

323. Under Article 20 of the *Horei*, the parent-child relationship was governed by the *lex patriae* of the father.[269] The constitutionality of this father-oriented rule was contested by academic circles and by some members of the Diet. In order to respond to them, the legislator in 1989 adopted the neutral criteria, the nationality and the habitual residence of the child. Article 32 of the current AGR which retains the provision made in 1989 contains the two choice-of-law rules which determine the law applicable to the parent-child relationships. This provision is designed to cover all the kinds of relationships which have arisen out of the parenthood established under the laws designated by the provisions as set out in Articles 28 to 31 (adoption). The choice-of-law rules are arranged in the form of cascade: the parent and child relationships are governed by the law of the child's *lex patriae* which coincides with the one of its parents; in the absence of such law, they are governed by the law of the country of the child's habitual residence. The preference for nationality over habitual residence is mainly due to the concern of the Legislative Council that the habitual residence may more easily lead to the corresponding change of the law applicable to the *ex lege* attribution or extinction of parental authority and custody. The application of the law of the child's habitual residence is conceivable in the following limited scenarios: e.g., a Japanese mother who gave birth to a Japanese child out of wedlock dies waiting for the acknowledgment by the foreign father; or a divorced Japanese mother to whom the divorce court granted the parental authority dies later. In such situations, where the child's welfare is

269. *See*, Yasuhiro Okuda, *Divorce, Protection of Minors, and Child Abduction*, in Basedow/Baum/Nishitani, 301.

likely to be at stake, protective measures may be taken pursuant to the law of the country where the child is habitually resident.

324. The law designated by Article 32 AGR governs the following matters: the attribution, exercise, termination, or restriction of parental authority; rights of custody as well as rights of contact. However, the provision does not cover the matter relating to the name and forename of the child. It is governed by the child's *lex patriae*. The guardianship, curatorship, and analogous institutions are governed by the law designated by Articles 5 and 35 AGR.

325. Even when Article 32 designates a foreign law as the child's *lex patriae*, the relevant provisions as contained in the Child Welfare Act apply mandatorily, as far as the child in question is resident in Japan. For example, pursuant to Article 27 of the said Act, a prefectural government shall take a measure necessary to protect a child, placing the child under a foster family or a child welfare institution.

III. Guardianship

326. Reflective of the arrangement by the Japanese Civil Code, the AGR stands upon the assumption that a guardian should be appointed according to the law designated by Article 35 AGR, namely the child's *lex patriae*, when there are no parents exercising their parental authority pursuant to the law applicable according to Article 32 AGR.[270] When the person in charge of a minor's personal or proprietary matters should be appointed by the court order, the court, which may assume jurisdiction on condition that the minor is domiciled or resident in Japan, or that he or she has Japanese nationality (Article 3-9 APFM), may appoint a guardian pursuant to the minor's *lex patriae* (Article 35 AGR).'[271] In addition, the court may appoint a guardian whose role is designed to protect an adult, in case that the child is very likely to be in no position to protect its interests even after reaching the age of majority. Such guardianship is governed by Japanese law referred to by Articles 5 and 35 AGR.

327. A guardian may be appointed *ex lege* or by a parent's last will pursuant to the child's *lex patriae*Unless a guardian is appointed *ex lege* or by a parent's last will, the court ought to exercise jurisdiction to appoint a guardian pursuant to the child's *lex patriae*. Article 35 AGR is silent about jurisdictional grounds for the

270. The applicable laws designated by those choice-of-law rules do not necessarily coincide with each other. It follows that a situation may arise where, whereas no parent is regarded any longer as entitled to the parental authority under the law applicable to the parental authority, the law applicable to guardianship allows a parent to continue exercising his or her parental authority. Academic writers have proposed the assimilation technique: courts may appoint a guardian under the law applicable to guardianship in favour of the child's interests, regardless of the conditions which that law requires for the appointment of guardian. *See*, Tameike, 528.

271. The court may also appoint a guardian according to Japanese law, when the person who is supposed to be a guardian determined *ex lege* or by a parent's will under a child's *lex patriae* cannot effectively exercise his rights and duties in Japan (Art. 35(2) AGR).

appointment of guardian. It is arguable that Article 5 AGR should be analogically applied to this matter. As a result, Japanese courts have jurisdiction to appoint a guardian, when a child concerned is domiciled or resident in Japan or has Japanese nationality.[272]

IV. Adoption

328. Japan is said to be the 'receiving country' rather than the 'country of origin' in respect of the intercountry adoption. Whereas some Asian states such as the Philippines, Thailand, China, Vietnam and Korea are the parties of the Hague Convention of 29 May 1993 on Protection of Children and Co-operation in Respect of Intercountry Adoption, Japan has not ratified it yet.

329. Irrespective of whether the adoption in question may be 'full' or 'limited' in its effects, Article 3-5 APFM confers jurisdiction upon a Japanese court over the establishment of adoption if either the prospective adoptive parent or the (minor) person to be adopted is domiciled in Japan.

330. Article 31 (1) AGR provides, in the first sentence, that the adopter's *lex patriae* governs the adoption at the time of the adoption. The *lex patriae* of the adopter was preferred, because most of newly established relationships are expected to be carried out in the adopter's home country. In view of the statistics displaying the tendency for Japan to be the receiving country, Japanese law is likely to be applicable to the intercountry adoption. The *lex patriae* of the adopter at the time of the adoption governs the questions concerning not only its conditions but also its effects such as a question as to whether the adopted child is completely integrated into the adopter's family. Article 31 (2) AGR provides, in particular, that the same law governs the questions whether and to what extent legal ties with the natural family are terminated, and whether the revocation of adoption should be permitted. The time fixed at the adoption are regarded as decisive for such effects of adoption, because they are interwoven with the question as to what types of adoption was created.

331. Article 31 AGR contains no specific choice-of-law rule dealing with the situation where the adopters are married. The legislator seems to have stood upon the assumption that, in such a situation, the two adoptions, the one between father and child and the other between mother and child, would be created. This idea of double adoption causes no difficulty, as far as the husband and wife are of the same nationality. Otherwise, namely, when they are a mixed couple, it is likely to lead to the assimilation problem difficult to be resolved: e.g., whereas the *lex patriae* of a spouse knows only the type of 'full adoption', only the 'limited adoption' is permissible under the other's *lex patriae*.

332. Article 31 (1) AGR provides, in the second sentence, that, if a child's *lex patriae* requires consent to be given by the child or by persons intervening in the

272. *See*, Yokoyama, 125.

adoption, or requires measures such as permission to be granted by authorities for the future adoption, such requirements should be also fulfilled in addition to the *lex patriae* of the adopter (cumulative application). The provision is designed to ensure that the informed consent should be given to the prospective adoption in order to prevent future disputes from arising in respect of the status of the child. Since it aims to establish the minimum safeguards for the best interests of the adopted child, the *renvoi* from the *lex patriae* of the child to Japanese law is not put in operation.

333. It appears that Japanese courts sometimes have had recourse to the *ordre public* for the purpose of granting the adoption. Given that Japan is a receiving country, the *lex patriae* of the adopter often coincides with Japanese law. However, this is not always the case. A Japanese family court excluded the application of the Chinese Adoption Law which, pursuing the so-called one-child policy, prohibited a married couple to adopt more than one child, on the ground that the denial of the adoption by a Sino-Japanese couple of two Japanese siblings habitually resident in Japan appeared to be intolerable in light of their interests.[273] Furthermore, a adjudication excluded the application of Iranian law prohibiting adoption.[274]

V. Artificial Insemination, Surrogacy

334. It seems that, whereas the artificial insemination, whether by a husband or by a donor, has given rise to legal problems in purely domestic cases,[275] there has been no reported cases with foreign elements. It is arguable that courts will apply the choice-of-law rules as set out in the AGR to questions involved in the artificial insemination. For example, they will have recourse to Article 28 AGR to determine the law applicable to the questions whether and under what conditions a child can be regarded as a legitimate child of a husband whose wife gave birth to the child.

335. To date, there has been formerly no regulation on surrogacy. However, the guidelines or codes of practice for the Japanese medical professionals have strictly prohibited the surrogate motherhood. As a consequence, it is said that a number of Japanese couples have had flown to foreign countries such as the US to have children through birth mothers resident there.[276] Such tendency brought the Supreme Court to face the question of whether a Nevada court order which had declared the legal parentage between a child and Japanese intending parents was recognizable in Japan. Although sympathetic with their course of action, the Court denied the recognition of the Nevada court order on the ground of the *ordre public* in the sense of Article 118 CCP, stating that the fundamental principle that the birth mother should always be the legal mother, *de lege lata*, underlay Japanese law.[277]

273. Adjudication of the Kobe Family Court, 10 May 1995, *Kagetsu* 47-12-91.
274. Adjudication of the Utsunomiya Family Court, 20 Jul. 2007, *Kagetsu* 59-12-106.
275. *See*, Mizuno, para. 42 *supra*.
276. Minamikata, 103.
277. Judgment of the Supreme Court, 23 Mar. 2007, 50 *J.A.I.L.552* (2008).

VI. Child Support

336. The child support is governed by the law applicable under the Act on the Law Applicable to Maintenance Obligations (incorporating the 1973 Hague Convention) and under the Convention of 24 October 1956 on the Law Applicable to Maintenance Obligations towards Children which was almost superseded by the former.

VII. Child Abduction

337. The Hague Convention of 25 October 1980 on the Civil Aspects of International Child Abduction entered in force since 1 April 2014. In order to implement the Convention, the Act for Implementation of the Convention on the Civil Aspects of International Child Abduction was enacted.[278]

§8. Protection of Adults

338. In 2000, the Japanese substantive law rules on guardianship were greatly reformed. The current system consists of the statutory guardianship and the continuing powers of attorney. The former takes the three forms of protection: the assistance, the curatorship, and the tutorship. The court may institute one of those protective forms of measures in accordance with the degree of impairment of his or her mental faculties, coupled with the appointment of an assistant, a curator, and a tutor pronounced in one set of proceedings. Whereas, although substantially modified in flexibility, the last two forms of protection derive from the '*interdiction*' and the lesser measure of restriction of capacity, the assistance is characterized by the idea far from deprivation of capacity and by arrangements tailor-made to needs of individual adults.

339. Article 5 AGR contains a jurisdictional rule and a unilateral choice-of-law rule with regard to the institution of the statutory guardianship for those who are not in a position to protect their interests. The jurisdictional approach being adopted, there is no room for the Japanese court to apply foreign laws in instituting the protective regimes. According to the said provision, the Japanese court may issue an

278. Act No. 48 of 19 Jun. 2013. For the Act, *see*, Jun Yokoyama, *A Japanese Implementation Bill for the 1980 Child Abduction Convention*, in *A Commitment to Private International Law* 661 et seq. (The Permanent Bureau of the Hague Conference on Private International Law (ed.), Intersentia 2013);. For the implementation, *see also*, Masayuki Tanamura, *International Child Abduction Cases and the Act for the Implementation of the Hague Convention*, 57 J.Y.B.I.L. 24 et seq. (2014); and Masako Murakami, '*Case Proceedings for the Return of an Abducted Child and the Compulsory Execution in Japan*', *ibid.*, 33 et seq. Judgment of the Supreme Court, 21 Dec. 2017, 61 *J.Y.B.I.L.*402 is the first judgment of the Court that applied the Act to admit the change of circumstances justifying the modification (refusal) of the return order.

order for commencement of such protective measures as laid down by the Civil Code, when the person concerned is domiciled or resident in Japan, or has Japanese nationality.[279]

340. Under the AGR, the court always applies Japanese law to determine whether the capacity of the person concerned should be restricted in his or her interests. Such deviation from the nationality principle is justifiable.[280] First, the current Japanese substantive law designed to give due respect to wishes of the person concerned seemed to reduce the necessity for the court to apply his or her *lex patriae.* Second, the Japanese substantive law has a form of protection, namely, the assistance, for those who should be classified into the 'vulnerable adults' rather than the 'incapable adults'. In contrast, the substantive laws of the neighbouring countries still maintain the traditional types of system consisting of the *interdiction* and analogous institutions. Consequently, if the legislator had adhered to the principle of nationality with respect to the causes of incapacity, vulnerable adults coming from those neighbouring countries who have accumulated more or less property in Japan would not be able to take advantage of the assistance. The application of Japanese law seems to be more beneficial to such persons. The Japanese substantive law rules which are to be applied pursuant to Article 5 AGR govern the direct effects of the pronouncements of the court which commence the tutorship, the curatorship, and the assistance. For example, the pronouncement of tutorship automatically triggers the restriction of the capacity in almost all matters. That of assistance may lead to the one-off restriction of the capacity limited to a particular matter.

341. Under applicable Japanese law, the court is not allowed to take any measures to restrict the capacity of an adult, unless it, at the same time, takes a measure to furnish the adult the protection proportional to the degree of mental faculties and tailored to the individual circumstances. It follows that the jurisdictional rules as enunciated in Article 5 AGR are also applicable to the question as to when the Japanese court may assume its jurisdiction for the appointment and the supervision of a person to represent or assist an incapable or vulnerable adult. The effective protection of the adult by the Japanese courts is only conceivable when they can apply the law familiar to them, namely, Japanese law. This is also the case with the adult of foreign nationality (Article 35 (2) (ii) of the AGR).

---

279. It is noteworthy that the situation of property situated in Japan does not found the jurisdiction for the Japanese court to commence the measures. This reflects the judges' strong opposition to this jurisdictional ground during discussions of the Legislative Council. They doubted that courts would be in a position to take appropriate measures for those who have no link with Japan other than the situation of property. They also expressed their concern over the ground of Japanese nationality, when it comes into play about a person not domiciled in Japan. However, situations where the Japanese nationality fails to be strengthened with other links with Japan do not seem to arise frequently. Further, the ground of jurisdiction should not discourage a family member of the person concerned to undertake his or her protection. Eventually, the Japanese nationality was adopted as a ground for jurisdiction.

280. Under the *Horei*, the causes which trigger the pronouncement of *interdiction* or of the lesser measure of restriction of capacity were governed by the *lex patriae* of the person.

342. For the purpose of promoting self-determination for the adults, the Act on Voluntary Guardianship Contract introduced the system of continuing powers of attorney.[281] By means of a mandate which remains in force or enters into force in the event that the adult's capacity becomes insufficient, he or she may make arrangements in advance while still fully capable. According to the Act, the mandate contract has to be made by the public notary and to be registered in a register kept by the Japanese administrative authorities. A power of attorney should become operative only when the court appoints a third person to supervise the attorney. However, neither the Act nor the AGR contains any black-letter rule on jurisdiction pursuant to which the court may appoint the supervisor or make interventions necessary in the interests of the adults, including the termination of the continuing powers of attorney. It is submitted that Article 5 AGR should be applied, by analogy, to the jurisdictional matters on the continuing powers of attorney. When a person who granted the continuing power of attorney is domiciled or resident in Japan, or has Japanese nationality, the Japanese court should have jurisdiction to take such a measure as the appointment of supervisor.

281. Act No. 150 of 8 Dec. 1999.

Chapter 6. Succession Law

§1. *Lex Successionis*

343. The choice-of-law rule on succession remains unaltered since 1898.[282] The current choice-of-law rule is contained in Article 36 AGR. It is faithful to the unitary system of succession. The applicable law is supposed to apply to all the assets of the deceased, whether moveable or immovable and to apply to the whole devolution process from the opening to the distribution. It is not, however, that the system of unity is thoroughly carried out under JPIL. First, combined with the *renvoi* clause (Article 41 AGR), the said choice-of-law rule may transform itself into a disjunctive rule. Second, as far as the immovable property is concerned, the *lex rei sitae* may have the last word so as to override the *lex successionis*.

344. The acceptance of the *renvoi* from the *lex patriae* of the deceased may be tantamount to the adoption of the disjunctive rule, depending upon the kinds of the assets to be inherited. Chinese PIL, in particular, designates the law of habitual residence of the deceased for the succession to the movable property and the *lex rei sitae* for the succession to the immovable property.[283] If JPIL accepts the *renvoi* in the first degree from Chinese PIL, it follows, for example, that, while the succession of the movable property owned by a deceased Chinese resident in Shanghai is governed by Chinese law, the immovable property situated at the China Town in Yokohama may be acquired by his heirs pursuant to Japanese law. The Japanese courts have, in fact, applied Japanese law, accepting the *renvoi* from Chinese PIL in the field of succession.

345. According to Articles 828(2) and 1151 of the Taiwanese Civil Code, the hereditary estate cannot be disposed before distribution without the agreement of all the heirs, namely, the hereditary property is subject to the joint ownership in undivided shares (*Eigentum zur gesamten Hand*). When Taiwanese law is the *lex successionis*, it follows that every heir is supposed to be incapable of disposing his share in favour of the third party without other heirs' consent to it. However, Japanese law which is applicable to the transfer of immovable property as the *lex rei sitae* knows no institutional framework which is designed to make known to the public something like the *Eigentum zur gesamten Hand*. Consequently, the hereditary property is subject to the ordinary form of co-ownership (*Miteigentum*) known to Japanese law.[284]

346. Article 36 AGR designates the *lex patriae* of the deceased at the time of his or her death. Preference for nationality over domicile or habitual residence has been explained by more stability and easier ascertainment inherent in the connecting factor of nationality. The habitual residence may be subject to the manipulation of the governing law by a Japanese testator who tries to evade Japanese provisions

282. *See*, Hayashi Takami, *International Succession in Japan*, 52 *J.Y.B.I.L.* 433 (2009).
283. Article 31 of Chinese PIL.
284. Judgment of the Supreme Court, 8 Mar. 1994, *Minshu* 48-3-835.

relating to legally reserved portion. Further, the notary public engaged in making the will might find it difficult to ascertain even his client's current habitual residence. In view of the present situation where the concept of habitual residence is far from unambiguously clear, there seems much to be said for the nationality. In addition to these arguments in favour of nationality, it is also worthy of noting that nationality is primarily chosen as the connecting factor of the choice-of-law rules on family matters.

347. The choice-of-law rule on succession which remains unaltered since the late nineteenth century seems to be still viable when we look at the fact that the number of Japanese people habitually resident in foreign countries has increased.[285] Most of their property and of family members are expected to be found in Japan. However, foreign people domiciled in Japan on the permanent basis, namely, Korean and Chinese people domiciled there for generations, might expect Japanese law to govern their succession.[286] The Legislative Council discussed the possibility of the *professio juris* in the field of succession law which enables a person to designate Japanese law to govern the succession as the law of habitual residence. However, the number of them has been decreasing year by year. This background seems to explain the silence of the Legislative Council with respect to the choice-of-law rule on *professio juris*.[287]

§2. Scope of Applicable Law

348. The *lex successionis* determined by Article 36 AGR governs when the succession opens. Whether and when a missing person is regarded as dead is governed by Article 6 on disappearance. According to the prevailing view, the presumption of simultaneous death in case the order of dying cannot be established is governed by the *lex successionis* rather than the *lex patriae* of the deceased, because such presumption is thought relevant only to the context of the succession.[288]

349. Who is entitled to inherit someone's hereditary estate?[289] In what order and to what extent is he so? Who may represent the heirs? To what extent is the free disposition by a testator limited (the forced heirship reserve)? These questions

285. They were around 1.31 million in 2015.
286. The number of them was 348,626 in 2015.
287. The demographic change taking place in Japan might lead to the reform of the choice-of-law rule on succession in the near future. *See*, Yokoyama, 298–299.
288. For example, Tameike, 256.
289. Article 3-11 APFM confers jurisdiction upon the Japanese courts over inheritance matters almost comprehensively.

relating to testate and intestate devolution are governed by the *lex successionis*. So are the questions as to whether, when, and how an heir may accept or waive the succession.[290]

350. The *lex successionis* also governs the administration of estate. It is the *lex successionis* to determine the method by means of which the inherited estate should be transferred from the deceased to beneficiaries and to determine the relationship between two or more heirs to which the inherited assets belong. When the estate is required to be administered by the executor or the personal representative of the deceased under the governing law, the Japanese courts have appointed such personal representatives pursuant to that law, availing themselves of the analogous proceedings available under the Japanese procedural law.[291]

351. The choice-of-law rules on matrimonial property regime and succession are not coordinated with each other. However, it seems that the Japanese courts have faced no case in which difficult problems arose out of the successive applications of the two different laws.

352. If the deceased left his estate in Japan without heirs under the *lex successionis*, Article 958-3 of the Japanese Civil Code may apply. According to the provision, the family court may, if it finds it reasonable, upon application by a person especially close to the deceased, such as a person who shared a livelihood with the deceased or a person who contributed to the medical treatment and nursing of the deceased, grant such a person the remaining amount of the inherited estate after liquidation, in whole or in part. When the inherited property is not disposed of pursuant to this provision, the estate is characterized as *bona vacantia* which eventually belongs to the National Treasury (Article 959 of the Civil Code).

353. The so-called joint bank accounts enabling the survivor to take the benefits of bank accounts on the death of the account holder is out of the range of the *lex successionis*. It is governed by the law of the contract concluded between the parties and the bank.[292]

---

290. When the *renvoi* is accepted, Japanese law applies. For example, Decree of the Tokyo Family Court, 15 Oct. 1999, *Kagetsu* 52-3-60 (*renvoi* from New Zealand law over a petition for waiving succession); Decree of the Kobe Family Court, 27 Jul. 1994, *Kagetsu* 47-5-60) (*renvoi* from Indian law over a petition for waiving succession).
291. *See*, Commentary II (Hayashi), 203.
292. Judgment of the Tokyo District Court, 8 Jul. 2014, *Hanta* 1415-283.

§3. TESTAMENTARY DISPOSITION

I. Legal Capacity

354. The capacity of the person making the disposition is understood to be governed by the law referred to by Article 37 AGR, not by Articles 4 and 5 on general capacity to act.[293]

II. Choice of Law

355. Whereas, as mentioned above, the Legislative Council discussed the *professio juris* in favour of the law of the person's habitual residence, they put off its introduction.[294]

III. Compulsory Portion

356. The *lex successionis* referred to by Article 36 AGR, not by Article 37, governs the question who is entitled to benefit from a reserved inheritance share irrespective of the deceased's disposition upon death. Consequently, the *lex successionis* to be finally fixed at the time of death turns out to be different from the law under which the deceased bore in mind in making the disposition. Although, pursuant to Article 37 (2), the testator has some chance to modify or revoke his or her earlier disposition after having changed his nationality, JPIL does not fully respect the testator's prediction about the fate of the inheritable property.[295]

IV. Interpretation

357. Each juridical act which the person intends to do by means of making the disposition upon death is governed by the law referred to by the corresponding choice-of-law rules.

V. Last Will

A. *Formal Validity*

358. The formal validity of wills is governed by the Act on Governing Laws Relating to the Form of Testamentary Dispositions. This Act is designed to incorporate the Hague Convention of 5 October 1961 on the Conflict of Laws Relating to the Form of Testamentary Dispositions.

---

293. Commentary II (Hayashi), 215.
294. *See*, paras 33, 348 *supra*.
295. *See*, para. 362 *infra*.

B. Substantive Validity

359. According to Article 37 (1) AGR whose content is also unaltered since 1898, the validity of a last will and its binding force are governed by the *lex patriae* of that person at the time of making the will. A later change of nationality will not affect the fate of substantive validity and binding force of the will, unless the revocation takes place under the choice-of-law rule as contained in Article 37 (2) AGR.

360. In addition to capacity to make a will, Article 37 AGR is said to cover the following matters: permissibility of a will made by two or more persons in one document; invalidity of the execution of a will on the ground of, e.g., fraud, duress, or mistake; the binding force of a will; and its operational time. However, the validity and effects of each juridical act which a testator intends to make by means of the last will is governed by each *lex causae* designated by each corresponding choice-of-law rule. For example, when a voluntary acknowledgment of a child is expressed in a last will, the validity and effects of the acknowledgment are governed by Article 29 AGR on the establishment of parentage of the child born out of wedlock.

361. The revocation of an earlier will is governed by the *lex patriae* of the testator at the time of the revocation (Article 37 (2) AGR). Where the revocation takes the form of a new will, the time of the execution of the new one is respected. Whereas there is no case law showing which time is relevant to the revocation by, e.g., the subsequent marriage of the testator, it is submitted that the time of marriage should be relevant to the determination of the governing law in the interests of the testator's expectations.

VI. Legacy

A. Formal Validity

362. The formal validity is governed by the Act on Governing Laws Relating to the Form of Testamentary Dispositions.

B. Substantive Validity

363. There is no specific choice-of-law rule dealing with the substantive validity of the legacy. It is understood to be governed by the *lex successionis* referred to by Article 36 AGR.

VII. Testamentary Contract

364. There is no choice-of-law rules dealing with an agreement which creates, modifies, or terminates rights to the future estate or estates of one or more persons such as the *Erbvertrag* of German law. There have been no cases on this matter.

§4. INHERITANCE AND LIABILITY

365. The *lex successionis* determines whether and to what extent beneficiaries are liable for debts owed by the deceased to his or her creditors. For example, the *lex successionis* applies to the following questions: who should pay debts, heirs or administrators; and whether and how the beneficiaries may accept the inheritance up to the value of the net assets. The law also governs the liability for debts arising in connection with the succession, such as costs involved in the administration of the inheritable estate.

Part III. International Civil Procedure

Chapter 1. Sources of ICP

366. The sources of JPIL regarding procedural matters, particularly, jurisdiction, and recognition and enforcement of foreign decisions, are found in Japanese statutes and case law. The latter source has been important until quite recently. The multilateral conventions available in the field of civil procedure are few.

Chapter 2. The Principle of *Lex Fori*

367. Matters of procedure are governed by the *lex fori*. As mentioned earlier, the principle seems to derive from the practical consideration that local judges should not be obliged to conduct the proceeding in accordance with foreign procedural rules unfamiliar to them.[296] This is probably the case with rules concerning burden of proof and evidence. However, Japanese judges have applied the foreign *lex causae* whose application would not cause much inconvenience to them, even if the foreign rules involved could be regarded, one way or another, as procedural, for example, rules concerning the persons eligible to apply to a court for acknowledgement of paternity and the limitation period for such application. There seem two kinds of Japanese procedural rules, namely, the ones replaceable with the applicable foreign rules and the ones whose reliance is mandatory. It seems to be difficult to draw dogmatically the demarcation line between the two.

368. Whereas Article 2 of the Personal Affairs Litigation Act enumerates the types of litigation over which a Japanese court may exercise jurisdiction, it refers to, for example, no litigation type of 'separation', because there is no such institution in the Civil Code to whose institutions the types of litigation as set out in the PALA are designed to correspond. It does not follow, however, that no Brazilian couple may apply for separation to the Japanese courts. It is widely agreed that the Act provides no black letter rules relating to some types of petitions simply because they are unknown to the Japanese Civil Code and that the legislator would not intend to preclude the analogical application of the Act to foreign institutions.

296. *See*, para. 74 *supra*.

Chapter 3. National Jurisdiction

369. The rules concerning internal venue (national jurisdiction) had played an important role in civil and commercial matters until the provisions on international jurisdiction were added to the CCP and to the Civil Interim Relief Act in 2012.[297]

370. When the first private international law was enacted in 1898, there was no provision which specifically dealt with the international jurisdiction in civil and commercial matters. Probably, the nineteenth century legislator followed the line of reasoning that the provisions of the CCP designed to 'distribute' national jurisdiction to each Japanese local court were also applicable to the question as to when international jurisdiction should be 'attributed' to the Japanese courts on the whole: for example, if a ground of national jurisdiction is located within the venue of the Tokyo District Court, it is taken for granted that the international jurisdiction has been already attributed to the courts of Japan on the whole. It is not until 1981 that the Supreme Court addressed the question when the Japanese courts might assume international jurisdiction in civil and commercial matters (*Malaysian Airline* case).[298] The Court showed the following line of reasoning: there was lacuna as regards international jurisdiction under Japanese law; it should be filled with norms deduced from the ends of justice; given that the ends of justice underlay the provisions on internal venue as set out in the CCP, the courts rely on such provisions in examining when they may assume international jurisdiction. In that way, the Court, in practical terms, maintained the principle that 'distribution', in principle, entailed 'attribution'. Inferior courts continued to follow this line of reasoning until the provisions on international jurisdiction were added to the CCP in 2012.

371. As regards the family matters, the courts have taken the position that the rules on national jurisdiction as set out in the Personal Status Litigation Act could not be applied to the issues on international jurisdiction even on the analogical basis. Everything has been left to the development of case law.

---

297. *See*, Koji Takahashi, *Japan's Newly Enacted Rules on International Jurisdiction: with a Reflection on Some Issues of Interpretation*, 13 *J.Y.B.I.L.* 146 (2011).

298. Judgment of the Supreme Court, 16 Oct. 1981, 26 *J.A.I.L.* 122 (1983). The judgment affirmed that the mere location of the defendant's establishment in Japan should be sufficient to confer jurisdiction on Japanese courts. The case which the Supreme Court dealt with was related to a contract which a Japanese tourist entered into with a Malaysian airline in Malaysia. He bought a round-trip ticket of flight from Kuala Lumpur to Penang. This was a purely domestic flight of Malaysia. The plane with him on board crashed somewhere on the way back from Penang to Kuala Lumpur. All the passengers were dead. Then, the family members of the deceased Japanese passenger raised an action for recovering damages against the airline in Japan. The court of the first instance denied entertaining jurisdiction over the action in light of the ends of justice. This denial of jurisdiction is understandable, because the defendant's principal office was situated in Malaysia and all the evidence was located there. Furthermore, whereas the Japanese branch of the defendant airline was in a position to sail such a ticket to the deceased, the branch had nothing to do with the contract *in casu*. Then, the plaintiffs made an appeal to the Nagoya High Court. In contrast to the judgment of the court of the first instance, the appellate court accepted jurisdiction on the ground that a business establishment of the defendant airline was situated in Japan, though the contract *in casu* had nothing to do with the establishment. The Supreme Court approved the appellate court's judgment.

Chapter 4. International Jurisdiction

§1. Statutory Forums

I. Civil and Commercial Matters

372. As mentioned above, the Japanese courts continued to rely on the provisions of the CCP on venue or national jurisdiction in examining when they might assume international jurisdiction. However, they soon began to face cases in which some rules on national jurisdiction did not work well in international situations. For example, the ground of the place of performance enabled Japanese courts to assume jurisdiction, even when Japan was hardly seen as an appropriate forum in light of the parties' expectations. In 1997, the Supreme Court itself held that the court was allowed to decline jurisdiction when they took account of circumstances of an individual case, even though its jurisdiction was founded pursuant to the venue rules as provided by the CCP. One might say that the Supreme Court introduced an idea inspired by the principle of forum non conveniens.[299] The introduction of such a principle is not blameable. Although it is certain that some elements of legal uncertainty are inherent in the principle, it is arguable that the general and abstract rule on jurisdiction does not always designate the appropriate forum under circumstances of a particular concrete case. What is really problematic with the position taken by the Supreme Court does not lie in the introduction of the principle of forum non conveniens as such but its introduction, leaving untouched the 'distribution entails attribution' rule. Unless jurisdictional rules suitable for international situations were at judges' disposal, they would be unnecessarily obliged to examine circumstances of a case even at the outset of the proceedings. Eventually, the new provisions on international jurisdiction were added to the CCP.[300]

373. The heading of Section 1, Chapter 2, Part 1 of the CCP reads 'Jurisdiction of the Courts of Japan'. The Section contains eleven Articles, dealing with general grounds of jurisdiction (Article 3-2), special grounds of jurisdiction varying with types of claims (Article 3-3), grounds for consumer and employment contracts (Article 3-4), exclusive jurisdiction (Articles 3-5 and 3-10), connected claims (Article 3-6), prorogation (Article 3-7), submission (Article 3-8), exception clause (Article 3-9), and examination as to jurisdiction (Article 3-11 and 3-12).

374. Article 3-2 CCP expresses the traditional rule of *actor sequitur forum rei.* This jurisdictional ground is available irrespective of the category of claims. In addition, and alternatively, the plaintiff may sue in the courts of Japan which does not coincide with the defendant's home country, when the heads of ground as listed in Article 3-3, 3-4, and 3-6 are found in Japan. By contrast, under Article 3-5 and 3-10, the plaintiff must sue in Japan as regards disputes which fall under the Japanese exclusive jurisdiction. Article 3-9 contains an exception clause which allows a

299. Judgment of the Supreme Court, 11 Nov. 1997, 41 *J.A.I.L.*, 117 (1998).

300. *See*, Masato Dogauchi, *New Japanese Rules on International Jurisdiction: General Observation*, 54 *J.Y.B.I.L.* 260 et seq. (2011).

court of Japan whose jurisdiction is founded by virtue of the other provisions as contained in the Section 1 to dismiss an action in individual circumstances of the case. Although the CCP had been originally inspired by the German CCP, the forum non conveniens has become an integral part of JPIL.[301]

A. General Grounds of Jurisdiction

375. The provision as contained in Article 3-2(1) CCP lays down the general ground of jurisdiction in relation to a natural person. A natural person may be sued in the courts of Japan, when he or she is domiciled in Japan at the time of the institution of the proceedings. When a person is found to have no domicile anywhere in the world, he or she may be sued as far as being resident in Japan. When the defendant is neither domiciled nor resident anywhere in the world, he or she may be sued in Japan when he or she is found to have had the domicile in Japan in the past. However, the last limb of the general jurisdiction does not apply, when it is established that the person who moved afterwards to a foreign country became domiciled there or in a third country.

376. According to Article 3-2(3) CCP, Japanese courts have jurisdiction over an action against a legal person or any other association or foundation, where the principal establishment, business or not, is situated in Japan. The defendant whose principal establishment is found nowhere in the world may be sued in Japan, where its representative or any other head officer is domiciled in Japan. The legal person etc. is regarded as having its principal establishment in Japan, either when it has its statutory seat in Japan under its articles of association or when the central administration, namely, its management and control is carried out in Japan. The alternative arrangement of these criteria is expected to avoid the negative conflict of jurisdictions.

377. A branch or other establishment in Japan, on its own, founds no jurisdiction of the Japanese courts. The additional connection with the forum as set out in Article 3-3(iv) is required for the Japanese courts to entertain jurisdiction, as mentioned below.[302]

B. Special Grounds of Jurisdiction Depending on Types of Claims

378. Article 3-3 CCP lists the heads of jurisdiction each of which corresponds to the *ratio materiae* of each claim. They are alongside and in parallel with the general ones. A plaintiff may raise an action in the courts of Japan which does not coincide with a defendant's home country as laid down in Article 3-2 CCP.

301. It should be noted that Art. 3-9 does not allow the courts of Japan to dismiss an action, when the parties made the exclusive choice of the Japanese courts or when a dispute falls under the exclusive jurisdiction.
302. *See*, para. 382 *infra*.

379. Experience tells that the place of performance has been one of the most important heads of jurisdiction in contractual matters.[303] The creditor often has legitimate interests in bringing an action in Japan, even when the defendant debtor has his or her home in a foreign country. Article 3-3(i) CCP, which purports to strike a fair balance between the interests of the parties, allows the plaintiff to sue in Japan as regards the claim for performance of a contractual obligation. As far as it arises out of a contract, every single obligation has its own place of performance as a jurisdictional ground, regardless of where the characteristic performance of the contract is or should be made. Besides, this head of jurisdiction is not limited to claims arising out of contractual obligations such as a claim for damages for the non-performance, but extends to claims arising in conjunction with an obligation. The head of jurisdiction may found the jurisdiction of the Japanese courts in relation to a claim based on a *negotiorum gestio* performed in connection with a contractual obligation as well as a claim based on unjust enrichment having arisen in connection with an obligation.

380. The jurisdictional ground of the place of performance is conditioned by elements relating to legal certainty and parties' expectations. The Japanese court may assume jurisdiction, when the parties, in their contract itself, agreed on Japan as a place of performance. In addition, the court may do so when the parties chose the law applicable to the contract by virtue of which Japan can be identified as the place of performance. As far as the choice of law by the parties is real, the implicit choice of law is sufficient in this context. However, in the situation where the law applicable to the contract is objectively determinable only by recourse to Article 8 AGR, the head of jurisdiction is not available for the plaintiff. In such a situation, it was feared that even the parties in business-to-business transactions could hardly predict the forum. Furthermore, the court should spare troubles to examine elements relevant to merits of a case at the outset of the proceedings.[304]

381. As mentioned earlier, Japanese courts have general jurisdiction over an action against a legal person or any other association or foundation, where the principal establishment, business or not, is situated in Japan (Article 3-2(3) CCP). In addition, special jurisdiction is conferred upon Japanese courts under the two conditions: the defendant's establishment is located in Japan; and the claim is connected with the operation of that establishment.[305] The following idea underlies this head of jurisdiction: a company or any other body which takes advantage of expanding its operation in Japan in the form of setting up its branches or other establishments should be prepared to take a risk of being a defendant before Japanese courts

303. For the previous court practice, Akira Saito, *International Civil Jurisdiction Based on the Place of Performance of Obligations Relating to a Contract*, 54 *J.Y.B.I.L.* 295 et seq. (2011).

304. Article 3-3(i) CCP says nothing about availability of this head of jurisdiction when the place of performance is determinable by an international agreement such as CISG. It is submitted that, since such an international agreement may afford as a certain and predictable legal basis as the law chosen by the parties, the place of performance to be designated, for example, by virtue of Art. 31 of the CISG may be the head of jurisdiction.

305. For a critical view of the provision, *see*, Yoshiaki Nomura, *Activity-Based Jurisdiction of Japanese Courts A Bold but Unnecessary Departure*, 55 *J.Y.B.I.L.* 263 et seq. (2012).

as regards claims arising out of the establishments' operations. It is immaterial whether claims are based on contracts or other relationships such as tort.

382. When a claim in question arises out of a contract, the contract in question must be, one way or another, one of the operations made by the establishment located in Japan. Two points should be noted. First, the operational reach of the establishment is not limited to the Japanese territory. For example, when an establishment administers the defendant's business to be carried out in the Far East on the whole, the fact that such establishment concluded a contract with a Korean plaintiff in Seoul does not preclude the Japanese courts from assuming jurisdiction.[306] Second, the fact that the establishment located in Japan was empowered to conclude the same kind of contract with that *in casu* does not trigger the assumption of jurisdiction by Japanese courts. This should be emphasized because Article 3-3(iv) CCP purports to abandon the case law established by the Supreme Court as regards the *Malaysian Airline* case.[307] If the same case should arise in the future, Japanese courts, pursuant to Article 3-3(iv) CCP, would not assume jurisdiction because such contract is out of the operation of the establishment located in Japan. It should be noted that, whereas the mere existence of a defendant's establishment cannot found Japanese jurisdiction on its own, Article 3-4(1) as referred to below, would ensure the consumer's access to Japanese courts.

383. There are many bodies which, particularly by electronic means, continuously operate their commercial activities in Japan without setting up their fixed bases such as branches. It follows that the head of jurisdiction as mentioned above would be only partially capable of attaining the goal that a person who tries to gain from his or her activities in Japan should be subject to the jurisdiction of Japan with respect to claims arising out of those activities. As far as the claim is connected with the operation continuously carried out in Japan, the legislator found it necessary to confer jurisdiction upon Japanese courts (Article 3-3(v) CCP). Whereas the underlying idea of this provision shares something with that of 'doing business' known in US, the provision is not designed to equate the business operation by the subsidiary with that by its parent company. If a local plaintiff made a contract with the Japanese subsidiary, he normally cannot sue the foreign parent company in relation to the claim arising out of that contract. The formal distinction between the subsidiary and the parent company, in principle, keeps significance in the current Japanese rules on jurisdiction.

384. Where the harmful event occurred in Japan, Japanese courts may assume jurisdiction (Article 3-3(viii) CCP).[308] They may do so, when Japan is either the place where the act giving rise to the damage took place or the place where the damage occurred. In practice and literature, the concept of the place where the damage occurred has been understood not to embrace the place where the consequential

306. *See*, Sato and Kobayashi, 52.
307. *See*, para. 370 *supra*.
308. *See*, Nozomi Tada, *International Civil Jurisdiction Based on the Place of the Tort*, 55 *J.Y.B.I.L.* 287 et seq. (2012).

damage was sustained. Such restrictive interpretation seems to hold good for that provision. Furthermore, a causal link between the act and the direct or primary damage is required for Japanese courts to assume jurisdiction: it must be reasonably foreseen that the result of the act which is committed in a foreign country may take place in Japan.

385. When Japanese companies whose products were exported to foreign countries applied for declaration of non-liability in product liability cases, Japanese courts often affirmed their jurisdiction. There is no provision in the current CCP which purports to alter such court practice. Consequently, given that the place of the act giving rise to the damage is likely to overlap with the place of domicile of the party responsible for the act, this limb of the *locus delicti* may be a genuine alternative to the defendant's forum with respect to declaration of non-liability in torts which take place at a distance.

386. When a ship collision or any other accident takes place within the Japanese territorial water, the Japanese courts may assume jurisdiction over an action relating to damage due to such accident as the *forum delicti* pursuant to Article 3-3(viii) CCP. The CCP contains a special rule which deals with actions for damages due to ship collisions or other events having taken place on the high seas. Pursuant to Article 3-3(ix) CCP, Japanese courts may assume jurisdiction where the first place at which the damaged ship docked was in Japan.[309]

387. As far as the subject matter of claim is related to rights in immovable property situated in Japan, Japanese courts may assume jurisdiction (Article 3-3(xi) CCP). Rights in immovable property in the sense of the provision embrace such rights as rights to restitution and tenancies of immovable property. Whereas disputes as to the registration of the immovable property to be made in the Japanese registry fall under the exclusive jurisdiction of Japan (Article 3-5(2)), Japan as the *forum rei sitae* has no exclusive jurisdiction. Nor Japanese courts seem to have jurisdiction, when the subject matter is related to rights *in personam* such as the right to the payment of rent.

388. The provision as set out in Article 3-3(iii) CCP allows Japanese courts to assume jurisdiction on the ground that Japan is the *forum rei sitae* in the two different situations: where the subject matter of a claim is connected with the property situated in Japan; and where the defendant's property to be seized is situated in Japan. In the former situation, the location of the property seems likely to indicate a sufficient link between the dispute and the forum. This special head of jurisdiction was undisputedly accepted by the Legislative Council. By contrast, the *forum rei*

309. The CCP contains no provision specifically dealing with claims related to unjust enrichment. On the other hand, there is one provision addressing a case of the *negotiorum gestio*, namely, salvage. Article 3-3(x) CCP provides that Japanese courts may entertain jurisdiction over an action as regards a claim relating to salvage, where either the place of salvage or the first place at which the salvaged ship docked is in Japan. Whereas this provision was enacted in line with Art. 5(xi) on national jurisdiction, the members of the Legislative Council doubted its legislative necessity because salvage cases have been mostly resolved by parties' agreements.

sitae in the latter situation aroused much debate within the Council, because it was the one widely labelled as exorbitant. Since the situation of the defendant's property to be seized in Japan does not ensure a sufficient link with the forum, no one believes that a Japanese judgment based on such a ground of jurisdiction is likely to be recognized in foreign countries. A large number of members of the Legislative Council opposed to, or were at least cautious about the *forum rei sitae* in that situation.[310] However, a voice was raised in its favour: the *forum rei sitae* might play a role akin to the *forum necessitatis*. Among other things, given that no Chinese judgment seems entitled to recognition and execution in Japan because of the absence of reciprocity between the two states, Japan, otherwise, would be a kind of execution heaven in relation to China. After all, the clause which enables the Japanese courts to assume jurisdiction on the ground of the mere existence of the defendant's property was accepted, but on condition that the property of the defendant to be seized is not valued significantly modest.[311]

389. As mentioned earlier, the *Malaysian Airline* case was the one in which the Supreme Court rendered the first judgment in relation to international jurisdiction in the civil and commercial matters. This judgment which affirmed the Japanese jurisdiction on the ground of the defendant's mere business establishment in Japan attracted the criticism that the head of jurisdiction was not capable of ensuring a sufficient nexus with the forum. Although due respect should be paid to such criticism, the wisdom of hindsight tells us that that case was not related to a claim arising out of a business transaction but a consumer contract. The truth seems to be that, whereas the Court was imperceptibly oriented towards the interests of the local consumer, the CCP contained no specific venue rules which the Court could rely on in favour of consumers' interests, and that, at that time, the idea of consumer protection was not matured enough for the Court to develop jurisdictional rules taking care of their interests.

390. Article 3-4(3) CCP makes clear that any special grounds of jurisdiction as set out in Article 3-3 are not applicable to the action brought against consumers.[312] Without the jurisdiction agreement as mentioned below, an operator of business may bring an action against a consumer before the Japanese courts only when the consumer is domiciled in Japan. Conversely, the consumer may bring an action against the other party to a contract before the Japanese courts, when one of the heads of jurisdiction, general or special, is found in Japan.

391. Furthermore, Article 3-4(1) CCP allows a consumer to bring an action against an operator of business where the consumer is domiciled in Japan at the time of bringing the action or where the consumer was domiciled in Japan at the time of the conclusion of the contract. It follows that the consumer who has moved into or

310. *See*, Kazuhiko Yamamoto, *International Jurisdiction Based on the Location of Property*, 54 *J.Y.B.I.L.* 311 et seq. (2011).

311. It is added that Japanese courts may assume jurisdiction as regards a claim based upon obligations secured by a ship where the ship is situated in Japan (Art. 3-3(vi) CCP).

312. Tadashi Kanzaki, *Jurisdiction over Consumer Contracts and Individual Labor-Related Civil Disputes*, 55 *J.Y.B.I.L.* 306 et seq. (2012).

out of Japan after the conclusion of the contract may institute proceedings before the Japanese courts when he or she is either currently domiciled in Japan or was domiciled there at the time of the conclusion of the contract.[313] The former alternative is justifiable because Japanese courts are normally expected to be the most accessible to consumers and because it is likely to ensure the convergence between the *forum* and the *ius* which is determined pursuant to the choice-of-law rule as laid down by Article 11 AGR. Whereas the latter alternative is less explainable in terms of the consumer's effective accessibility to the judicial remedy in Japan, its addition militates in favour of more protection of the consumer and is unlikely to betray the expectation of the operator of business who was aware of or should have been aware of the consumer's domicile at the time of the conclusion of the contract.

392. Article 3-4(1) CCP defines the 'consumer' as an individual who does not become a party to the contract as a business or for the purpose of business, and defines the 'business operator' as a legal person, any other association or foundation or an individual who becomes a party to the contract as a business or for the purpose of business. The provision does not categorize as the consumer contract a certain type of contract under which one of the parties is likely to be in need of protection. As far as a person is regarded as the consumer in the sense of Article 3-4(1) CCP, the person may rely on the judicial remedy in the current and former home country, whatever the contract may be. In addition, the said provision requires no link between the contract and activities pursued in Japan or directed to Japan by the operator of business. As the Supreme Court in the *Malaysian Airline* case probably did so, the legislator thought that, however active local consumers might be, it would be difficult for them to raise their actions in foreign countries. It should be noted, however, that such regulation in favour of consumers are subject to the exception clause of Article 3-9 CCP (forum non conveniens). It would seem that the total absence of activities by the operator of business in Japan might trigger the application of that clause.

393. Articles 3-4 CCP also contains the rules on individual contracts of employment. The jurisdictional regulation in favour of employees is arranged in a manner parallel to that in favour of consumers. This seems to be justifiable because the employee and the consumer are both in the weaker position in terms of the bargaining power and the level of legal information. However, the forum most accessible to the employee may be different from that of the consumer. Besides, given the special connecting factor being adopted by the choice-of-law rule as set out in Article 12 AGR, the convergence between the *forum* and the *ius* would necessitate the heads of jurisdiction tailored to the employment contract. These considerations led the legislator to adopt the workplace as a jurisdictional ground in the proceedings instituted by the employee. The workplace also conditions the scope of the jurisdiction agreement, as mentioned below.[314]

313. The jurisdiction of the Japanese court over the *Malaysian Airline Case* would be explainable in terms of the consumer's domicile in Japan at the time of the conclusion of the contract. *See*, Sato and Kobayashi, 33.

314. *See*, paras 422 *infra*.

394. When the employer raises an action against the employee, any special grounds of jurisdiction as set out in Article 3-3 do not apply to individual employment-related civil disputes. Without a jurisdiction agreement, only the general ground of jurisdiction as set out in Article 3-2(1) CCP is available for the employer: the employer may bring an action against the employee before the Japanese courts only when the employee is domiciled in Japan. Conversely, the employee may bring an action against the employer before the Japanese courts, when one of the heads of jurisdiction, general or special, as laid down in Article 3-2 and 3-3 CCP, is found in Japan. In addition, pursuant to Article 3-4(2) CCP, the employee may bring an action against the employer, where the place at which the work is carried out under the contract of employment is in Japan. Such extension of Japanese jurisdiction enables the employee to carry out his or her procedural activities less costly. In addition, it would not betray the expectation of the employer under whose direction the employee is supposed to work in a particular country. If one specific workplace cannot be identified, the place of the establishment which engaged the employee in Japan becomes the criterion for the Japanese jurisdiction.

395. Furthermore, Article 3-4(2) extends the Japanese jurisdiction in the sense that the employee may bring an action when the workplace was situated in Japan sometime in the past. The provision enables the Japanese courts to assume jurisdiction in favour of the employee not only after the employment contract was already terminated, but also after, under the employer's direction, the workplace shifted from Japan to a foreign country.

396. The Supreme Court, in its judgment of 8 June 2001, affirmed that the venue rule on objective joining claims before a single local court was capable of being, by analogy, applied to international jurisdiction on condition that the claims are closely connected with each other.[315] This requirement of 'close connection between the claims' seems to have been needed, given that the machinery of transference which should work between competent local courts is unavailable in the international context. The legislator, basically, endorsed the Court's holding in the first sentence of Article 3-6 CCP which reads as follows: '[w]here two or more claims are to be made by a single action and the courts of Japan have jurisdiction over one claim but not the other(s), such action may be brought in the courts of Japan only when the former claim is closely connected with the latter'.

397. There has been no Supreme Court judgment addressing subjective joining claims in the field of direct international jurisdiction. Some of the inferior courts

315. 45 *J.A.I.L.* 151 (2002). The provisions on venue as contained in the CCP allow the joining of claims before a single local court. A local court which is not otherwise competent to hear a particular claim is allowed to do so, when it is competent to hear another claim (objective joining of claims): for example, the *forum delicti* attracts contractual claims; the *forum contractus* attracts claims in matters of tort. The derived competence of a local court, in principle, is not unfavourable to the defendant in that he or she would be obliged to appear in any event before another local court competent to hear a claim for which the *forum attractivitatis* is otherwise incompetent. When, under individual circumstances of a case, the *forum attractivitatis* turns out to be inappropriate, the court may transfer the whole or part of the action to another competent local court.

affirmed the Japanese jurisdiction on the ground of subjective joining claims.[316] In a case, some heirs of the deceased Japanese, who had got involved in a collision in Spain between two airplanes operated by two different Spanish airlines, brought an action before Tokyo District Court against those airlines as joint tortfeasors. Whereas one of the defendant airlines had no link with Japan, the court assumed jurisdiction over the claim against that airline, particularly referring to the fact that the burden which the defendant airline should bear in appearing before the Japanese court would be outweighed by that which the plaintiff should bear otherwise.[317] Generally speaking, however, Japanese courts have been extremely cautious about assuming derived jurisdiction against the multiple defendants. Undoubtedly, such jurisdiction may be excessively to the detriment of the defendant(s). Some of the judgments went so far as to say that they might exceptionally assume such jurisdiction when, under individual circumstances of a case, the Japanese court appeared to be a *forum conveniens*. It may safely be said that they have denied jurisdiction when the claims to be joined were not based on the same factual or legal causes. The following second sentence of Article 3-6 CCP should be read against the background of such court practice: the action may be brought by or against two or more persons only when the requirements set out in the first sentence of Article 38 CCP are met, namely, when the claims to be joined were based on the same factual or legal causes. It should be noted that, even in a case where such requirements are met, the exception clause as set out in Article 3-9 CCP is applicable under circumstances of a case.

398. Even if the Japanese courts have no jurisdiction over the claim that is the subject matter of the counterclaim, the defendant may sue on the counterclaim, in so far as such claim is closely connected with the one that is the subject matter of the original claim or with the defendant's allegations and evidence as defence. However, according to Article 146 (3) CCP, this rule does not apply when the Japanese courts have no jurisdiction over the claim whose subject matter would belong to the exclusive jurisdiction of a foreign court pursuant to Article 3-5 CCP. Besides, in the context of the counterclaim, the exception clause as set out in Article 3-9 may also prevent the Japanese courts from exercising jurisdiction.

---

316. Under the venue rules of the CCP, the *forum attractivitatis* is available for a plaintiff, when he or she brings a single action against two or more defendants such as co-debtors or joint tortfeasors (subjective joining of claims). In contrast to objective joining claims against the same defendant, joining claims against multiple defendants is allowed only when the claims to be joined are common to those defendants (co-debtors) or are based on the same factual or legal causes (joint tortfeasors): the *forum attractivitatis* must be the *forum connexitatis* in relation to the subjective joining claims. The existence of connection between claims does not necessarily ensure that a local court entertaining its derived competence is appropriate under individual circumstances of a case: the court may transfer the whole or part of the action to another competent local court, if the ends of justice require it to do so.

317. Judgment of the Tokyo District Court, 8 May 1985, *Hanji* 1232-40.

C. Exclusive Jurisdiction

399. The rules on exclusive jurisdiction are contained in Article 3-5 CCP. As far as they are applicable, the other grounds of jurisdiction, whether general or special, do not come into operation. The jurisdiction agreement cannot supersede those provisions, either. Foreign judgments which are concerned with a matter over which the Japanese courts have exclusive jurisdiction are not entitled to recognition and enforcement in Japan. The heads of exclusive jurisdiction are three. All of them are explainable in light of a close link between the dispute and Japanese public interests. First, if companies and other legal persons were established under Japanese law, the Japanese courts have exclusive jurisdiction over specific actions concerning, in particular, their fates and their internal affairs (Article 3-5(1) CCP).[318] Second, where the public registration must be made in Japan, the Japanese courts have exclusive jurisdiction over actions as regards claims for entries in one of the public registers such as the immovable property register (Article 3-5(2) CCP). The practical meaning of this provision is that the Japanese public registration offices are not obliged to make or alter registrations in such ways as foreign judgments may order. In this sense, it sticks to the principle of *auctor regit actum*. It seems worth noting that the situation of the immovable property is simply a head of special jurisdiction (Article 3-3(xi) CCP). Third, when the intellectual property right was created by virtue of entry in the Japanese register, the Japanese courts have exclusive jurisdiction over actions as regards its existence or validity (Article 3-5(3) CCP). The intellectual property rights, such as copyright, which come into existence without any formalities, are not covered by this provision. Consequently, the following intellectual property rights are, in matters of their existence or validity, subject to the exclusive jurisdiction of the Japanese courts: patent right, utility model right, plant breeder's right, design right, and trade mark right.[319] The exclusive jurisdiction of the Japanese courts does not extend to disputes other than those over existence or validity of the intellectual property right, for example, to a dispute over the infringement of an intellectual property right. It should be added that the exclusive jurisdiction over disputes on regularity of the registration of such rights is not covered by this provision but by the preceding paragraph on public registry.

318. Those actions are, under the venue rules of the CCP, also subject to exclusive jurisdiction of each local court within whose venue the principal establishment is situated. It should be noted that, under the Japanese substantive law rules, legal persons to be established pursuant to Japanese law are required to have their principal establishments in Japan.

319. Under the current Japanese law, disputes over existence or validity of those rights created by virtue of entry in the Japanese registry are subject to material jurisdiction of the administrative authorities, not the courts in civil litigation. It follows that the practical meaning of the provision lies in the context of recognition and enforcement of foreign judgments: no judgment rendered by a foreign court over such a dispute is entitled to recognition in Japan, even if the foreign civil court is materially competent under the foreign law.

D. Exception Clause (Forum Non Conveniens and Lis Pendens)

400. Except when Japanese courts exclusively assume jurisdiction either on the basis of the parties' jurisdiction agreement or by virtue of Article 3-10 CCP, they may decline their jurisdiction, taking account of individual circumstances of a case. In proposing the provision of Article 3-9 CCP, the Legislative Council may be said to have adopted a kind of forum non conveniens known in Scotland and common law countries. We should refer to the background against which such proposal was made. First, as mentioned earlier, the Supreme Court already showed the attitude that individual circumstances of a case would allow the court to decline jurisdiction in the interests of the ends of justice.[320] The inferior courts followed it since 1997. Second, Article 17 CCP on national jurisdiction, which came into force in 1998, enables a locally competent court to transfer an action to another locally competent court in the similar interests under circumstances of a case. In view of the fact that judges have been experienced in construing and applying such open-ended clause as expressed in Article 17 CCP, some members of Legislative Council believed that the canons of construction learnt through the application of that provision would serve for judges in applying the exception clause of Article 3-9 CCP.

401. According to Article 3-9 CCP, the court may dismiss the whole or part of such action when it finds exceptional circumstances under which a trial and judicial decision by the Japanese courts would lead to the impairment of the fairness between the parties or to the obstacle to the due and prompt administration of trial. The provision exemplarily lists some factors which the court should take into consideration in assessing such exceptional circumstances: the nature of the case; the extent of the burden to be borne by the defendant; and the location of the evidence. Whereas no reference is given to the parties' expectations, this factor is undoubtedly one of such factors, probably the most important one, account being taken of the *ratio legis* that the exclusive jurisdiction of the Japanese courts founded on the parties' agreement is not subject to the exception clause of Article 3-9 CCP.[321] It is worth noting that the provision does not refer to the applicability of a foreign law to the merits as one of those factors.

402. As a matter of course, the Japanese courts may decline its jurisdiction, only when possible alternative forum or fora are available to the plaintiff. It does not mean, however, that the court is allowed to evaluate which forum would be more appropriate for the trial. Such a comparative evaluation of possible alternative fora seems to be hardly consistent with the exceptional nature of the provision. It is submitted that it requires the court to decide whether it is manifestly inappropriate for the Japanese court to exercise jurisdiction. While it remains to be seen under what exceptional circumstances the Japanese courts will decline jurisdiction, there is one scenario in which a Japanese court is manifestly inappropriate: given no diplomatic relationship between Japan and Taiwan, which entails no judicial assistance between

320. *See*, para. 373*supra*.
321. Yokoyama, 368.

the two countries, the Japanese court is likely to decline jurisdiction in favour of the Taiwanese courts when most of relevant evidence is located in Taiwan.

403. It was most debated whether the international lis pendens rule should be introduced to the CCP.[322] A proposal was made to the Legislative Council to enact a provision to the effect that a Japanese court may stay the proceedings for the period of time shorter than four months, when the action having the same subject matter is pending between the same parties in a foreign court. The proposal was not based on the *prior tempore* rule but on the prospects for the recognition of the foreign judgment: according to the proposal, a Japanese court should mandatorily take into account such circumstances as the progress of the proceedings running in a foreign court and the likelihood of its rendering a judgment capable of being recognized in Japan. The judge members of the Council strongly opposed to such a proposal, asserting as follows: without such a lis pendens rule, the courts have, in practice, taken into account the progress of proceedings in foreign courts by means of flexible application of the rules on the designation of date of the proceedings; and, if an appeal was permissible against the stay of proceedings, it would unnecessarily delay the proceedings. In addition to such opposition, the proposal seemed hardly convincing to those who doubted that the judge was percipient enough to find a foreign judgment concerned passing the *ordre public* test for the recognition in the future. The view was also expressed to the effect that, under the proposed lis pendens rule, a 'torpedo' might be launched from a neighbouring country. The proposal was finally rejected. Consequently, it is anticipated that the parallel proceedings in a foreign court may be taken into account in the context of application of the exception clause as set out in Article 3-9 CCP.[323]

II. Family Matters

404. Neither the Personal Status Litigation Act (Act No.109 of 16 July 2003) nor the Act on Procedure in Family Matters (Act No.52 of May 25, 2011) contained any provisions on international jurisdiction. The determination of jurisdiction over the family matters has been left to the development of case law. However, it can hardly be said that the courts have fully developed rules on jurisdiction with respect to those matters. This legislative inertia and the undeveloped case law in the field of jurisdiction over the family matters seems basically due to the fact that Japan was in the homogeneous and immobile situation for the four decades before the early 1990s: foreign nationals domiciled in Japan for a prolonged period of time accounted for only around 0.7 % of the total Japanese population, and most of them were people of Korean or Chinese origin who had been domiciled in Japan on the permanent basis. Given the steady increase of foreigners domiciled in Japan from the last three decades, notably, people from China, Vietnam and other neighbouring countries in Asia, it has been strongly desired that the rules on jurisdiction be enacted to cope with such change of demographic situation. In 2018, the number of

322. *See*, Yoshihisa Hayakawa, *Lis Pendens*, 54 *J.Y.B.I.L.* 324 et seq. (2011).
323. Judgment of the Supreme Court, 10 Mar. 2016, *Hanta* 1424-110.

foreigners domiciled in Japan is estimated at around 25000,000. On 18 April 2018, the Diet passed an Act designed to introduce those rules both into the Personal Status Litigation Act (PSLA) and into the Act on Procedure in Family Matters (APFM).

405. The former Act, namely, the Personal Status Litigation Act, envisages the following types of litigations: divorce of married couples; dissolution of the adoptive relation between adoptive parents and an adopted child; filiation of a child; declaration of the existence of a parent-child relationship; and formation or declaration of the existence of other family relationships. A petitioner or a respondent in such a litigation is necessarily a 'party to the family relationship' in the sense of such substantive law rules as set out in the Civil Code. Articles 3-2 to 3-5 PSLA are the provisions laying down the jurisdictional grounds of Japanese courts in relation to those litigations.

406. However, the Act on Procedure in Family Matters envisages the following matters: the predominantly non-contentious groups of cases which the family courts are expected to interfere in for public interests; the disputes which, although in an adversarial relationship, the parties are primarily expected to resolve on the basis of their voluntary agreements; and the conciliation matters. Articles 3-2 to 3-12 APFM are the provisions laying down the jurisdictional grounds of Japanese courts for the first two matters, and Article 3-13 APFM is exclusively concerned with the jurisdictional ground for the conciliation proceedings.

407. For the reason of space, the author would like to refer to those new provisions only in connection with divorce. According to Article 3-2 PSLA, Japanese courts may assume jurisdiction in matters relating to divorce: (a) the respondent is domiciled in Japan (item 1); (b) both spouses are of Japanese nationality (item 5); (c) the petitioner is domiciled in Japan, if both spouses were last domiciled in Japan (item 6); or (d) the petitioner is domiciled in Japan, if there are special circumstances under which the assumption of jurisdiction by Japanese courts would ensure the fairness between the parties or the due and prompt administration of justice, in particular, when the respondent's whereabouts are unknown or when the final divorce decree having been rendered by a court of a foreign country where the respondent is domiciled has no effects in Japan (item 7). Except the last open-ended jurisdictional ground (d) which is oriented towards individual and concrete circumstances of a case, Articles 3-2 PSLA is subject to the new Article 3-5 PSLA expressing the forum non conveniens rule. Japanese courts may dismiss the proceedings, if there are special circumstances under which the assumption of jurisdiction would impair the fairness between the parties or hinder the due and prompt administration of justice, account being taken of the nature of the case, the burden of appearance to be borne by the respondent, the location of evidence and the best interests of a minor child born between the parties. [324]

324. Under the PALA, a petition for divorce in Japan is not barred by a petition concerning the same subject matter lodged abroad earlier by a respondent to the Japanese petition. The parallel proceedings in a foreign country would be taken into account in the context of application of Article 3-5 as mentioned in the next section.

408. Where an action concerning divorce seeks compensation for damages arising from the facts which constitute the statement of claims for divorce, the court which, otherwise, would have no jurisdiction to hear the claim on tort is allowed to do so (Article 3-3 PSLA). The divorce court attracts claims in matters of tort.[325]

409. According to Article 3-4 (1) PSLA, the *forum attractivitatis* is also available for a judicial adjudication designating a person to have custody or parental authority over the parties' child(ren) after their divorce or any other ancillary disposition regarding the custody of their child(ren) including contacts.[326] Whereas the child's domicile should be the primary ground of jurisdiction as shown by Article 3-8 APFM, a Japanese court exercising jurisdiction to decide upon a petition for divorce may assume jurisdiction to take such measures for their child domiciled in a foreign country.[327] This *forum attractivitatis* is, as a matter of course, subject to the forum non conveniens rule as provided in Article 3-5 which explicitly refers to 'the best interests of the child'.

410. The reformed PSLA made explicit the conditions on counterclaim and alteration of claims. If the Japanese courts have no jurisdiction over the claim that is the subject matter of the counterclaim, the respondent may sue on the counterclaim (annulment of marriage), in so far as the subject matter of the original claim is the divorce. The both claims are concerned with the same family relationship (Article 18 (3)(i) PSLA).[328] The criterion of the 'the same family relationship' also applies to the alteration of claims (Article 18 (2) PSLA).

411. As mentioned earlier, the court, in principle, is required to stick to the 'conciliation first' rule, when the parties fail to reach any agreement on divorce under the law applicable to the divorce.[329] They have to undergo the conciliation proceedings before bringing litigation, through which a 'family court conciliation committee' consisting of a judge and two commissioners help the parties to reach an amicable settlement of disputes. The decision-making process being essentially consensual, Article 3-13 (iii) APFM allows the parties to confer conciliation jurisdiction on a Japanese family court.

325. The Japanese divorce court may assume jurisdiction over the distribution of property between the divorcing spouses, taking advantage of one of the almost identical jurisdictional grounds as enumerated in Article 3-12 APFM.
326. The PSLA is silent about whether the *forum attractivitatis* is available for a petitioner, when he or she lodges a single petition against two or more respondents such as a husband and his concubine as a joint tortfeasor. This silence implies the prohibition of such subjective joining of claims. One feared that the joining claims against multiple respondents would be likely to cause hardship to at least one of them.
327. According to Article 32 (4) PSLA, when taking protective measures, the court shall hear the child(ren)'s statements if the child(ren) is at least 15 years of age.
328. The counterclaim is also permissible, when the respondent claims compensation for damages arising from the facts which constitute the statement of original claim (Article 18 (ii) PSLA).
329. *See*, paras 88, 288, 295 *supra*.

§2. Choice of Forum Agreement

I. Civil and Commercial Matters

412. The Supreme Court, in its judgment on 18 November 1975, showed its view as regards several aspects on validity and effects of an agreement on jurisdiction.[330] Article 3-7 CCP was enacted in line with almost all the remarks made in this judgment. Yet, its material scope of operation is not far reaching.

413. First, Article 3-7(1) allows the parties to confer jurisdiction by their agreement on the courts of one country, or one or more specific courts of one country, in parallel with or to the exclusion of the jurisdiction which either all courts or certain courts would assume in the absence of the agreement. If the Japanese courts are prorogated or derogated by virtue of a valid agreement, the Japanese procedural rules govern the questions as to whether and how they give effects to such prorogation or derogation. It should be noted, with respect to the prorogation, that the exception clause as set out in Article 3-9 does not come into operation, when an agreement confers exclusive jurisdiction upon the Japanese courts.

414. In line with the judgment by the Supreme Court in 1975, the CCP lays down the three requirements whose fulfilments validate the choice of forum agreement.[331] First, Article 3-7(2) CCP requires, in the interests of the parties' expectations, that such agreement be connected with a specific legal relationship. Second, it should be made in writing.[332] The Supreme Court, which sustained a jurisdiction clause contained in a bill of lading, did not require that both the offer and acceptance be made in a particular document signed by the parties. It seems that under the current CCP also, the formal requirements would be satisfied, when the agreement is evidenced by a certain document prepared by either of the parties. Third, such agreement is not permissible where the dispute in question falls under the exclusive jurisdiction of Japan (Article 3-10 CCP).

415. The CCP does not contain any other rule as to the validity of the jurisdiction agreement except in relation to consumer contracts and employment contracts. It seems probable that questions of substantive validity such as those of capacity, fraud etc., are governed by the laws applicable pursuant to the choice-of-law rules

330. 20 *J.A.I.L.* 106 (1976). The facts were as follows. Crude sugar was shipped from Brazil to Japan on the Dutch defendant's ship. When bags of sugar were unloaded in Japan, many of them were found damaged by sea water. A Japanese insurance company which succeeded to the rights of the original holder of a bill of lading raised an action for damages against the Dutch defendant. The defendant relied on the bill of lading which contained a clause submitting the dispute in question to the exclusive jurisdiction of the court of Amsterdam. The Supreme Court approved the judgment of the appellate court which had dismissed the action, relying on the jurisdiction agreement. For more details of the case, *see*, Koji Takahashi, *Law Applicable to Choice-of-Court Agreements*, 58 *J.Y.B.I.L.* 384 et seq. (2015).

331. *See*, Shunichiro Nakano, *Agreement on Jurisdiction*, 54 *J.Y.B.I.L.* 278 et seq. (2011).

332. Its para. 3 ranks an electronic form as equivalent to 'writing'.

as provided by the AGR. In addition, whereas there is no explicit provision concerning the reasonable test or the *ordre public* test that the Supreme Court in 1975 set out for the validity of the jurisdiction agreement, it seems that the silence of the legislator does not preclude such tests from coming into operation under circumstances of a case.[333]

416. The jurisdiction agreement is severable from the main contract. When a choice-of-court agreement is valid, the Japanese courts may entertain the prorogated jurisdiction despite invalidity of a main contract. It entails that, when the judgment of a foreign court whose jurisdiction was prorogated invalidated a main contract, such judgment may be recognized in Japan.

417. Some important effects of the jurisdiction agreement are believed to be left to the parties' intention. First, while being circumscribed by the requirement of the specific connection between the agreement and the legal relationship as set out in Article 3-7(2) CCP, the scope of a jurisdiction agreement depends on the parties' intention: non-contractual claims may be subsumed into an agreement. Second, there is no presumptive rule working in favour of the agreement being for exclusive jurisdiction. The legislative silence about such presumption is intentional. During discussions of the Legislative Council, the members from the business circles indicated that Japanese companies, big or small, usually used the explicit terminology showing exclusivity if they really wanted to make exclusive jurisdiction agreements. Consequently, the Council decided to leave all to the parties' intention without any presumption. Third, the parties' intention is also decisive in determining whether a jurisdiction agreement extends to a counterclaim or whether a counterclaim may be raised only in the agreed court.

418. Article 3-7(4) CCP allows Japanese courts to assume jurisdiction in spite of a valid agreement exclusively conferring jurisdiction upon the courts of a foreign country, when the foreign courts are found unable to exercise, factually or legally, their jurisdiction. This provision, which was inspired by the above-mentioned Supreme Court judgment in 1975, purports to avoid the situation where the parties would, otherwise, be placed under the denial of justice.

419. The statutory jurisdictional rules in favour of consumers as mentioned above may be departed when the consumer and the operator of business made the jurisdiction agreement. When the operator of business enters into the jurisdiction agreement after the dispute has arisen, the agreement is honoured: it is treated as if it were made in a business-to-business transaction. Even though a jurisdiction agreement was entered into before the disputes have arisen, such agreement is valid, when the consumer is regarded as having ratified it after the dispute has arisen, namely, when the consumer, on his own initiative, has raised an action before the agreed court of a country, or when, by invoking the agreement, the consumer has

333. *See*, Judgment of the Tokyo High Court, 25 Oct. 2017, 61 *J.Y.B.I.L.* 416 (2018). It holds that the Japanese Antimonopoly Act does not automatically make void the agreement exclusively conferring jurisdiction upon the courts of Michigan.

contested jurisdiction of the court before which the operator of business raised an action (Article 3-7(5)(ii) CCP). Consequently, even when an operator of business instituted proceedings against a consumer in a country where the consumer is currently domiciled, the latter can rely on the prior jurisdiction agreement, if he or she so wishes.

420. In addition to such subsequent ratification given by the consumer, the agreement which purports to confer jurisdiction upon the courts of Japan or any other countries in the future is valid when it is agreed that an action may be brought in a court or courts of the country where the consumer was domiciled at the time of the conclusion of the contract (Article 3-7(5)(i) CCP). This provision purports to avoid totally invalidating the prior jurisdiction clause which seems likely to appear in the consumer contract. The two points should be noted. First, the provision redundantly works in favour of the consumer because, even in the absence of such agreement, Article 3-4(1) CCP allows the consumer to bring an action before the courts of Japan where he or she was domiciled at the time of the conclusion of the contract. Second, Article 3-7(5)(i) CCP does not promote the interests of the operator of business about the forum so much as it appears. The bracketed sentence of the said provision deems such agreement to be not exclusive but facultative: even an explicit agreement to the effect that an action should be brought to the exclusion of courts of any other countries does not preclude the consumer from instituting proceedings in another court, particularly in the court of the country where he or she is currently domiciled.

421. During discussions of the Legislative Council, the members who spoke in the interests of business circles consistently expressed their concerns about consequences which the statutory jurisdictional rules in favour of the employee as mentioned above would entail (Article 3-4(2)(3) CPC). Suppose that a Japanese engineer, who wanted to terminate his contract with a Japanese company and was going to take up employment with a competing Korean company, made to the Japanese company a contractual promise not to reveal a particular technological secret to the new Korean employer. Nevertheless, he broke that promise with the result that the Japanese company sustained damage. Referring to such a scenario, the members on the side of business circles consistently asserted that the Japanese employer would have legitimate interests in instituting proceedings against his former employee in Japan. Most of the members of the Legislative Council seemed to think at the early stage of their discussions that only the jurisdiction agreement could be a tool for counterbalancing the disadvantage at which the provisions as set out in Article 3-4(2) and (3) CCP would place the employer. Then, the discussions became focused upon what would be the conditions on which the jurisdiction agreement should be valid. It may safely be said that Article 3-7(6) CCP as mentioned below showed a result of compromise between the members from the business circles and those from the trade union.

422. The provision as set out in Article 3-7(6)(i) CCP only deals with the validity of the jurisdiction agreement entered into between the employer and the employee prior to the time when the dispute has arisen. It means that the validity of the jurisdiction agreement, made after the dispute has arisen, is subject to the general rules on the jurisdiction agreement. After the dispute has arisen, the employee seems unlikely to be forced to agree in a manner as the employer wishes. Furthermore, pursuant to Article 3-7(6)(ii) CCP, the jurisdiction agreement, made before the disputes has arisen, is valid when the employee is regarded as having tacitly ratified it: when the employee on his own initiative has raised an action before the agreed court; or when, by invoking the agreement, the employee has contested jurisdiction of the country before whose court the employer raised an action.

423. In relation to the situation where the employee refuses to make such subsequent agreement or to ratify the previous agreement, the debate arose as to whether and under what conditions the jurisdiction agreement should be valid. The Legislative Council finally reached the conclusion that such agreement should be valid but subject to the two limitations in terms of the time of the agreement and the courts to be chosen: the parties may agree on jurisdiction at the time of termination of the employment contract, and they may choose a court or courts of the country in which the work has been carried out at that time. Although subject to such limitations, the possibility of agreeing on jurisdiction led to mitigating the concern of the business circles. Whereas, as the members from the trade union did, one may doubt that such time limitation would really prevent the employer from abusing the force he actually has in the contractual relationship of employment, the conclusion of the Council came to be expressed in Article 3-7(6)(i) CCP.

424. Article 3-8 CCP regards 'submission' as a tacit jurisdiction agreement: Japanese courts may assume jurisdiction, when a defendant, without contesting the jurisdiction of the Japanese courts, has presented oral arguments on the merits or made statements in preparatory proceedings pursuant to the CCP. It should be noted, here again, that Article 3-10 CCP on exclusive jurisdiction supersedes the said provision.

II. Family Matters

425. As far as the family matters are concerned, the parties are not allowed to prorogate or derogate Japanese courts by virtue of their agreement on jurisdiction. There are, however, two exceptional scenarios in which the parties are allowed to make jurisdictional agreement in writing (Articles 3-11 (5) and 3-13 (1) (iii) and (3) APFM). First, the divorcing parties, in particular, may allow themselves to take advantage of the Japanese conciliation proceedings, expecting to reach an agreement on the amicable and voluntary basis (Article 3-13 (1) (iii) and (3) APFM).[334] Second, when disputes are concerned with the division of an estate to be inherited or the reserved inheritance share, the parties can make jurisdictional agreement, in

334. If the conciliation proceeding turns out to be unsuccessful and a party lodges a petition for divorce, the family court might take into consideration the parties' jurisdictional agreement on conciliation when it decides whether the assumption of jurisdiction over the petition would ensure the fairness between the parties.

parallel with or to the exclusion of the jurisdiction which either all courts or certain courts would assume in the absence of the agreement (Article 3-11 (4) APFM). Those disputes seem to be hardly distinguishable from ordinary civil or commercial ones because purely economic interests are likely to be involved in those disputes. It may be added that, when they confer exclusive jurisdiction upon the Japanese courts in this scenario, Article 3-14 APFM expressing the forum non conveniens rule does not come into operation.

§3. Procedural Requirements

426. Whereas the plaintiff is expected to allege and prove the ground of jurisdiction except those of exclusive jurisdiction, the court may conduct examination of evidence on its own motion in matters relating to jurisdiction (Article 3-11 CPC, Article 29 (1) PSLA and Article 56 APFM). It is immaterial whether the defendant has contested the Japanese jurisdiction.

427. In torts, factual elements which are relevant for founding jurisdiction are interwoven with those related to the merits of a case. The court should not examine all elements relevant for the judgment on the merits at the outset of the proceedings. However, the court should not be satisfied with the mere consistency of the plaintiff's allegations in deciding its jurisdiction. Otherwise, the alleged tortfeasor who turns out to be not liable might be unnecessarily obliged to appear before the court. The Supreme Court, which was called on to verify the ground of jurisdiction on tort, took a middle course when it only required the plaintiff to prove the objective elements giving rise to the damage.[335]

428. Article 3-12 CCP provides that the jurisdiction of a court of Japan shall be determined by reference to the time that an action is brought in the court. The provision expresses the principle of *perpetuatio fori*: the Japanese courts, whose jurisdiction has been once founded by virtue of a jurisdictional ground at the time of the institution of the proceedings, will not lose its jurisdiction, irrespective of whether factual elements determining such ground alter after that time. The same applies in family matters (Article 29 (1) PSLA and Article 3-15 APFM). The principle does not say that one of the jurisdictional grounds must necessarily exist at the time of proceedings in the sense that the proceedings would, otherwise, result in nothing. It is sufficient that one of the jurisdictional grounds comes into existence sometime before the dismissal of action.

335. Judgment of the Supreme Court, 8 Jun. 2001, 45 *J.A.I.L.* 151 (2002).

§4. International Service

429. Japan is a party to the Hague Convention of 15 November 1965 on the Service Abroad of Judicial and Extrajudicial Documents in Civil or Commercial Matters.[336]

430. In the absence of other international instruments such as bilateral consular treaties with the US and the United Kingdom, Japan is ready to assist foreign authorities under the Act Relating to the Reciprocal Judicial Assistance to be Given at the Request of Foreign Courts.[337]

§5. Rules of Evidence

431. Japan is not a party to the Hague Convention of 18 March 1970 on the Taking of Evidence Abroad in Civil or Commercial Matters. Apart from relevant consular treaties, the above-mentioned Reciprocal Judicial Assistance Act allows Japanese authorities to assist foreign counterparts in evidentiary matters.

§6. Temporary Relief

432. In 2011, a new provision on jurisdiction for provisional measures was added to the Civil Provisional Remedies Act,[338] in association with the provisions on jurisdiction as contained in the CCP. Article 11 of the Act provides that a petition for a temporary restraining order may be filed with the courts of Japan, when an action on the merits may be brought in the courts of Japan or when the property to be provisionally seized or the object in dispute is situated in Japan. The provision is not subject to the exception clause as contained in Article 3-9 CCP.

433. First, when the Japanese courts may entertain jurisdiction over the proceedings on the merits, the Japanese courts may take provisional measures. This head of jurisdiction is justified by the ancillary nature of the provisional measures. It follows, for example, that, when the proceedings on the merits are already pending in a Japanese court, the court may issue an order of provisional seizure over the debtor's ship which is still outside the Japanese territorial water but is expected to call a Japanese port a few days later. The provision gives no indication of whether the Japanese courts may take measures to be enforced in a foreign country such as a provisional seizure over immovable property situated in a foreign country. The

336. Japan is also a party to the Hague Convention of 1 Mar. 1954 on Civil Procedure. These conventions are implemented by the Act on Special Provisions Concerning Civil Procedure Attendant upon Implementation of the 'Convention on Civil Procedure' and Other Conventions (Act No. 115 of 5 Jun. 1970).

337. Act No. 63 of 13 Mar. 1905.

338. Act No. 91 of 22 Dec. 1989.

court is expected to address the question within the framework of Article 20 of the Act which allows courts to decide the necessity of issuing an order of provisional seizure.

434. Second, the Japanese courts may take provisional measures, when the property to be provisionally seized or the object in dispute is situated in Japan. The head of jurisdiction is explainable by the urgent nature inherent in such measures. Given that the Japanese court can be the *forum rei sitae* as regards the proceedings on the merits pursuant to Article 3-3(iii) CCP, the head of jurisdiction laid down by Article 11 of the said Act is likely to coincide with that of jurisdiction on the merits.[339] The head of jurisdiction in question is expected to play its role, when a foreign court has exclusive jurisdiction on the parties' agreement or when the arbitration agreement has been entered into between the parties.

435. Article 30 (1) PSLA used to deny the application of Article 11 of the Civil Provisional Remedies Act to the case in which the action on the merits was related to matters envisaged by the PSLA. That provision was deleted by the Act of 2018. Consequently, Article 11 of the Civil Provisional Remedies Act is now applicable to the personal and family litigations: e.g., when the divorce proceedings are already pending in a Japanese family court, the court may issue a provisional custody order to ensure the return of the child; and, when the foreign divorce decree definitely terminating a dispute is entitled to recognition in Japan, the Japanese courts may take provisional measures on the ground that the matrimonial property to be provisionally seized or the object in dispute is situated in Japan.

339. *See*, para. 389 *supra*.

Chapter 5. Recognition and Enforcement of Foreign Decisions

436. Japan is not a party to any comprehensive international agreement on recognition and enforcement of foreign decisions. The principal rule on the matter is laid down in Article 118 CCP. It sets out the automatic recognition of the foreign decision which fulfils the listed conditions. The decision recognized pursuant to the said provision should be declared enforceable according to Article 24 of the Civil Execution Act.[340]

437. The Supreme Court defined the foreign decision as 'the final one passed by a foreign court, regardless of the name, procedures, or form of court, as far as it was rendered under the assurance of due process for both parties with regard to legal relationships in private law'.[341] The concept embraces divorce decrees and negative declarations. A 'summary judgment' as known in Australian law[342] and a decision of Hong Kong High Court in respect of the costs and expenses of the litigation[343] were held to fall under the notion of such foreign decision. So are the private acts granting divorce passed by the parliament of Quebec.[344] An administrative act by the 'Chinese Adoption Centre' permitting adoption is said to qualify for the judgment to be recognized. However, authentic instruments or 'in-court' settlements are excluded from the scope of Article 118 CCP.

438. The decision is required to have effects of definitely terminating a dispute. Neither decisions still subject to appeal nor interlocutory decisions of procedural nature are entitled to recognition. The absence of diplomatic relations between Japan and the foreign sate of origin, for example, Taiwan, does not affect the recognition of the judgment of such state.

§1. Recognition

439. Whereas Article 118 CCP itself does not explicitly declare the principle that there shall be no review of the merits, the principle is taken for granted. The Japanese courts do not, as a rule, re-examine the conclusions as to fact or law reached by the foreign court or the law applied by it. However, the principle is subject to some exceptions, in particular, in relation to the *ordre public* test. The said provision lays down the four conditions for recognition.[345]

340. Act No. 4 of 30 Mar. 1979.
341. Judgment of the Supreme Court, 28 Apr. 1998, 42 *J.A.I.L.* 155 (1999).
342. Judgment of the Tokyo District Court, 25 Feb. 1998, *Hanji* 1664-78.
343. Judgment of the Supreme Court, 28 Apr. 1998, 42 *J.A.I.L.*155 (1999).
344. Circular No. 1349 dated 7 July 1955 and Circular No. 280 dated 14 January 1976 issued by the Ministry of Justice.
345. It is applied by analogy in the family matters (Article 79-2 APFM).

I. Grounds of Jurisdiction

440. Whereas Article 118 CCP requires the foreign court to have had the jurisdiction over the dispute, it contains no provision specifically designed to define what is called the 'indirect jurisdiction'. As far as the civil and commercial matters are concerned, the Supreme Court is said to have adopted the 'mirror-image' method: the jurisdictional grounds for the Japanese courts to hear the case should also serve for the criteria for judging whether a foreign judgment is entitled to recognition in Japan with respect to its jurisdiction.[346] In drafting the provisions on direct jurisdiction, the Legislative Council, indeed, had to be imaginative about how each jurisdictional ground would reflect on the phase of the recognition. For example, the required connection between the claim and the operation of the defendant company as set out in Article 3-3(iv) and (v) CCP were thought to be necessary for blocking effects of American judgments founded on the mere 'doing business' test. Furthermore, some of the heads of jurisdiction are practically meaningful only in the context of recognition: for example, the exclusive jurisdiction on intellectual property as provided in Article 3-5(3) CCP.[347]

441. The 'mirror-image' method was said to be also valid in family matters. For example, the Tokyo Family Court refused to recognize a decree of an Australian court whose jurisdiction was founded merely upon the petitioner's Australian nationality.[348] However, a judgment of the Supreme Court recently held that the indirect jurisdiction should be determined by means of the 'mirror-image' method only in the matters other than the family matters.[349] Although it is still unclear why the Court so held, it is certain that a foreign court's decree should be recognized irrespective of its jurisdictional ground, when a new family relationship such as a remarriage of an ex-spouse has been established on the basis of that decree in the country of origin.

II. Service of Process

442. The second condition of the recognition is that the defendant who lost the case had been duly served with the document instituting the proceedings (Article 118 (ii) CCP). As far as the defendant actually appeared before the original foreign court without receiving such service, the condition was met. The service must have been given to the defendant in accordance with the international agreements to which both the foreign state in question and Japan are the parties, for example, the Hague Convention of 15 November 1965 on Service Abroad of Judicial and Extrajudicial Documents in Civil or Commercial Matters.[350]

346. Judgment of the Supreme Court, 28 Apr. 1998, 42 *J.A.I.L.*155 (1999).
347. Disputes over existence or validity of intellectual property rights created by virtue of entry in the Japanese registry are subject to the material jurisdiction of the administrative authorities, not the courts in civil litigation. *See*, para. 400 *supra*.
348. Decree of the Tokyo Family Court, 11 Sept. 2007, 52 *J.A.I.L.*697 (2009).
349. Judgment of the Supreme Court, 24 Apr. 2014, 58 *J.A.I.L.*463 (2015).
350. Judgment of the Supreme Court, 28 Apr. 1998, 42 *J.A.I.L.*155 (1999).

443. Japan originally did not oppose the direct transmission of judicial documents by postal channels as set out in Article 10a) of the Hague Convention on the Service Abroad. As a result, the service was supposed to be proper, for example, when an American plaintiff mailed the document instituting the proceedings directly to a Japanese defendant. However, on 21 December 2018, the Japanese government informed the Ministry of Foreign Affairs of the Netherlands of the opposition to the use of such method of transmission, pursuant to Article 21 of the said Convention.

III. Ordre Public

444. According to the provision as set out in Article 118 (iii) CCP, the foreign judgment contrary to the *ordre public* cannot be recognized. Experience tells that the recognition of a foreign decision seems to be refused, when the recognition brings about effects inconsistent with the basic institutional frameworks of Japanese law. Since Japanese courts have tendency to take such institutional framework as more or less domestic, they are likely to estimate the hypothetical effects of recognition unendurable only when the case has a close link with Japan. The institutions relevant to the recognition have been substantive or procedural.

A. *Substantive Ordre Public*

445. In court practice, it has been taken for granted that foreign decisions might be different from those which the Japanese courts would have rendered if they had dealt with the same case. To date, as far as the institutions on which foreign judgments were based are known in Japan, they have been recognized: for example, given that Japanese law knows the statutory interest rate, a Korean judgment which ordered the payment of damages calculated at the statutory rate of 20% per annum was recognized, whereas the statutory rate to which the Japanese court would have had recourse was 6% per annum.[351] Conversely, a foreign judgment based upon the institution totally unknown to Japanese law seems likely to be regarded as repugnant to the Japanese *ordre public*. The two judgments of the Supreme Court illustrate this attitude. They are related to the punitive damages and the surrogate motherhood.

446. The Supreme Court refused to recognize and enforce the award of punitive damages as contrary to the *ordre public*.[352] The foreign judgment was from California. The plaintiff had been awarded USD 425,251 in compensatory damages and more than USD 1 million in punitive damages. The Court found an institutionally wide gulf lying between the Californian punitive damages system inspired by the

351. Judgment of the Tokyo District Court, 12 Feb. 2009, *Hanji* 2068-95. A judgment of the Tokyo High Court, 20 May 2015, 59 *J.Y.B.I.L.*490 (2016) says that changes in the exchange rate which turned out to aggravate a maintenance debtor's financial position would not make the content of a foreign judgment ordering maintenance for his child contrary to public policy of Japan.
352. Judgment of the Supreme Court, 11 Jul. 1997, 41 *J.A.I.L.*104 (1998).

idea of punishment or deterrence and the Japanese system of damages of compensatory nature. A few points should be noted with regard to this judgment. First, the punitive damages awarded by the Californian court were regarded as falling under the concept of the 'decision' in the sense of Article 118 CCP. Second, the Court did not address the issue as to how disproportionate the awarded amount was to the damage actually sustained. Rather, it concentrated on whether the punitive damages awards were designed to fulfil a function similar to penal sanction. It does not seem, however, that its penal nature can always justify the refusal of recognition and enforcement. It is said that costs and expenses incurred in a law suit, which are to be classified into the concept of the compensatory damages under Japanese law, are occasionally included in the punitive damages. If such compensatory items had been specifically mentioned in the award in question, then the Court might have examined how exorbitant the relevant part of damages was.

447. The other Supreme Court judgment was related to the surrogate motherhood.[353] A Japanese couple had found a surrogate mother in Nevada who gave birth to their twin babies. A court of Nevada made an order to the effect that the Japanese couple was the children's biological and legal parents. After the couple returned to Japan, they tried to register the children's births with their family registry, but the Japanese administrative authorities refused their application. The Tokyo Family Court approved the refusal. In contrast, the appellate court ordered the authorities in charge of family registration to accept the application, overturning the adjudication of the family court. Then, the authorities appealed to the Supreme Court. In addressing the issue as to whether the order of the Nevada court was entitled to recognition, the Court showed the following line of reasoning. What types of parent-child relationship can be legally established is not a matter at private persons' disposal. The public interests and the child's welfare involved require that the matter be uniformly regulated and clearly defined by certain rules of law. The Civil Code which provides such rules stands upon the basic assumption that the mother-child relationship can be established between a child and a woman who conceived and delivered that child. In view of surrogate births being constantly occurring, there must be room to accept, *de lege ferenda*, a certain types of parent-child relationship other than those types as provided for in the current Civil Code. However, the establishment of such relationship as confirmed by the Nevada court is, *de lege lata*, unacceptable as contrary to the fundamental idea underlying the Civil Code, even if the alleged mother donated the eggs. It should be noted that the judgment seems to have stood on the implicit assumption that the commissioning parents were of Japanese nationality. The Court might have recognized the Nevada order, for example, if the parents had been American citizens.

353. Judgment of the Supreme Court, 23 Mar. 2007, 51 *J.Y.B.I.L.* 552 (2008). *See*, Dai Yokomizo, *Recognition of a Foreign Judgment on Children Born Through Surrogate Pregnancy*, 60 *J.Y.B.I.L.* 399 et seq. (2017).

B. Procedural Ordre Public

448. The Supreme Court stated, albeit *obiter*, in its judgment of 7 June 1983, that the judicial procedure on the basis of which a foreign decision was rendered should be subject to the control of the *ordre public*.[354] However, there has been no case in which the Supreme Court refused the recognition on the ground of the infringement of the procedural *ordre public*. It seems that the procedural aspects hardly trigger the application of the *ordre public* clause, given that the means of redress must have been available to the defendant in the country of origin.[355]

IV. Reciprocity

449. Reciprocity is the fourth threshold which the foreign decision is required to pass. In response to criticism of academic writers against the case law established in the 1930s,[356] the Supreme Court lowered the threshold in 1983.[357] According to it, the reciprocity is regarded as existing between Japan and the foreign country whose court rendered the decision in question, when that foreign country is ready to recognize the equivalent decision by the Japanese courts under the conditions not different in important points. There was, in the past, one judgment which rejected the recognition of a judgment of a court of Belgium whose law knew the *révision au fond*. Today, the reciprocity requirement does not seem to be practically harmful to judgment creditors except those from the Chinese courts. There seems to be no reciprocity between China and Japan. The Chinese Supreme Court expressed the view, on 26 June 1994, that their courts should recognize and enforce no Japanese decisions. In response, the Japanese appellate courts refused to recognize the Chinese judgments on the ground of the absence of reciprocity between the two states.[358]

§2. Enforcement

450. According to Article 24 (5) CEA, a foreign judgment whose finality has been established by the judgment creditor is only enforceable when a judgment of

354. 27 *J.A.I.L.* 119 (1984).,
355. There has been an isolated judgment in which the court refused the recognition of a Korean divorce decree on the ground that the decree was obtained by fraud (Judgment of the Tokyo High Court, 27 Feb. 1990, 34 *J.A.I.L.*166 (1991)).
356. The Supreme Court, in its judgment on 5 Dec. 1933, held: 'the original state is required to recognise the judgment of Japan under the conditions that are the same as or more liberal than those prescribed' in the provision equivalent to current Art. 118 CCP (*Shinbun* 3670-16).
357. 27 *J.A.I.L.*119 (1984).
358. Judgment of the Osaka High Court, 9 Apr. 2003, 48 *J.A.I.L.*171 (2005); Judgment of the Tokyo High Court, 25 Nov. 2015 (unpublished). Cf. Satoshi Watanabe, *A Study of a Series of Cases Caused Non-recognition of a Judicial Judgment Between Japan and Mainland China*, 57 *J.Y.B.I.L.* 287 et seq. (2014). For the Sino-Japanese relation, Béligh Elbalti, 'Reciprocity and the Recognition and Enforcement of Foreign Judgments: a Lot of Bark But Not Much Bite', 13 *Journal of Private International Law* 184, 201 et seq. (2017).

enforcement is rendered by a Japanese court which has ascertained the fulfilment of all the requirements as set out in Article 118 CCP. The *révision au fond* is prohibited in the proceedings (paragraph 2 of the said Provision).

Chapter 6. International Insolvency Law

451. In the early 1990s, Japan began to go into economic recession, followed by the increase of insolvency cases. It was believed in the middle of the 1990s that the inefficiencies and costs involved in the liquidation proceedings were partly circumventing lenders' swift collection of outstanding debts.[359] In response, the Ministry of Justice began to reform the insolvency system in a comprehensive way in 1996 and ended its legislative works with the amendment of the Bankruptcy Act in 2005.[360] In a series of legislative reforms, the new rules relating to cross-border insolvency were made.[361] Particularly, the Act on Recognition and Assistance for Foreign Insolvency Proceedings (ARAFIP) was enacted in 2000 for the purpose of ensuring liquidation or rehabilitation of debtors in an internationally coordinated manner.

§1. International Jurisdiction

452. Bankruptcy or civil rehabilitation proceedings may be opened either when the debtor, a natural person, has a business establishment, domicile, residence, or assets in Japan or when the debtor, a legal person, has an establishment or assets in Japan.[362] This scope of the direct jurisdiction is wider than that of indirect one as provided in the ARAFIP to the extent that the former lists the debtor's assets located in Japan. This is due to the necessity of protecting local creditors' interests linked with those assets. However, Article 4 of the Corporate Reorganization Act allows the reorganization proceedings to be opened only when a debtor company has an establishment in Japan in that such proceedings are aimed at formulating the reorganization plan of the debtor company and are likely to affect even the interests of secured creditors for implementing such a plan. All the three proceedings, liquidation, or rehabilitation, have universal scope and encompass all the debtor's assets wherever they are situated.[363] It follows that, in light of Japanese law, an administrator or a debtor in possession appointed by a Japanese court may administer debtors' assets in foreign countries, whereas it is needless to say that all depends upon whether the relevant foreign laws allow them to do so.[364]

---

359. For the overview of international insolvency law in Japan, *see*, Kent Anderson, *Japanese Insolvency Law after a Decade of Reform*, 43 Canadian Business Law Journal 2 (2006); Kazuhiko Yamamoto, *New Japanese Legislation on Cross-Border Insolvency*, 43 *J.A.I.L.* 83 (2000).
360. It is noteworthy here that the legislative work of PIL originally started with the piecemeal revision of a choice-of-law rule for assignment of a claim against a debtor.
361. The Civil Rehabilitation Act (Act No.2255 of 22 Dec. 1999), the Corporate Reorganization Act (Act No.172 of 1952, amended by Act No.154 of 13 Dec. 2002), and Bankruptcy Act (Act No.71, 1922, amended by Act No.75 of 2004).
362. Article 4 of the Bankruptcy Act and Art. 4 of the Civil Rehabilitation Act.
363. Article 34(1) of the Bankruptcy Act, Art. 38(1) of the Civil Rehabilitation Act and Art. 32(1) of the Corporate Reorganization Act.
364. The so-called hotchpot rule is adopted. A creditor who, in the insolvency proceedings, has obtained a dividend may not receive a final distribution made in other proceedings until any other creditor

453. The jurisdictional grounds being founded, the existence of concurrent proceedings in a foreign country does not preclude Japanese courts form opening the local insolvency proceedings. The Japanese insolvency law takes it for granted that plural proceedings may be opened at home and abroad. It allows a foreign insolvency practitioner to file a petition for opening the local insolvency proceedings on behalf of creditors participating in the foreign proceedings and to participate in local creditors' meetings.[365]

§2. Recognition

454. The ARAFIP was enacted, heavily inspired by the UNCITRAL Model Law on Cross-Border Insolvency. The ARAFIP purports to give effect to foreign insolvency proceedings in Japan by means of providing for recognition and assistance proceedings in relation to such foreign insolvency proceedings. While the Act uses the term of 'recognition', it does not mean that the foreign insolvency proceedings which satisfy the prerequisites of recognition can, *ex lege*, enjoy their authority in Japan to which they are entitled in that foreign country.[366] It requires an insolvency practitioner appointed in the foreign insolvency proceedings to file a petition with a Japanese court (in principle, exclusively the Tokyo District Court) for recognition of the foreign insolvency proceedings (Article 4 ARAFIP). The recognition decision by the Japanese court does not automatically trigger any effects. In other words, the foreign decision having opened insolvency proceedings does not extend to Japan the effects to be produced under the foreign law. On recognition, it is left to the Japanese judge's discretion what measures listed by the Act should be taken, such as staying individual actions or prohibiting the transfer of assets.[367]

455. As stated above, the Japanese insolvency law presupposes the possible coexistence of plural proceedings home and abroad. However, the Japanese insolvency law stands on the principle of 'one running proceeding for one debtor'. Whereas, between plural foreign proceedings, the main proceedings have priority over the secondary ones,[368] the Act, in principle, gives preference to the local proceedings when the plural proceedings are running home and abroad. However, the

with the same priority obtains an equivalent dividend in those other proceedings (Art. 201(4) of the Bankruptcy Act, Art. 89(2) of the Civil Rehabilitation Act and Art. 137(2) of the Corporate Reorganization Act).

365. Japanese insolvency practitioners may also participate in foreign insolvency proceedings on behalf of local creditors participating in the foreign insolvency proceedings (Arts 246 and 247 of the Bankruptcy Act, Arts 209 and 210 of the Civil Rehabilitation Act, and Arts 244 and 245 of the Corporate Reorganization Act).

366. The jurisdictional grounds for recognition are as follows: the debtor's domicile, residence or establishment in the country where foreign insolvency proceedings are petitioned against the debtor (Art. 17(1) of the ARAFIP). It is irrelevant whether the foreign insolvency proceedings are main or secondary.

367. Articles 25 to 55 of the ARAFIP.

368. Article 62(1) of the ARAFIP. A judgment of the Tokyo High Court dated 2 Nov. 2012 (*Hanji* 2174-55) relies on the concept of the centre of the debtor's main interests in deciding which foreign insolvency proceedings should be regarded as main, Italian or Texan in the case.

court may recognize the foreign main proceedings and stay the local ones when the recognition of the foreign main proceedings serves the general interests of a body of creditors and when it will not prejudice the interests of local creditors.[369]

§3. Applicable Law

456. The *lex fori concursus,* namely, the law of the country in which the proceedings have been opened, govern the insolvency proceedings and their effects. However, in a series of reform works as stated above, it does not seem to have been fully explored to what extent the *lex fori concursus* should predominate over the laws, for example, applicable to contract and property pursuant to the choice-of-law rules contained in the AGR.

---

369. Article 57(1) of the ARAFIP.

Chapter 7. International Arbitration

457. The number of cases which the Japan Commercial Arbitration Association (JCAA) has settled, that of commercial disputes, international or domestic, are quite few, less than thirty new cases annually. Compared with the counterparts of Hong Kong (Hong Kong International Arbitration Centre) and Singapore (Singapore International Arbitration Centre), the JCAA has been remarkably less frequently used. In view of arbitration clauses being commonly incorporated into international contracts involving Japanese companies, the fact implies that Japan has seldom been chosen as a site of arbitration. One of the reasons for such unpopularity was said to be that the relevant provisions of arbitration were obviously out-of-date.[370] In order to ameliorate the situation, the Arbitration Act whose content, for the most part, derives from the 1985 version of the UNCITRAL Model Law on International Commercial Arbitration (the Model Law), was enacted in 2003.[371] The Act forms one of the main Japanese legal sources of arbitration, together with the multilateral conventions such as the New York Convention of 1958 and the International Center for Settlement of Investment Disputes (ICSID) Convention of 1966.[372]

§1. Law Governing the Arbitration Agreement

458. The validity and effects of the arbitration agreement can be relevant in different contexts: e.g., (i) whether courts should dismiss its proceedings in favour of arbitration; (ii) whether arbitrators may assume jurisdiction; (iii) whether courts should give assistance in taking evidence; (iv) whether the resulting award should be set aside or enforceable. In line with the New York Convention and the Model Law, the Act explicitly refers to the law governing the arbitration agreement only in the last context (iv): the law chosen by the parties and, in the absence of such choice, the law of the place of arbitration (Articles 44(1)(ii) and 45(2)(ii) of the Act).[373] It is arguable that the choice-of-law rule expressed in those provisions should apply to other contexts as mentioned above. It is worth noting that the Act contains the mandatory rules in the Supplement to the Act for the weaker party protection. It provides that the consumer should be entitled to cancel the arbitration agreement made with the business (Article 3) and that no arbitration agreement previously made over employment disputes should be valid (Article 4).

---

370. Those provisions set forth in the Japanese CCP were enacted in 1890, modelled upon the German *Zivilprozessordnung* at that time.

371. Act No.138 of 1 Aug. 2003. The Act covers arbitrations, domestic and international. It is not limited to 'international' arbitrations as set force by Art. 1(1) of the Model Law.

372. For the Act, *see*, Shunichiro Nakano, *International Commercial Arbitration under the New Arbitration Law of Japan*, 47 *J.A.I.L.* 96 et seq. (2004); Keiichiro Nakabayashi, *Applicable Law of International Arbitration Agreement*, 52 *J.Y.B.I.L.* 598 et seq. (2009).

373. In a case where there was no explicit choice of law, a judgment of the Supreme Court applied the law of the place of the arbitration as the implicitly chosen law to the question whether the court proceedings should be dismissed because of the arbitration agreement (Judgment of the Supreme Court, 4 Sept. 1997, 41 *J.A.I.L.* 109 (1998)). In the absence of explicit and implicit choice, a judgment of the Tokyo High Court dated 21 Dec. 2010, applied the law of the chosen place of arbitration, Japanese law (55 *J.A.I.L.* 566 (2012)).

§2. Law Governing the Arbitration Procedure

459. In line with Article 1(2) of the Model Law, the Act encompasses, with some exceptions, all the matters on arbitral proceedings where the place of arbitration is in Japan, such as the appointment of arbitrators, the grounds for challenge, and the commencement and termination of arbitration proceedings (Article 3 of the Act). The agreed place of arbitration does not necessarily mean the seat of arbitration where hearings are conducted but is understood to express the choice of the law governing the arbitral proceedings (the *lex arbitri*).

460. Whether the *lex arbitri* is foreign or not is irrelevant to the questions relating to the recognition and enforcement of the arbitral award. By contrast, when one tries to set aside an arbitral award before a Japanese court, the *lex arbitri* must be Japanese law (Article 3(1) and (3) of the Act). In addition, the *lex arbitri* is said to govern the question whether the agreement to arbitrate should be regarded as an agreement separate and distinct from other parts of the agreement of which it forms part, because the rule as expressed in Article 13 (6) of the Act purports to prevent the party unwilling to be subject to the arbitration from delaying the arbitration proceedings by claiming the invalidity of the main contract.[374]

§3. Law Governing the Substance of the Dispute

461. Article 36 (1) of the Act provides that the arbitral tribunal shall decide the dispute in accordance with such a set of rules of law as chosen by the parties as applicable to the substance of the dispute and that any designation of the law or legal system of a given country shall be construed, unless otherwise expressed, as directly referring to the substantive law rules of that country and not to its choice-of-law rules.[375] Under the Act, the parties may also choose a non-state set of rules such as the 1994 UNIDROIT Principles of International Commercial Contracts or the *lex mercatoria*. If the parties fail to make such choice, the arbitral tribunal should apply the law of the country with which the dispute is most closely connected (Article 36 (2) of the Act). The legislator gave preference to the formulation of the choice-of-law rule as adopted by the national provisions such as Article 187 (1) of the Swiss Private International Law and Article 29 of the Korean Arbitration Act rather than Article 28 (2) of the Model Law. In the absence of choice, the arbitrators should apply a state law which they consider appropriate without recourse to any choice-of-law rule. There is no room for them to apply a set of non-state rules. Lastly, if the parties explicitly so wish, the arbitrators should decide the case *ex aequo et bono*.

374. Nakano, *supra*, 106–107.
375. This provision appears to be a literal translation of Art. 28(1) of the Model Law.

§4. Recognition and Enforcement of Foreign Arbitral Awards

462. It was discussed which of the two legal sources should prevail with respect to the recognition and enforcement of foreign arbitral awards, the New York Convention or the Japanese domestic law. Article VII (1) of the New York Convention does not seem to be decisive in determining this priority problem. Whereas the majority of authors seem to opine that the parties seeking recognition and enforcement of foreign arbitral awards may choose one of those two legal sources, the problem is practically of little significance. Article 45 of the Act closely follows Article 36 of the Model Law which, in turn, enumerates the grounds for refusal of recognition identical to those listed in Article V of the New York Convention.

463. Whereas, pursuant to Article 3(1) of the Act, an arbitral award can be set aside if the place of arbitration was in Japan, the said Article 45, which lists the grounds for refusal of recognition, applies irrespective of the place of arbitration (Article 3(3) of the Act). Consequently, the question of whether or not a particular arbitral award is foreign is irrelevant to the recognition.

Annex: National Legal Sources

Act on General Rules for Application of Laws[376]

(Act No. 78 of June 21, 2006)

Chapter III General Rules for Governing Law

Section 1 Person

(Person's Capacity to Act)

Article 4 (1) The legal capacity of a person to act shall be governed by his/her national law.

(2) Notwithstanding the preceding paragraph, when a person who has performed a juridical act is subject to the limitation of his/her capacity to act under his/her national law but has full capacity to act under the law of the place where the act is done (lex loci actus), that person shall be deemed to have full capacity to act, only in cases where all the parties were present in a place governed by the same law at the time of the juridical act.

(3) The preceding paragraph shall not apply to a juridical act to be governed by the provisions of family law or inheritance law, or a juridical act relating to real property situated in a place governed by a different law from the law of the place where the act was done.

(Ruling for Commencement of Guardianship, etc.)

Article 5 The court may make a ruling for commencement of guardianship, curatorship or assistance (hereinafter collectively referred to as a 'Ruling for Commencement of Guardianship, etc.') under Japanese law where a person who is to become an adult ward, person under curatorship or person under assistance has domicile or residence in Japan or has Japanese nationality.

(Adjudication of Disappearance)

Article 6 (1) The court may make an adjudication of his/her disappearance under Japanese law where an absentee had domicile in Japan or had Japanese nationality, at the latest point of time when he/she was found to be alive.

(2) Even in the case where the preceding paragraph does not apply, if an absentee's property is situated in Japan, or if an absentee's legal relationship should be governed by Japanese law or is connected with Japan in light of the nature of the legal relationship, the domicile or nationality of the party and any other

376. This translation is based on the one translated by the 'Japanese Law Translation Database System' available at home page of the Ministry of Justice of Japan (http://www.moj.go.jp).

circumstances concerned, the court may, by applying Japanese law, make an adjudication of the absentee's disappearance only with regard to said property or said legal relationship, respectively.

Section 2 Juridical Acts

(Choice of Governing Law by the Parties)

Article 7 The formation and effect of a juridical act shall be governed by the law of the place chosen by the parties at the time of the act.

(In the Absence of Choice of Governing Law by the Parties)

Article 8 (1) In the absence of a choice of law under the preceding Article, the formation and effect of a juridical act shall be governed by the law of the place with which the act is most closely connected at the time of the act.

(2) In the case referred to in the preceding paragraph, if only one of the parties is to provide a characteristic performance involved in a juridical act, the law of the habitual residence of the party providing said performance (in cases where said party has a place of business connected with the juridical act, the law of the place of business; in cases where said party has two or more such places of business which are connected with the juridical act and which are governed by different laws, the law of the principal place of business) shall be presumed to be the law of the place with which the act is most closely connected.

(3) In the case referred to in paragraph (1), if the subject matter of the juridical act is real property, notwithstanding the preceding paragraph, the law of the place where the real property is situated (lex rei sitae) shall be presumed to be the law of the place with which the act is most closely connected.

(Change of Governing Law by the Parties)

Article 9 The parties may change the law otherwise applicable to the formation and effect of a juridical act; provided, however, that if such change prejudices the rights of a third party, it may not be asserted against the third party.

(Formalities for Juridical Act)

Article 10 (1) The formalities for a juridical act shall be governed by a law applicable to the formation of the act (the initially applicable law prior to the change shall govern if the law was changed under the preceding Article after the juridical act).

(2) Notwithstanding the preceding paragraph, the formalities that comply with the law of the place where said act was done shall be valid.

(3) For the purpose of the application of the preceding paragraph, with regard to a manifestation of intention to a person in a place governed by a different law, the place from where the notice of such manifestation was dispatched shall be deemed to be the place where said act was done.

(4) The preceding two paragraphs shall not apply to the formalities for a contract concluded between persons in places governed by different laws. In this case, notwithstanding paragraph (1), the formalities for a contract that comply with either the law of the place from where the notice of offer was dispatched or the law of the place from where the notice of acceptance was dispatched shall be valid.

(5) The preceding three paragraphs shall not apply to the formalities for a juridical act to establish or dispose of a real right (a right in rem) with regard to movable or immovable, or any other right requiring registration.

(Special Provisions for Consumer Contracts)

Article 11 (1) Even when the law applicable to the formation and effect of a contract (excluding a labour contract: hereinafter referred to as a 'Consumer Contract' in this Article) between a consumer (meaning an individual, excluding an individual who becomes a party to a contract as a business or for a business; hereinafter the same shall apply in this Article) and a business operator (meaning a juridical person and any other association or foundation and an individual who becomes a party to a contract as a business or for a business; hereinafter the same shall apply in this Article) as a result of a choice or a change of law under Article 7 or Article 9 is a law other than the law of the consumer's habitual residence, if the consumer has manifested his/her intention to the business operator that a specific mandatory provision from within the law of the consumer's habitual residence should be applied, such mandatory provision shall also apply to the matters stipulated by the mandatory provision with regard to the formation and effect of the Consumer Contract.

(2) Notwithstanding Article 8, in the absence of a choice of law under Article 7 with regard to the formation and effect of a Consumer Contract, the formation and effect of the Consumer Contract shall be governed by the law of the consumer's habitual residence.

(3) Even where a law other than the law of a consumer's habitual residence is chosen under Article 7 with regard to the formation of a Consumer Contract, if the consumer has manifested his/her intention to the business operator that a specific mandatory provision from within the law of the consumer's habitual residence should be applied to the formalities for the Consumer Contract, such mandatory provision shall exclusively apply to the matters stipulated by the mandatory provision with regard to the formalities for the Consumer Contract, notwithstanding paragraphs (1), (2) and (4) of the preceding Article.

(4) Where the law of a consumer's habitual residence is chosen under Article 7 with regard to the formation of a Consumer Contract, if the consumer has manifested his/her intention to the business operator that the formalities for the Consumer Contract should be governed exclusively by the law of the consumer's habitual residence, the formalities for the Consumer Contract shall be governed exclusively by the law of the consumer's habitual residence, notwithstanding paragraphs (2) and (4) of the preceding Article.

(5) In the absence of a choice of law under Article 7 with regard to the formation of a Consumer Contract, notwithstanding paragraphs (1), (2) and (4) of the

preceding Article, the formalities for the Consumer Contract shall be governed by the law of the consumer's habitual residence.

(6) The preceding paragraphs of this Article shall not apply in any of the following cases:

(i) where a business operator's place of business that is connected with a Consumer Contract is located in a place governed by a different law from the law of a consumer's habitual residence, and the consumer proceeds to a place governed by the same law as the law of the place of business and concludes the Consumer Contract there; provided, however, that this shall not apply where the consumer has been, in the place of his/her habitual residence, solicited by the business operator to conclude the Consumer Contract in a place governed by the same law as the law of the place of business;

(ii) where a business operator's place of business that is connected with a Consumer Contract is located in a place governed by a different law from the law of a consumer's habitual residence, and the consumer has received or has been supposed to receive the entire performance of the obligation under the Consumer Contract in a place governed by the same law as the law of the place of business; provided, however, that this shall not apply where the consumer is, in the place of his/her habitual residence, solicited by the business operator to receive the entire performance of the obligation in a place governed by the same law as the law of the place of business;

(iii) where at the time of conclusion of a Consumer Contract a business operator did not know a consumer's habitual residence, and had reasonable grounds for not knowing that; or

(iv) where at the time of conclusion of a Consumer Contract a business operator misidentified the counterparty as not being a consumer, and had reasonable grounds for making such misidentification.

(Special Provisions for Labour Contracts)

Article 12 (1) Even where the applicable law to the formation and effect of a labour contract as a result of a choice or change under Article 7 or Article 9 is a law other than the law of the place with which the labour contract is most closely connected, if a worker has manifested his/her intention to an employer that a specific mandatory provision from within the law of the place with which the labour contract is most closely connected should be applied, such mandatory provision shall also apply to the matters stipulated in the mandatory provision with regard to the formation and effect of the labour contract.

(2) For the purpose of the application of the preceding paragraph, the law of the place where the work should be provided under the labour contract (in cases where such place cannot be identified, the law of the place of business at

which the worker was employed; the same shall apply in paragraph (3)) shall be presumed to be the law of the place with which the labour contract is most closely connected.

(3) In the absence of a choice of law under Article 7 with regard to the formation and effect of a labour contract, notwithstanding Article 8, paragraph (2), the law of the place where the work should be provided under the labour contract shall be presumed to be the law of the place with which the labour contract is most closely connected with regard to the formation and effect of the labour contract.

Section 3 Real Rights (Rights in rem), etc.

(Real Right and Other Right Requiring Registration)

Article 13 (1) A real right to movables or immovables and any other right requiring registration shall be governed by the law of the place where the subject property of the right is situated.

(2) Notwithstanding the preceding paragraph, acquisition or loss of a right prescribed in said paragraph shall be governed by the law of the place where the subject property of the right is situated at the time when the facts constituting the cause of the acquisition or loss were completed.

Section 4 Claims

(Negotiorum Gestio and Unjust Enrichment)

Article 14 The formation and effect of a claim arising from management without mandate (negotiorum gestio) or unjust enrichment shall be governed by the law of the place where the facts constituting the cause of it occurred.

(Exception for Cases Where Another Place Is Obviously More Closely Connected)

Article 15 Notwithstanding the preceding Article, the formation and effect of a claim arising from management without mandate or unjust enrichment shall be governed by the law of the place that is obviously more closely connected with the management without mandate or unjust enrichment than the place indicated in the said Article, in light of that the parties had their habitual residence in the places governed by the same law at the time of the occurrence of the facts constituting the cause of the management without mandate or unjust enrichment, that management without mandate was performed or unjust enrichment arose in connection with a contract concluded between the parties, or any other circumstances concerned.

Annex

(Change of Governing Law by the Parties)

Article 16 The parties to the management without mandate or unjust enrichment may change a law applicable to the formation and effect of a claim arising from the management without mandate or unjust enrichment after the facts constituting the cause of it occurred; provided, however, that if such change prejudices the rights of a third party, it may not be asserted against the third party.

(Tort)

Article 17 The formation and effect of a claim arising from a tort shall be governed by the law of the place where the result of the wrongful act occurred; provided, however, that if the occurrence of the result at said place was ordinarily unforeseeable, the law of the place where the wrongful act was committed shall govern.

(Special Provisions for Product Liability)

Article 18 Notwithstanding the preceding Article, where a claim arises from a tort involving injury to life, body or property of others, caused by a defect in a product (meaning a thing produced or processed; hereinafter the same shall apply in this Article) that is delivered, against a producer (meaning a person who has produced, processed, imported, exported, distributed or sold a product in the course of trade; hereinafter the same shall apply in this Article) or a person who has provided a representation on the product in a manner which allows the others to recognize such person as its producer (hereinafter collectively referred to as a 'Producer, etc.' in this Article), the formation and effect of such claim shall be governed by the law of the place where the victim received the delivery of the product; provided, however, that if the delivery of the product at said place was ordinarily unforeseeable, the law of the principal place of business of the Producer, etc. (in cases where the Producer, etc. has no place of business, the law of his/her habitual residence) shall govern.

(Special Provisions for Defamation)

Article 19 Notwithstanding Article 17, the formation and effect of a claim arising from a tort of defamation of others shall be governed by the law of the victim's habitual residence (in cases where the victim is a juridical person or any other association or foundation, the law of its principal place of business).

(Exception for Cases Where Another Place Is Obviously More Closely Connected)

Article 20 Notwithstanding the preceding three Articles, the formation and effect of a claim arising from a tort shall be governed by the law of the place with which the tort is obviously more closely connected than the place indicated in the preceding three Articles, in light of that the parties had their habitual residence in the places governed by the same law at the time of the occurrence of the tort, that the tort was committed in breach of the obligation under a contract between the parties, or any other circumstances concerned.

(Change of Governing Law by the Parties)

Article 21 The parties to a tort may, after the tort occurs, change a law applicable to the formation and effect of a claim arising from the tort; provided, however, that if such change prejudices the rights of a third party, it may not be asserted against the third party.

(Restriction by Public Policy Regarding Tort)

Article 22 (1) In the case where a tort shall be governed by a foreign law, if facts to which the foreign law should be applied do not constitute a tort under Japanese law, no claim under the foreign law may be made for damages or any other remedies.

(2) In the case where a tort shall be governed by a foreign law, even if facts to which the foreign law should be applied constitute a tort both under the foreign law and Japanese law, the victim may make a claim only for damages or any other remedies that may be permitted under Japanese law.

(Assignment of Claim)

Article 23 The effect of an assignment of a claim, against the obligor and a third party, shall be governed by the law applicable to the claim assigned.

Section 5 Family

(Formation and Formalities of Marriage)

Article 24 (1) The formation of a marriage shall be governed by the national law of each party.

(2) The formalities for a marriage shall be governed by the law of the place where the marriage is celebrated (lex loci celebrationis).
(3) Notwithstanding the preceding paragraph, the formalities that comply with the national law of either party to a marriage shall be valid; provided, however, that this shall not apply where a marriage is celebrated in Japan and either party to the marriage is a Japanese national.

(Effects of Marriage)

Article 25 The effects of a marriage shall be governed by the national law of the husband and wife if their national law is the same, or where that is not the case, by the law of the habitual residence of the husband and wife if their law of the habitual residence is the same, or where neither of these is the case, by the law of the place most closely connected with the husband and wife.

Annex

(Marital Property Regime)

Article 26 (1) The preceding Article shall apply mutatis mutandis to the marital property regime.

(2) Notwithstanding the preceding paragraph, if a husband and wife have designated one of the laws listed in the following as the governing law by means of a document signed by them and dated, their marital property regime shall be governed by the law thus designated. In this case, the designation shall be effective only for the future:
   (i) the law of the country where either husband or wife has nationality;
   (ii) the law of the habitual residence of either husband or wife; or
   (iii) with regard to marital property regime regarding real property, the law of the place where the real property is situated.

(3) The marital property regime to which a foreign law should be applied pursuant to the preceding two paragraphs may not be asserted against a third party without knowledge, to the extent that it is related to any juridical act done in Japan or any property situated in Japan. In this case, in relation to such third party, the marital property regime shall be governed by Japanese law.

(4) Notwithstanding the preceding paragraph, a contract on marital property concluded under a foreign law pursuant to paragraph (1) or (2) of this Article may be asserted against a third party when it is registered in Japan.

(Divorce)

Article 27 Article 25 shall apply mutatis mutandis to divorce; provided, however, that if either husband or wife is a Japanese national who has habitual residence in Japan, their divorce shall be governed by Japanese law.

(Formation of Parent-Child Relationship with Child Born in Wedlock)

Article 28 (1) If a child shall be treated as a child born in wedlock under the national law of either the husband or wife at the time of the child's birth, the child shall be deemed to be a child born in wedlock.

(2) If a husband has died before his child's birth, the husband's national law at the time of his death shall be deemed to be the husband's national law set forth in the preceding paragraph.

(Formation of Parent-Child Relationship with Child Born Out of Wedlock)

Article 29 (1) In the case of a child born out of wedlock, the formation of a parent-child relationship with regard to the father and the child shall be governed by the father's national law at the time of the child's birth, and with regard to the mother and the child by the mother's national law at said time. In this case, when establishing a parent-child relationship by voluntary acknowledgment of parentage of a child, if obtaining the acceptance or consent from the child or a third party is required for voluntary acknowledgement under the child's national law at the time of the acknowledgement, such requirement shall also be satisfied.

(2) Establishment of parentage of a child shall be governed by the law designated in the first sentence of the preceding paragraph, or by the national law of the parent or of the child at the time of the establishment. In this case, if the voluntarily acknowledging person's national law is to govern, the second sentence of the preceding paragraph shall apply mutatis mutandis.

(3) If a father has died before his child's birth, the father's national law at the time of his death shall be deemed to be the father's national law set forth in paragraph (1). If the person referred to in the preceding paragraph has died before the acknowledgment, the person's national law at the time of his/her death shall be deemed to be the person's national law set forth in said paragraph.

(Legitimation)

Article 30 (1) A child shall acquire the status of a child born in wedlock if the child is legitimated under the national law of the father or the mother or of the child at the time when the facts constituting the requirements for legitimation are completed.

(2) If a person referred to in the preceding paragraph has died before the facts constituting the requirements for legitimation are completed, the person's national law at the time of his/her death shall be deemed to be the person's national law set forth in said paragraph.

(Adoption)

Article 31 (1) Adoption shall be governed by the national law of an adoptive parent at the time of the adoption. In this case, if obtaining the acceptance or consent from the person to be adopted or a third party, or obtaining permission or any other decision from a public authority is required for adoption under the national law of the person to be adopted, such requirement shall also be satisfied.

(2) The termination of a family relationship between an adopted child and his/her natural relatives by blood and dissolution of adoption shall be governed by the law applicable under the first sentence of the preceding paragraph.

(Legal Relationship between Parents and Child)

Article 32 The legal relationship between parents and their child shall be governed by the child's national law if it is the same as the national law of either the father or mother (in cases where one parent has died or is unknown, the national law of the other parent), or in other cases by the law of the child's habitual residence.

(Other Family Relationships, etc.)

Article 33 Family relationships or rights and obligations arising therefrom other than those provided for in Article 24 to Article 32 shall be governed by the national law of the party concerned.

(Formalities for Juridical Act Regarding Family Relationships)

Article 34 (1) The formalities for a juridical act regarding family relationships provided for in Article 25 to Article 33 shall be governed by the law applicable to the formation of the juridical act.

(2) Notwithstanding the preceding paragraph, the formalities that comply with the law of the place where the act was done shall be valid.

(Guardianship, etc.)

Article 35 (1) Guardianship, curatorship or assistance (hereinafter collectively referred to as 'Guardianship, etc.') shall be governed by the national law of a ward, person under curatorship or person under assistance (collectively referred to as a 'Ward, etc.' in paragraph (2)).

(2) Notwithstanding the preceding paragraph, in the following cases where a foreign national is a Ward, etc., a ruling of appointment of a guardian, curator or assistant and other ruling concerning Guardianship, etc. shall be governed by Japanese law:
   (i) where the grounds for commencement of Guardianship, etc. of the foreign national exist under his/her national law, and there is no person to conduct the affairs of Guardianship, etc. in Japan; or
   (ii) where a Ruling for Commencement of Guardianship, etc. of the foreign national is made in Japan.

Section 6 Inheritance

(Inheritance)

Article 36 Inheritance shall be governed by the national law of the decedent.

(Will)

Article 37 (1) The formation and effect of a will shall be governed by the national law of a testator at the time of the formation.

(2) The rescission of a will shall be governed by the national law of a testator at the time of the rescission.

Section 7 Auxiliary Provisions

(National Law)

Article 38 (1) Where a party concerned has two or more nationalities, the party's national law shall be the law of the country of his/her nationality where he/she has habitual residence, or, the law of the country with which the party is most closely connected if there is no such country of his/her nationality where the party has habitual residence; provided, however, that if one of those nationalities is Japanese, Japanese law shall be the party's national law.

(2) In cases where the national law of a party concerned shall govern, if the party has no nationality, the law of his/her habitual residence shall govern; provided, however, that this shall not apply with regard to the application of Article 25 (including cases where it is applied mutatis mutandis pursuant to Article 26, paragraph (1) and Article 27) and Article 32.

(3) Where a party concerned has nationality in a country where different laws are applied in different regions, his/her national law shall be the law designated in accordance with the rules of the country (in the absence of such rules, the law of the region with which the party is most closely connected).

(Law of Habitual Residence)

Article 39 In cases where the law of a party's habitual residence shall govern, if his/her habitual residence is unknown, the law of his/her residence shall govern; provided, however, that this shall not apply with regard to the application of Article 25 (including cases where it is applied mutatis mutandis pursuant to Article 26, paragraph (1) and Article 27).

(Law of Country or Place Where Different Laws Are Applied According to Person's Status)

Article 40 (1) Where a party concerned has nationality in a country where different laws are applied according to a person's status, his/her national law shall be the law designated in accordance with the rules of the country (in the absence of such rules, the law with which the party is most closely connected).

(2) The preceding paragraph shall apply mutatis mutandis to the law of a party's habitual residence that is applicable under Article 25 (including cases where they are applied mutatis mutandis pursuant to Article 26, paragraph (1) and Article 27), Article 26, paragraph (2), item (ii), Article 32 or Article 38, paragraph (2) in cases where different laws are applied according to a person's status in the place of the party's habitual residence, and to the law of the place with which a husband and wife are most closely connected in cases where different laws are applied according to a person's status in the place with which the husband and wife are most closely connected.

(Renvoi)

Article 41 In cases where the national law of a party concerned shall govern, if Japanese law shall govern in accordance with the law of the country of the national law, Japanese law shall govern; provided, however, that this shall not apply where the national law of a party shall govern under Article 25 (including cases where it is applied mutatis mutandis pursuant to Article 26, paragraph (1) and Article 27) or Article 32.

(*Ordre Public*)

Article 42 In cases where a foreign law shall govern, if the application of those provisions of the foreign law is against public policy, those provisions shall not apply.

(Exclusions from Application)

Article 43 (1) The provisions of this Chapter, except for the main clause of Article 39, shall not apply to the obligations to support arising from the relationship between a husband and wife, parents and their child, and other family relationships.

(2) The provisions of this Chapter, except for the main clause of Article 38, paragraph (2), the main clause of Article 39, and Article 40, shall not apply to the formalities for a will.

Supplementary Provisions [Extract]

(Effective Date)

Article 1 This Act shall come into effect from the day specified by Cabinet Order within a period not exceeding one year from the date of promulgation.

(Transitional Measures)

Article 2 The provisions of the Act on General Rules for Application of Laws after the revision (hereinafter referred to as the 'New Act'), except under the next Article, shall also apply to matters that have arisen prior to the date of the effectuation of this Act (hereinafter referred to as the 'Date of Effectuation').
Article 3 (1) With regard to the capacity of a person to perform a juridical act done prior to the Date of Effectuation, the provisions then in force shall remain applicable, notwithstanding Article 4 of the New Act.

(2) With regard to a Ruling for Commencement of Guardianship, etc. and adjudication of disappearance based on a petition filed prior to the Date of Effectuation, the provisions then in force shall remain applicable, notwithstanding Article 5 and Article 6 of the New Act.

(3) With regard to the formation and effect of a juridical act done prior to the Date of Effectuation and the formalities for such act, the provisions then in force shall remain applicable, notwithstanding Article 8 to Article 12 of the New Act.
(4) With regard to the formation and effect of a claim arising from management without mandate and unjust enrichment for which the facts constituting the cause occurred prior to the Date of Effectuation, and a claim arising from a tort for which the result of the wrongful act occurred prior to the Date of Enforcement, notwithstanding Article 15 to Article 21 of the New Act, the provisions then in force shall remain applicable.
(5) With regard to the effect of an assignment of a claim done prior to the Date of Effectuation against the debtor and third parties, the provisions then in force shall remain applicable, notwithstanding Article 23 of the New Act.
(6) With regard to the formalities for a juridical act concerning a family relationship (excluding the family relationships prescribed in Article 14 to Article 21 of the Act on General Rules for Application of Law prior to revision) done prior to the date of Effectuation, the provisions then in force shall remain applicable, notwithstanding Article 34 of the New Act.
(7) With regard to a ruling of appointment of a guardian, curator or assistant or any other ruling concerning Guardianship, etc. based on a petition filed prior to the Date of Effectuation, the provisions then in force shall remain applicable, notwithstanding Article 35, paragraph (2) of the New Act.

Annex

Code of Civil Procedure[377]

Act No. 109 of June 26, 1996 (as amended by Act No.36 of 2011)

Part I General Provisions

Chapter I General Rules

....

Section 1 Jurisdiction of Courts of Japan

(Jurisdiction Based on the Defendant's Domicile, etc.)

Article 3-2 (1) A court shall have jurisdiction over an action brought against a person if the person has domicile in Japan, if the person has no domicile or his/her domicile is unknown but he/she has residence in Japan, or if the person has no residence or his/her residence is unknown but he/she had domicile in Japan before the filing of the action (excluding the case where the person had domicile in a foreign country after he/she last had domicile in Japan).

(2) Notwithstanding the provisions of the preceding paragraph, a court shall have jurisdiction over an action brought against an ambassador, minister or any other Japanese national in a foreign country who enjoys immunity from the jurisdiction of that country.

(3) A court shall have jurisdiction over an action brought against a juridical person or any other association or foundation if its principal office or business office is located in Japan, or if it has no business office or other office or the location thereof is unknown but its representative or any other principal person in charge of its business has domicile in Japan.

(Jurisdiction over Action Relating to Contractual Obligation, etc.)

Article 3-3 Actions listed in the following items may be filed with a court of Japan in the cases specified in the respective items:

(i) An action to claim performance of a contractual obligation or an action to make a claim relating to management without mandate conducted or unjust enrichment arising in connection with a contractual obligation, a claim for damages for non-performance of a contractual obligation or any other claim relating to a contractual obligation: Where the place of performance of the obligation determined by the contract is located in Japan, or where the place

377. This translation is based on the one translated by the 'Japanese Law Translation Database System' available at home page of the Ministry of Justice of Japan (http://www.moj.go.jp).

of performance of the obligation is supposed to be located in Japan in accordance with the law chosen under the contract.

(ii) An action to claim payment of money for a bill or note or a check: Where the place of payment of the bill or note or the check is located in Japan.

(iii) An action on a property right: Where the subject matter of claim is located in Japan, or where the action is to claim payment of money, and any seizable property of the defendant is located in Japan (excluding the case where the value of such property is extremely low).

(iv) An action against a person who has a business office or other office, which relates to the business conducted at such business office or other office: Where the business office or other office is located in Japan.

(v) An action against a person who conducts business in Japan (including a foreign company (meaning a foreign company prescribed in Article 2, item (ii) of the Companies Act (Act No. 86 of 2005)) which carries out transactions continuously in Japan): Where the action relates to the business conducted by the person in Japan.

(vi) An action based on a ship claim or any other claim secured by a ship: Where the ship is located in Japan.

(vii) The following actions relating to a company or any other association or foundation: Where the association or foundation is a juridical person and it is incorporated under the laws and regulations of Japan, or where the association or foundation is not a juridical person and its principal office or business office is located in Japan.

 (a) An action brought by a company or any other association against its member or a person who was its member, an action brought by a member against another member or a person who was a member or an action brought by a person who was a member against a member, which is based on his/her status as a member

 (b) An action brought by an association or foundation against its officer or a person who was its officer, which is based on the status as an officer

 (c) An action brought by a company against its incorporator or a person who was its incorporator or against its inspector or a person who was its inspector, which is based on the status as an incorporator or inspector

 (d) An action brought by a creditor of a company or any other association against its member or a person who was its member, which is based on his/her status as a member

(viii) An action relating to a tort: Where the place where the tort took place is located in Japan (excluding the case where the result of a wrongful act committed in a foreign country occurred in Japan, and the occurrence of such result in Japan was ordinarily unforeseeable).

(ix) An action for damages due to ship collision or any other accident at sea: Where the first place where the damaged ship docked is located in Japan.

(x) An action relating to salvage: Where the place where the salvage was performed or the first place where the salvaged ship docked is located in Japan;

(xi) An action relating to real property: Where the real property is located in Japan.

(xii) An action relating to a right of inheritance or statutory reserved share or an action relating to a testamentary gift or any other act that shall become effective upon death: Where the decedent has domicile in Japan at the time of commencement of inheritance, where the decedent has no domicile or his/her domicile is unknown but he/she has residence in Japan at the time of commencement of inheritance, where the decedent has no residence or his/her residence is unknown but he/she had domicile in Japan before commencement of inheritance (excluding the case where the decedent had domicile in a foreign country after he/she last had domicile in Japan).

(xiii) An action relating to a claim on the decedent or other burden on inherited property, which does not fall under the category of action set forth in the preceding item: As specified in said item.

(Jurisdiction over Action Relating to Consumer Contract and Labour Relations)

Article 3-4 (1) An action relating to a contract concluded between a consumer (meaning an individual (excluding an individual who becomes a party to a contract as a business or for a business); the same shall apply hereinafter) and a business operator (meaning a juridical person or any other association or foundation or an individual who becomes a party to a contract as a business or for a business; the same shall apply hereinafter) (such contract shall exclude a labour contract; hereinafter referred to as a 'consumer contract'), which is brought by the consumer against the business operator, may be filed with a court of Japan if the consumer has domicile in Japan at the time of the filing of an action or at the time of conclusion of the consumer contract.

(2) An action relating to a civil dispute arising between an individual worker and his/her employer with regard to the existence or absence of a labour contract or any other matters concerning labour relations (hereinafter referred to as an 'individual civil dispute in labour relations'), which is brought by the worker against the employer, may be filed with a court of Japan if the place of provision of labour determined by the labour contract pertaining to the individual civil dispute in labour relations (if such place is not determined, the location of the place of business office at which the worker is employed) is located in Japan.

(3) The provisions of the preceding Article shall not apply to an action relating to a consumer contract, which is brought by a business operator against a consumer, or an action relating to an individual civil dispute in labour relations, which is brought by an employer against a worker.

(Exclusive Jurisdiction)

Article 3-5 (1) Actions prescribed in Part VII, Chapter II of the Companies Act (excluding those prescribed in Sections 4 and 6 of said Chapter), actions prescribed in Chapter VI, Section 2 of the Act on General Incorporated Associations and General Incorporated Foundations (Act No. 48 of 2006), and other actions relating to associations or foundations incorporated under laws and regulations of Japan other than said Acts which are equivalent to those actions specified herein shall be under the exclusive jurisdiction of a court of Japan.

(2) An action relating to a registration shall be under the exclusive jurisdiction of a court of Japan if the place where registration should be made is located in Japan.
(3) An action relating to the existence or absence or effect of an intellectual property right (meaning an intellectual property right prescribed in Article 2, paragraph (2) of the Intellectual Property Basic Act (Act No. 122 of 2002)) which is established upon registration of establishment shall be under the exclusive jurisdiction of a court of Japan.

(Jurisdiction over Joint Claim)

Article 3-6 Where two or more claims are to be made by a single action, and a court of Japan has jurisdiction over one of those claims and has no jurisdiction over other claim(s), such action may be filed with a court of Japan only if said one claim is closely connected with the other claim(s); provided, however, that with regard to an action brought by two or more persons or an action brought against two or more persons, this shall apply only in the case specified in the first sentence of Article 38.

(Agreement on Jurisdiction)

Article 3-7 (1) The parties may determine, by an agreement, the country in which they may file an action with a court.

(2) The agreement set forth in the preceding paragraph shall not become effective unless it is made with respect to an action based on certain legal relationships and made in writing.
(3) If the agreement set forth in paragraph (1) is made by means of an electromagnetic record (meaning a record made in an electronic form, a magnetic form or any other form not recognizable to human perception, which is used in information processing by computers; the same shall apply hereinafter) in which the content of such agreement is recorded, the provisions of the preceding paragraph shall be applied by deeming such agreement to have been made in writing.
(4) An agreement to the effect that an action may be filed only with a court of a foreign country may not be invoked if such court is unable to exercise its jurisdiction by law or in fact.
(5) An agreement as set forth in paragraph (1) which covers a dispute on a consumer contract that may arise in the future shall be effective only in the following cases:
    (i) Where the agreement provides that an action may be filed with a court of a country where a consumer had domicile at the time of conclusion of a consumer contract (except in the case set forth in the following item, any agreement to the effect that an action may be filed only with a court of

such country shall be deemed to be providing that it does not preclude the filing of an action with a court of any other country).

(ii) Where a consumer, in accordance with the agreement, has filed an action with a court of the country determined by the agreement, or where a business operator has filed an action with a court of Japan or a foreign country and the consumer has invoked the agreement.

(6) An agreement as set forth in paragraph (1) which covers an individual civil dispute in labour relations that may arise in the future shall be effective only in the following cases:

(i) Where the agreement has been made at the time of termination of a labour contract, and it provides that an action may be filed with a court of the country in which the place of provision of labour as of that time is located (except in the case set forth in the following item, any agreement to the effect that an action may be filed only with a court of such country shall be deemed to be providing that it does not preclude the filing of an action with a court of any other country).

(ii) Where a worker, in accordance with the agreement, has filed an action with a court of the country determined by the agreement, or where a business operator has filed an action with a court of Japan or a foreign country and the worker has invoked the agreement.

(Jurisdiction by Appearance)

Article 3-8 If a defendant, without filing a defence of lack of jurisdiction of a court of Japan, has presented oral arguments on the merits or made statements in preparatory proceedings, a court shall have jurisdiction.

(Dismissal of Action without Prejudice due to Special Circumstances)

Article 3-9 Even where a court of Japan is to have jurisdiction over an action (excluding the case where an action is filed in accordance with an agreement to the effect that an action may be filed only with a court of Japan), a court may dismiss without prejudice the whole or part of the action when it finds that there are special circumstances under which, if a court of Japan conducts a trial and makes a judicial decision on the action, it would lead to the impairment of the fairness between the parties or to the obstacle to the due and prompt administration of justice, in consideration of the nature of the case, the degree of burden that the defendant is to bear by making an appearance, the location of evidence, and other circumstances.

(Exclusion from Application in the case of Exclusive Jurisdiction)

Article 3-10 The provisions of Articles 3-2 through Article 3-4 and Article 3-6 through the preceding Article shall not apply where exclusive jurisdiction of a court of Japan over an action in question is provided for in laws or regulations.

(Examination of Evidence by Court's Own Authority)

Article 3-11 A court may conduct examination of evidence by its own authority with regard to the matters concerning jurisdiction of a court of Japan.

(Base Time for Determining Jurisdiction)

Article 3-12 The jurisdiction of a court of Japan shall be determined on the basis of the time of the filing of an action.

…

Article 118 A final and binding judgment rendered by a foreign court shall be effective only where it meets all of the following requirements:

(i) The jurisdiction of the foreign court is recognized under laws or regulations or conventions or treaties.
(ii) The defeated defendant has received a service (excluding a service by publication or any other service similar thereto) of a summons or order necessary for the commencement of the suit or has appeared without receiving such service.
(iii) The content of the judgment and the court proceedings are not contrary to public policy in Japan.
(iv) A mutual guarantee exists.................................

(Counterclaims)

Article 146 (1) The defendant may file a counterclaim with the court where the principal action is pending up until such time as oral arguments have reached a conclusion, but only if the subject matter of the counterclaim is a claim with a bearing on the claim that is the subject matter of the principal action or with a bearing on the means of defence; provided, however, that this does not apply in the following cases:

(i) if the claim that is the subject matter of the counterclaim is subject to the exclusive jurisdiction of another court (excluding one determined by an agreement between the parties pursuant to the provisions of Article 11);
(ii) if the filing of a counterclaim would substantially delay litigation proceedings.

(2) If the principal action is pending before a court specified in any of the items of Article 6, paragraph (1), and the claim that is the subject matter of the counterclaim is subject to the exclusive jurisdiction of another court pursuant to the provisions of paragraph (1) of that Article, the provision of item (i) of the preceding paragraph does not apply.
(3) If the Japanese courts have no jurisdiction over a claim that is the subject matter of a counterclaim, the defendant may file a counterclaim pursuant to the provisions of paragraph (1) only if the subject matter of the counterclaim is a

claim with a close bearing on the claim that is the subject matter of the principal action or with a close bearing on the means of defence; provided, however, that this does not apply if the Japanese courts have no jurisdiction over the claim that is the subject matter of the counterclaim pursuant to the provisions on exclusive jurisdiction.

The Personal Status Litigation Act

(Act No. 109 of July 16, 2003)

Chapter I General Provisions

Section 1 General Rules

...

(Jurisdiction over Petition of Personal Litigation)

Article 3-2 A Japanese court shall have jurisdiction over a petition of personal status litigation where -

(i) the respondent who is either party to a family relationship is domiciled in Japan (or resident in Japan when he or she is not domiciled in Japan or when his or her domicile is unknown);
(ii) if a petition is filed against both of the parties to a family relationship, either is or both are domiciled in Japan (or resident in Japan when none of the parties is domiciled in Japan or when their domiciles are unknown);
(iii) if a party to a family relationship is a petitioner, the respondent was domiciled in Japan at the time of his or her death;
(iv) if the parties to a family relationship are both dead, either was or both were domiciled in Japan at the time of death;
(v) both of the parties to a family relationship have Japanese nationality (including the case that either or both had Japanese nationality at the time of death);
(vi) a petitioner who is a party to a family relationship is domiciled in Japan, when the parties to the family relationship were, both, domiciled in Japan lastly; or
(vii) a petitioner who is a party to a family relationship is domiciled in Japan, in case that there are special circumstances under which the assumption of jurisdiction by Japanese courts would ensure the fairness between the parties or the due and prompt administration of justice, in particular, when the respondent's whereabouts are unknown or when the final decree over the same family relationship with the one concerning the said petition rendered by a court of a foreign country where the respondent is domiciled has no effects in Japan.

(Jurisdiction over Joint Claim)

Article 3-3 When both a claim concerned with personal status litigation and a claim concerning compensation for damages arising from the facts which constitute the statement of the claim (limited to the petitioner's claim concerned with personal status litigation against the respondent) are brought in a single petition, a Japanese court has jurisdiction only in so far as the court has jurisdiction over a claim pertaining to the personal status litigation.

(Jurisdiction over Custody of Child, etc.)

Article 3-4 (1) A court shall have jurisdiction over a case concerned with a judicial decision designating a person to have custody over their child(ren) or any other disposition regarding custody of the child(ren) as set forth in Article 32 (1) and with a judicial decision on the designation of a person who will have parental authority as set forth in the said Article (3), when a Japanese court has jurisdiction over an petition seeking the revocation of a marriage or a divorce.

(2) A court shall have jurisdiction over a case concerned with a judicial decision about a disposition regarding the distribution of property as set forth in Article 32 (1), when a Japanese court has jurisdiction over a petition seeking the revocation of a marriage or a divorce and when the case falls under any item as set forth Article 3-12 of the Act on Procedure in Family Matters (Act No. 52 of 2011).

(Dismissal of Petition without Prejudice Due to Special Circumstances)

Article 3-5 Even where a Japanese court is to have jurisdiction over a petition filed with the court, it may dismiss without prejudice the whole or part of the petition when it finds that there are special circumstances under which, if a Japanese court conducts a trial and makes a judicial decision on the petition, it would lead to the impairment of the fairness between the parties or to the obstacle to the due and prompt administration of justice in consideration of the nature of the case, the degree of burden that the other related persons than the petitioner are to bear, the location of evidence, the best interests of a minor child of the parties of a family relationship concerned with a petition and other circumstances.

…

(Amendment of Claims and Counterclaims)

Article 18 (1) Notwithstanding the provisions of Article 143 (1) and (4), Article 146 (1) and Article 300 of the Code of Civil Procedure, a petitioner may amend a claim or statement of claims and a respondent may file a counterclaim until the conclusion of the oral arguments in the first or second instance with regard to the procedures for personal status litigation.

(2) If a Japanese court has no jurisdiction over the amended claim for personal status litigation, a petitioner may amend the claim pursuant to the provision as set forth in the preceding paragraph only in so far as it also seeks the formation, or a declaration of the existence of the same family relationship with that concerned with the one to be amended.

(3) If a Japanese court has no jurisdiction over one of the claims listed in the following items which are the subject matter of a counterclaim, a respondent may file a counterclaim pursuant to the provision as set forth in the preceding paragraph only in either case as set forth in the following items:

(i) A claim concerned with personal status litigation: Where a counterclaim seeks the formation, or a declaration of the existence, of the family relationship which is also the subject matter of the original claim; and

(ii) A claim concerning compensation for damages arising from the facts which constitute the statement of the claim concerned with personal status litigation: Where the petition of the personal status litigation is pending in a Japanese court.

Annex

The Act on Procedure in Family Matters

(Act No. 52 of May 25, 2011)

Part I General Provisions

Chapter I General Rules

(Jurisdiction over Adjudication Matter for Dispositions Regarding Administration of Property of Absentee)

Article 3-2 A court shall have jurisdiction over an adjudication matter for a disposition regarding the administration of the property of an absentee (meaning an adjudication matter regarding the particulars set forth in Appended Table 1, row (55)), when the absentee's property is situated in Japan.

(Jurisdiction over Adjudication Matter for Revocation of Adjudication of Disappearance)

Article 3-3 A court shall have jurisdiction over an adjudication matter for the revocation of an adjudication of disappearance (meaning an adjudication matter regarding the particulars set forth in Appended Table 1, row (57));

(i) when a Japanese court issued an adjudication declaring the person to be missing, or
(ii) when an absentee is domiciled in Japan or has Japanese nationality, or
(iii) when an absentee was domiciled in Japan or had Japanese nationality, at the point when he or she was known to be alive.

(Jurisdiction over Adjudication Matter for Appointment of a Special Agent in a Petition to Rebut Presumption of a Child in Wedlock)

Article 3-4 A court shall have jurisdiction over an adjudication matter for the appointment of a special agent in a petition to rebut presumption of a child in wedlock (meaning an adjudication matter regarding the particulars set forth in Appended Table 1, row (59); the same shall apply in Article 159 (1) and (2)), when a Japanese court has jurisdiction over a petition to rebut the presumption of a child in wedlock.

(Jurisdiction over Adjudication Matter for Permission to Adopt)

Article 3-5 A court shall have jurisdiction over an adjudication matter for permission to adopt (meaning an adjudication matter regarding the particulars set forth in Appended Table 1, row (61); the same shall apply in Article 161 (1) and (2)) and for the establishment of a special adoption (meaning an adjudication matter regarding the particulars set forth in Appended Table 1, row (63); the same shall apply in the Article 164 (1) and (2)), when either the prospective adoptive parent or the person to be adopted is domiciled in Japan (or resident in Japan when none of them are domiciled in Japan or when their domiciles are unknown).

(Jurisdiction over Adjudication Matter for Permission for the Dissolution of an Adoptive Relationship after the Death of a Party to Adoption)

Article 3-6 A court shall have jurisdiction over an adjudication matter for permission for the dissolution of an adoptive relationship after the death of a party to an adoption (meaning an adjudication case regarding the particulars set forth in Appended Table 1, row (62); the same shall apply in Article 162 (1) and (2));

(i) when either an adoptive parent or an adopted child is domiciled in Japan (or resident in Japan when none of them are domiciled in Japan or when their domiciles are unknown), or
(ii) when either an adoptive parent or an adopted child was domiciled in Japan at the time of his or her death, or
(iii) when either an adoptive parent or an adopted child has Japanese nationality and when the other party had Japanese nationality at the time of his or her death.

(Jurisdiction over Adjudication Matter for Dissolution of Special Adoption)

Article 3-7 A court shall have jurisdiction over an adjudication matter for the dissolution of a special adoption (meaning an adjudication matter regarding the particulars set forth in Appended Table 1, row (64); the same shall apply hereinafter);

(i) when an adoptive parent is domiciled in Japan (or resident when he or she is not domiciled in Japan or when his or her domicile is unknown), or
(ii) when an adopted child is domiciled in Japan (or resident when he or she is not domiciled in Japan or when his or her domicile is unknown), in case of a petition by a natural parent or a public prosecutor, or
(iii) when either an adoptive parent or an adopted child has Japanese nationality, or
(iv) when both an adoptive parent and an adopted child had the last domicile in Japan, in case of a petition by the adopted child domiciled in Japan, or
(v) in case of a petition by an adopted child in Japan, if there are special circumstances under which the assumption of jurisdiction by Japanese courts would ensure the fairness between an adoptive parent and the adopted child or the due and prompt administration of justice, in particular, when the adoptive parent's whereabouts are unknown or when the final decree concerned with the dissolution of adoption rendered by a court of a foreign country where he or she is domiciled has no effects in Japan.

Annex

(Jurisdiction over Adjudication Matter for Parental Authority, etc.)

Article 3-8 A court shall have jurisdiction over an adjudication matter regarding parental authority (meaning adjudication matters regarding the particulars set forth in Appended Table 1, rows from (65) to (69) and in Appended Table 2, rows (7) and (8)), disposition concerned with the custody of a child (meaning an adjudication matter regarding the particulars set forth in the same Table, row (3); the same shall apply in Article 150 (iv) and Article 151 (ii)), to the exclusion of a ruling of a disposition regarding the sharing of expenses required for the custody of a child), and loss of the right of administration of property upon the commencement of bankruptcy proceedings against a person who exercises parental authority (meaning an adjudication matter regarding the particulars set forth in Appended Table 1, row (132); the same shall apply in Article 242 (1)(ii) and (3)), when a child is domiciled in Japan (or resident when he or she is not domiciled in Japan or when his or her domicile is unknown).

(Jurisdiction over Adjudication Matter for Appointment of a Person Who Is to Be a Guardian of an Adopted Minor after the Dissolution of an Adoptive Relation)

Article 3-9 A court shall have jurisdiction over a ruling of the appointment of a person who is to be a guardian of a minor after the dissolution of an adoptive relationship (meaning an adjudication matter regarding the particulars set forth in Appended Table 1, row (70); the same applies in Article 176 and Article 177 (i)) or a ruling of the appointment of a guardian of a minor (meaning an adjudication matter regarding the particulars set forth in Appended Table 1, row (71); the same applies in the same Article (ii)), when a minor to be made a ward or a minor ward (hereinafter referred to as 'minor ward, etc.' in this Article) is domiciled or resident in Japan, or when a minor ward, etc. has Japanese nationality.

(Jurisdiction over Adjudication Matter Regarding Maintenance Obligations Arising from Such Family Relationships as Husband and Wife, and Parents and Child)

Article 3-10 A court shall have jurisdiction over an adjudication matter for the establishment of a maintenance obligation (meaning an adjudication matter regarding the particulars set forth in Appended Table 1, rows (84) and (85), and Appended Table 2, rows (1) to (3), (9) and (10). The row (3) is limited to a ruling of a disposition regarding the sharing of expenses required for the custody of a child), when a maintenance debtor who is not a petitioner (a person to be a maintenance debtor in relation to an adjudication matter regarding the particulars set forth in Appended Table 1, row (84)) or a maintenance creditor (a person who has custody of a child or the child in relation to a ruling of a disposition regarding the sharing of expenses required for the custody of a child) is domiciled in Japan (or resident when he or she is not domiciled in Japan or when his or her domicile is unknown).

(Jurisdiction over Adjudication Matter Regarding Succession)

Article 3-11 (1) A court shall have jurisdiction over an adjudication matter for the inheritance (meaning an adjudication matter regarding the particulars set forth in Appended Table 1, rows (86) to (110), (133) and Appended Table 2, rows (11) to (14)), when, at the time when the succession opened, the deceased person was domiciled in Japan, or, if he or she was not domiciled in Japan or his or her domicile at the time is unknown, when he or she was resident in Japan at that time, or, if he or she was not resident in Japan or his or her residence at the time is unknown, when he or she had been domiciled before the succession opened (excluding the case where he or she was domiciled in a foreign country after he or she had been lastly domiciled in Japan).

(2) When a petition was filed with an adjudication matter for the disinheritance of a presumptive heir (meaning an adjudication matter regarding the particulars set forth in Appended Table 1, row (86); the same shall apply hereinafter), an adjudication matter for the revocation of a ruling of the disinheritance of a presumptive heir (meaning an adjudication matter regarding the particulars set forth in the same Table, row (87); the same shall apply in Articles 188 (1) and 189(1)), an adjudication matter for the confirmation of a will (meaning an adjudication matter regarding the particulars set forth in the same Table, row (102); the same shall apply in Article 209 (2)), or an adjudication matter for the permission for an heir's renunciation of the said heir's legally reserved portion (meaning an adjudication matter in the same Table row (110); the same shall apply in Article 216 (1)), the terms 'the deceased person at the time when the succession opened' and 'before the succession was opened' deem to be replaced with 'the deceased person' and 'before a petition', respectively.

(3) In addition to the jurisdictional grounds as provided by paragraph (1), a court shall have jurisdiction when the property to be inherited is situated in Japan, with respect to an adjudication matter for a disposition regarding the administration of an estate for a period before a ruling of the disinheritance of a presumptive heir or a ruling to revoke such ruling becomes final and binding (meaning an adjudication matter regarding the particulars set forth in Appended Table 1, row (88); the same shall apply in Article 189 (1) and (2)), an adjudication matter for a disposition regarding the preservation or administration of inherited property (meaning an adjudication matter regarding the particulars set forth in the same Table, row (90; the same shall apply in the Article 201 (10)), an appointment of an administrator of inherited property upon acceptance of the qualified acceptance of inheritance (meaning an adjudication matter regarding the particulars set forth in the same Table (94), an adjudication matter for a disposition regarding the administration of inherited property after the request for the separation of property (meaning an adjudication matter regarding the particulars set forth in the same Table (97); the same shall apply in Article 202 (2) and (3)), and an adjudication for a disposition regarding the administration of inherited property in the event of non-existence of an heir (meaning an adjudication matter regarding the particulars set forth in the same Table, row (99); the same shall apply hereinafter).

(4) The parties may determine, by an agreement, the country in which they may file a petition with a court, with respect to adjudication matters regarding the division of an estate (meaning the adjudication matters regarding the particulars set forth in Appended Table 2, rows (12) to (14); the same shall apply in Articles 3-14 and 191 (1)).

(5) The provisions as set forth in Article 3-7 (2) to (4) of the Code of Civil Procedure (Act No. 109 of 1996) applies mutatis mutandis to the agreement as set forth in the preceding paragraph.

(Jurisdiction over Adjudication Matter Regarding Distribution of Property)

Article 3-12 A court shall have jurisdiction over an adjudication matter for a disposition regarding the distribution of property (meaning an adjudication matter regarding the particulars set forth in Appended Table 2, row (4); the same applies in Article 150 (5));

(i) when, in case that a person who has been a husband or wife files a petition, the other is domiciled in Japan (or resident when he or she is not domiciled in Japan or when his or her domicile is unknown), or
(ii) when both persons who have been a husband or a wife have Japanese nationality, or
(iii) when, if a person domiciled in Japan who has been a husband or wife files a petition, both were domiciled in Japan lastly, or
(iv) when there are special circumstances under which the assumption of jurisdiction by Japanese courts would ensure the fairness between the parties or the due and prompt administration of justice, in particular, when, if a person domiciled in Japan who has been a husband or wife files a petition, the other's whereabouts are unknown or the final decree for a disposition regarding the distribution of property rendered by a court of a foreign country where the other is domiciled has no effects in Japan.

(Jurisdiction over Family Conciliation)

Article 3-13 (1) A court has jurisdiction over a family conciliation case;

(i) when a Japanese court would have jurisdiction over a litigation or an adjudication case with respect to the matter for which a petition for family conciliation has been filed, or
(ii) when the respondent is domiciled in Japan (or resident in Japan when he or she is not domiciled in Japan or when his or her domicile is unknown), or
(iii) when the parties made an agreement that they might file a petition with a Japanese court.

(2) The provisions as set forth in Article 3-7 (2) and (3) of the Code of Civil Procedure applies mutatis mutandis to the agreement as set forth in item (iii) of the preceding paragraph.

(3) The provision as set forth in paragraph 1 (limited to items (ii) and (iii)) shall not apply to a conciliation case over the matter for which a petition regarding personal status (excluding a petition for divorce and a petition for the dissolution of an adoptive relationship) may be filed pursuant to Article 2 of the Personal Status Litigation Act (Act No. 109 of 2003).

(Dismissal of Petition without Prejudice Due to Special Circumstances)

Article 3-14 Even where a Japanese court is to have jurisdiction over a petition filed with the court pursuant to the provisions as set forth in Articles 3-2 to 3-13 (excluding the case where a petition is filed in accordance with an agreement to the effect that a petition may be filed exclusively with a Japanese court in relation to an adjudication matter regarding the division of an estate), it may dismiss without prejudice the whole or part of the petition when it finds that there are special circumstances where, if a Japanese court conducts a trial and makes a judicial decision on the petition, it would lead to the impairment of the fairness between the parties or to the obstacle to the due and prompt administration of justice in consideration of the nature of the case, the degree of burden that the other related persons than the petitioner are to bear, the location of evidence, the best interests of a minor child and other circumstances.

(Time Standards for Determining Jurisdiction)

Article 3-15 The jurisdiction of a Japanese court shall be determined based on the time when a petition for adjudication or conciliation over family matters is filed or when a court commences the proceedings concerned with family matters by its own authority.

...

(Effects of Final and Binding Decree of Foreign Court in Family Matters)

Article 79-2 Article 118 of the Code of Civil Procedure applies mutatis mutandis to a final and binding decree rendered by a foreign court over family matters (including determinations equivalent to such decrees by foreign public organs).

Selected Bibliography

Since 1989, when the Horei underwent thorough revision, Japanese PIL have altered itself considerably. American-Japanese Private International Law written by Albert. A. Ehrenzweig, Sueo Ikehara and Norman Jensen (Oceana Publications 1964) is obsolete today. There is no comprehensive and updated book on Japanese PIL in English. Apart from Minamikata's, most of the works mentioned below are related to Japanese PIL and written in Japanese. New case law relating to PIL is presented in English by Japanese Yearbook of International Law and its predecessor, Japanese Annual of International Law.

Basedow, J, Baum, H. and Nishitani Y. (ed.), Japanese and European Private International Law in Comparative Perspective. Tübingen: Mohr Siebeck, 2008. Cited as Basedow/Baum/Nishitani.

Basedow, J, Kono, T. and Metzger, A. Intellectual Property in the Global Arena. Tübingne: Mohr Siebeck, 2010. Cited as Basedow/Kono/Metzger.

Dougauchi, M. 'Four-Step Analysis of Private International Law', 315 Recueil des Cours 9 (2005).

Ikehara, S. Private International Law, General Part (Kokusai Shiho, Souron). Tokyo: Yuhikaku, 1973. Cited as: Ikehara.

Kidana, S. (ed.) Private International Law (Kokusai Shiho), Tokyo: Seibundo, 2016. Cited as: Kidana.

Koide, K. (ed.) Commentary on the Act on General Rules for Application of Law (Ho no Tekiyo nikansuru Tsusokuho). Tokyo: Shojihomu, 2015. Cited as: Koide.

Kono, T. (ed.), Intellectual Property and Private International Law. Oxford: Hart Publishing, 2012. Cited as: Kono.

Matsuoka, H. (ed.) Introduction to Private International Law (Kokusai Kankei Shiho Nyumon). 4th ed., Tokyo: Yuhikaku, 2019.

Minami, T. Commentary on the Amended Horei (Kaisei Horei no Kaisetsu). Tokyo: Housoukai, 1992.

Minamikata, S. Family and Succession Law in Japan. Wolters Kluwer, 2015. Cited as: Minamikata.

Nakanishi, Y., Kitazawa A., Yokomizo, D. and Hayashi, T. Private International Law (Kokusai Shiho). 2nd ed., Tokyo: Yuhikaku, 2018.

Okuda, Y. International Family Law (Kokusai Kazokuho). Tokyo: Akashi Shoten, 2015.

Orimo, Y. Private International Law, Special Part (Kokusai Shiho, Kakuron). Tokyo: Yuhikaku, 1972.

Selected Bibliography

Sakurada, Y. Private International Law (Kokusai Shiho). 6th ed., Tokyo: Yuhikaku, 2012. Cited as: Sakurada.

Sakurada, Y, and Dogauchi, M. (ed.) Commentary on Private International Law (Chushaku Kokusai Shiho), vol.1. Tokyo: Yuhikaku, 2011. Cited as: Commentary I (author).

Sakurada, Y, and Dogauchi, M. (ed.) Commentary of Private International Law (Chushaku Kokusai Shiho), vol.2. Tokyo: Yuhikaku, 2011. Cited as: Commentary II (author).

Sato, T and Kobayashi, Y, Explanatory Note on the Reform of the Code of Civil Procedure and the Civil Provisional Remedies Act in 2011 (Ichimon Itto Heisei 23 Nen Minji Soshoho to Kaisei), Tokyo: Shojihomu, 2012. Cited as: Sato/Kobayashi.

Sawaki, T. and Dogauchi M., Introduction to Private International Law (Kokusai Shiho Nyumon). 8th ed., Tokyo: Yuhikaku, 2018.

Tameike, Y. Private International law Course (Kokusai Shiho Kogi). 3rd ed., Tokyo: Yuhikaku, 2005. Cited as Tameike.

Uchino, M. Explanatory Note on the Reform of the Personal Status Litigation Act and the Act on Procedure in Family Matters in 2018 (Ichimon Itto Heisei 30 Nen Minji Soshoho to Kaisei), Tokyo: Shojihomu, 2019.

Yamada, R. Private International Law (Kokusai Shiho). 3rd.ed., Tokyo: Yuhikaku, 2014.

Yokoyama, J. International Family Law (Kokusai Kazokuho no Kenkyu). Tokyo: Yuhikaku, 1997.

Yokoyama, J. Private International Law (Kokusai Shiho), Tokyo: Sanseido, 2012.

Table of Cases

Referees Are to Paragraphs in the Text, Not to Pages.

The Supreme Court

The High Court (Appellate Court)

Table of Cases

The District Court

The Family Court

Table of Principal Japanese PIL Statutes

The Bills of Exchange Act (Act No. 20 of 15 July 1932).
The Cheques Act (Act No. 57 of 29 July 1933).
Act on Governing Laws Relating to the Form of Testamentary Dispositions (Act No. 100 of 10 June 1964).
Act on Special Provisions Concerning Civil Procedure Attendant upon Implementation of the 'Convention on Civil Procedure' and Other Conventions (Act No. 115 of 5 June 1970).
Act on the Law Applicable to Maintenance Obligations (Act No.84 of 12 June 1986).
Act on Recognition and Assistance for Foreign Insolvency Proceedings (Act No.129 of 29 November 2000)
Arbitration Act (Act No.138 of 1 August 2003)
Act on General Rules for Application of Laws (Act No.78 of 21 June 2006).
Act on the Civil Jurisdiction of Japan with Respect to a Foreign State, etc. (Act No. 24 of 24 April 2009).

Table of Principal Japanese PIL Statutes

Table of International Treaties

Hague Conventions

Convention of 5 October 1961 on the Conflicts of Laws Relating to the Form of Testamentary Dispositions (1964.8.2).
Convention of 5 October 1961 Abolishing the Requirement of Legalisation for Foreign Public Documents (1970.6.5).
Convention of 1 March 1954 Civil Procedure (1970.7.26).
Convention of 15 November 1965 on the Service Abroad of Judicial and Extrajudicial Documents in Civil or Commercial Matters (1970.7.27).
Convention of 24 October 1956 on the Law Applicable to Maintenance Obligations towards Children (1977.9.19).
Convention of 2 October 1973 on the Law Applicable to Maintenance Obligations (1986.9.1).
Convention of 25 October 1980 on the Civil Aspects of International Child Abduction (2014.4.1).

Other Conventions and Protocols

Protocol on Arbitration Clauses (1928.9.24).
Convention for the Settlement of Certain Conflict of Laws in Connection with Bills of Exchange and Promissory Notes (1934.1.1).
Convention for the Settlement of Certain Conflicts of Laws in Connection with Cheques (1934.1.1).
Convention on the Execution of Foreign Arbitral Awards (1952.10.11).
Convention on the Recognition and Enforcement of Foreign Arbitral Awards (1961.9.18).
ICSID (International Center for Settlement of Investment Disputes) Convention (1967.9.16).
Protocol to Amend the International Convention for the Unification of Certain Rules of Law Relating to Bills of Lading (1977.6.23).
Convention Relating to the Status of Refugees (1982.1.1).
Convention for the Unification of Certain Rules for International Carriage by Air (2003.11.4).
Convention on Contracts for the International Sales of Goods (2009.8.1).

Index

The numbers here refers to paragraph numbers.

Index

Index

www.ingramcontent.com/pod-product-compliance
Lightning Source LLC
Chambersburg PA
CBHW071443230926
51846CB00001B/328
* 9 7 8 9 4 0 3 5 1 9 4 2 5 *